FEMINIST INTERNATIONAL RELATIONS

Exquisite Corpse

This book offers a contemporary intervention in the field of feminism/international relations. Partly inspired by Surrealism, the book is written in a series of vignettes and draws on a variety of approaches inviting readers in to inhabit the text. It is a politically engaged book, though one which does not direct readers in conventional ways, visiting global politics, the classroom, poetry, institutional violence, cartoons, feminist violence, films, violent white men, angry black women, blood and 'English' puddings. Working imaginatively with epistemology and methodology, and embedding theory throughout the text, the book can be considered part of the current genre of scholarship which attends to complexity, uncertainty, disruption, affect and the creative possibilities of randomness.

Feminist International Relations: Exquisite Corpse will be of interest to students and scholars of International Politics, Gender and Feminist Studies, International Studies, Political Theory, Globalization Studies and further afield.

Marysia Zalewski is Professor and Head of School of Social Science at the University of Aberdeen, Scotland, UK.

Interventions

Edited by:

Jenny Edkins, *Aberystwyth University and Nick Vaughan-Williams, University of Warwick*

'As Michel Foucault has famously stated, "knowledge is not made for understanding; it is made for cutting." In this spirit the Edkins–Vaughan-Williams Interventions series solicits cutting edge, critical works that challenge mainstream understandings in international relations. It is the best place to contribute post disciplinary works that think rather than merely recognize and affirm the world recycled in IR's traditional geopolitical imaginary'
Michael J. Shapiro, University of Hawai'i at Mānoa, USA

The series aims to advance understanding of the key areas in which scholars working within broad critical post-structural and post-colonial traditions have chosen to make their interventions, and to present innovative analyses of important topics.

Titles in the series engage with critical thinkers in philosophy, sociology, politics and other disciplines and provide situated historical, empirical and textual studies in international politics.

Critical Theorists and International Relations
Edited by Jenny Edkins and Nick Vaughan-Williams

Ethics as Foreign Policy
Britain, the EU and the other
Dan Bulley

Universality, Ethics and International Relations
A grammatical reading
Véronique Pin-Fat

The Time of the City
Politics, philosophy, and genre
Michael J. Shapiro

Governing Sustainable Development
Partnership, protest and power at the world summit
Carl Death

Insuring Security
Biopolitics, security and risk
Luis Lobo-Guerrero

Foucault and International Relations
New critical engagements
Edited by Nicholas J. Kiersey and Doug Stokes

International Relations and Non-Western Thought
Imperialism, colonialism and investigations of global modernity
Edited by Robbie Shilliam

Autobiographical International Relations
I, IR
Edited by Naeem Inayatullah

War and Rape
Law, memory and justice
Nicola Henry

Madness in International Relations
Psychology, security and the global governance of mental health
Alison Howell

Spatiality, Sovereignty and Carl Schmitt
Geographies of the nomos
Edited by Stephen Legg

Politics of Urbanism
Seeing like a city
Warren Magnusson

FEMINIST INTERNATIONAL RELATIONS

Exquisite Corpse

Marysia Zalewski

LONDON AND NEW YORK

First published 2013
by Routledge
2 Park Square, Milton Park, Abingdon, Oxon OX14 4RN

Simultaneously published in the USA and Canada
by Routledge
711 Third Avenue, New York, NY 10017

Routledge is an imprint of the Taylor & Francis Group, an informa business

British Library Cataloguing in Publication Data
A catalogue record for this book is available from the British Library

Library of Congress Cataloging-in-Publication Data
Zalewski, Marysia.
Feminist international relations: exquisite corpse / Marysia Zalewski.
p. cm.
Includes bibliographical references and index.
1. Feminist theory. 2. Feminism. 3. International relations. I. Title.
HQ1190.Z354 2013
305.42—dc23
2012036138

ISBN13: 978-0-415-44921-2 (hbk)
ISBN13: 978-0-415-44922-9 (pbk)
ISBN13: 978-0-203-37458-0 (ebk)

Typeset in Bembo
by Book Now Ltd, London

Printed and bound in Great Britain by MPG Printgroup

For my daughters, Tessa and Laura, with love.

CONTENTS

ILLUSTRATIONS

Cover image: *Eine Kleine Nachtmusik*

Figures

ACKNOWLEDGEMENTS

First of all, my heartfelt thanks to Jindy Rosa Pettman. Her intellectual and personal support has been limitless and absolutely wonderful. This book would not have been completed without her. And life would have been a lot less fun too. Thank you a million times over Jindy.

There are many others who have also helped me weave my way through this book and life around it. *Always* Cynthia Enloe, so too Spike Peterson, Anne Sisson Runyan, Maria Stern, Helen Kinsella and Jill Steans (you were so right about the 'business card scene' Jill). My thanks also to others who have helped me on my way: Shirin Rai, Sandy Whitworth, Ann Tickner, Kimberly Hutchings, Lisa Prügl, Moya Lloyd, Georgina Waylen, Hilary Charlesworth, Ruth Seifert, Jane Parpart, Laura Shepherd, Laura Sjoberg and Penny Griffin. I am also deeply grateful to the wonderful Fionas, both profound intellects in their different ways: Fiona McNally (you'll never know how important the red bag has been), and Fiona Sampson (my file labelled 'FS inspirations' has been invaluable). Thank you also to Jenny Edkins and Nick-Vaughan Williams for their encouragement and patience, and indeed to Routledge for their patience. Many thanks to Mairi Stewart for such wise counsel; thanks also to Catriona McAra and our shared admiration for Dorothea Tanning, and to Merlyn Riggs for being fantastically energetic (and for being my *alter ego*). And special thanks to Heather Morgan who has been an enormous and brilliant help in so many ways, not least with the permissions and references. Thank you Heather and I hope our collaborations go on for a long time. Thanks also to Zephyrine Barbarachild (who'd have thought from the long-ago Swansea days?), and to Pip Buckingham (go for the writing!).

And my thanks to the many nameless students and colleagues whose thoughts and lives are scattered throughout these pages. Finally, I want to express deep gratitude to Bernie Hayes for her sterling and steadfast commitment and for the quiet but profound ways in which she has made it possible for me to finish this book (and I promise I won't make you watch the *Song of Bernadette*!).

Marysia Zalewski
Aberdeen, May 2012

FIGURE CREDITS

Front cover (also appears as Figure 9): Permission kindly granted by DACS/Tanning estate. © ADAGP, Paris and DACS, London 2012.

Figure 1: Author's photograph (© Marysia Zalewski).

Figure 2: Author's photograph (© Marysia Zalewski).

Figure 3: © Victoria and Albert Museum.

Figure 4: © Punch Ltd.

Figure 5: Author's photograph (© Marysia Zalewski), Memento Park, Hungary (www.mementopark.hu).

Figure 6: Author's photograph (© Marysia Zalewski), Memento Park, Hungary (www.mementopark.hu).

Figure 7: http://en.wikipedia.org/wiki/File:Cheshire_Cat_Tenniel.jpg

Figure 8: © Cartoon Stock.

Figure 10: © Getty Images.

Figure 11: © Shelendra Kumar.

Figure 12: 'Gender Equality Duty' images. From Zalewski, M., '"I don't even know what gender is". A discussion of the relationship between gender mainstreaming and feminist theory', *Review of International Studies*, 2010, 36, 3–27. http://journals.cambridge.org/action/displayAbstract?fromPage=online&aid=7103388

Figure 13: 'Apa Itu Gender', Women's Empowerment Office, Indonesia. From Jauhola, M., 'Building back better? – negotiating normative boundaries of gender mainstreaming and post-tsunami reconstruction in Nanggroe Aceh Darussalam, Indonesia', *Review of International Studies*, 2010, 36, 29–50. http://journals.cambridge.org/action/displayAbstract?fromPage=online&aid=7103400

Figure 14: © Leeds Postcards.

Figure 15: Author's photograph (© Marysia Zalewski).

Figure 16: Author's photograph (© Marysia Zalewski).

Figure 17: Public domain

Figure 18: © Associated Press.

Figure 19: Author's photograph (© Marysia Zalewski), Canberra War Museum.

Figure 20: © Getty Images.

Grateful thanks to The Carnegie Trust for the Universities of Scotland for financial support to cover the cost of reproducing Figures 4, 8, 9/front cover image.

The trouble with normal is that it always gets worse.[1]

Bruce Cockburn

The things that trigger wars are totally absurd details, the stuff of village gossip and taxi-ride chit chat. And yet they can be enough to kill you.[2]

Hélène Cixous

Isn't that like a bridge consisting only of the first and last pillar,
and yet you walk over it securely as though it was all there? ...
But the really uncanny thing about it
is the strength that exists in such a calculation,
holding you so firmly that you land safely in the end.[3]

Giovanni Vignale

PRELUDE

But feminist theory – that's the place where the questions stop.[4]

This book is composed of a series of vignettes. I chose not to write conventional chapters as I thought they would fail to achieve what I wanted. Chapters (at least the way in which I imagined chapters might be written) so often, like conventional conclusions, end up being too neat, too tidy, too restricting, too closing, too suffocating. I wanted to write something more anarchic, more eclectic, more opening and perhaps a little disquieting. I also wanted to write about the everyday, not the detail or content of any particular (every)day, but rather to work with and pay attention to the flows and ripples of ordinary life.

I have been inspired by a range of ways of thinking that have helped me shape this book. Some of these I find in conventional forms of writing (academic books, novels, print media and digitally produced forms of writing), but also through the form and content of art, poetry and popular culture. But it remains the everyday, more than anything, that I notice and am moved by, and I don't think I am alone in this. The everyday as it emerges through the varying texts I read, and fields and sites I move through.

Figure 1 shows the memorial dedicated to Australian Service Nurses, one of many memorials on the Anzac Parade in Canberra, Australia.[5] Delicately ingrained in the glass (barely visible here) are very traditional images of nursing, not least in that the nurses are all seemingly female and the soldiers they care for are all seemingly male. It is quite beautiful though, especially in the Australian sunshine; cool, curving and evocative of fluidity. It is formally described as taking the form of interlocking glass walls representing nurturing hands, symbolic of nursing.[6] The frontispiece, as shown in Figure 1, bears the caption 'beyond all praise'. Really? *Beyond* all praise? An everyday instance of the artful 'fictioning of femininity'.[7]

FIGURE 1 'Beyond all praise'

Author's photograph (© Marysia Zalewski)

Whether prostitutes, presidents or popes; academics, miners or cleaners, what ends up mattering most is moving through and being in the day. Listening to the radio, travelling, walking into a room, reading, preparing food, listing to music, gardening, watching a plasma screen, checking *Facebook*, feeding animals, staring into space, shopping, talking, listening and noticing (however absent-mindedly) what's in the street, the shops, a billboard, a museum, a holiday spot, a class, a meeting. This image of the everyday is perhaps not much like a regular academic representation of international politics, which is seemingly far removed from the mundanity of everyday life. It may also seem far removed from what feminist international relations is imagined to be. What I see though, when I think of feminist international relations, is more of a story, more like a life. And one where I hope the questions don't stop.

> Everywhere there are starting points, intersections and junctions if we refuse ... the boundaries between territories[8]

EXQUISITE CORPSE

Nothing will unfold for us unless we move toward what looks to us like nothing:[9]

Alice Fulton

A poet's way of thinking suggests that '*Exquisite Corpse*' is the most glamorous of dis/junctions, though an artist describes *Exquisite Corpse* as something dreamt up one night by some of the Surrealist 'drunken boys'[10] who came up with the phrase 'the *Exquisite Corpse* will drink the new wine'.[11] '*Cadavre exquis*'[12] might be more popularly recognised as the children's game of consequences where one child writes or draws something at the top of a piece of paper, then folds it over so the next child can't see the preceding image/word, they then add their word/image and so on, hopefully ending up with – well for children – something ridiculously strange and funny.

We can think about *Exquisite Corpse* as helping us to imagine the production of a composite image through collective means, though more interestingly, I think, it offers a glimpse of the language of the unconscious invoking and working with Freudian concepts of the unconscious and the interpretation of dreams. Or more precisely, the way the unconscious, or symbol, has a grammar which persists even when logical content is disrupted. *Exquisite Corpse* is certainly not the preserve of male artists. Women, perhaps particularly women working with Surrealist ideas, also use the muse of *cadavre exquis*. The *Femme Maison* works of Louise Bourgeois, for example 'recall the Surrealist *Exquisite Corpse*'.[13] But my engagement with the idea and practice of *Exquisite Corpse* is not focused on artists' use of it, or indeed their art *per se*. Nor do I directly engage Freudian analysis. Rather, I use the idea of *Exquisite Corpse* as a kind of methodological muse conjoined with a heterodox and allegorical deployment of a range of techniques drawn from critical theory.

I hope to enact or performatively produce something of an *Exquisite Corpse* in this book, and invite readers to join in. The folds of the narrative, the tantalising links left by the trace of the previous mark(er) and the ensuing contingency of connections is richly methodological.

Yet what does it mean to work with (an) *Exquisite Corpse*, and how might readers join in? And how can this work within the academic endeavour? It's not appropriate simply to toy with artistic, imaginative and creative devices. And it's surely not right to think that imagination and creativity, things perhaps evoked by *Exquisite Corpse*, imply the collation of an unethically random collage of 'things'. In international relations, borrowing from the jewels of artistic imaginations,[14] or foraging through aesthetic treasures,[15] or indeed deploying poetic license and form[16] are not new (if not widespread). Though they perhaps become a new format to commodify, to write 'state-of-the-art' articles about, to demonstrate their 'international relations-ness', to create a new publishing niche or to augment citation indexes. All of which feels some distance from the epistemological and political promise of the lines of poetry that opened this vignette. Film, art and poetry might all be disciplinarily and methodologically graspable, but not nothing. It seems impossible; impossible to see or hold the shape and form of nothing.

> *Nothing will unfold for us unless we move toward what*
> *looks to us like nothing:*[17]

Alice Fulton

An ordinary man

> ...the average white guy, a mere image trace of an always incipient violence.[18]

Austria holds something of an enigmatic place in the European popular imagination, at least as far as that imagination is represented through the media. When the details of the case of an Austrian man named Josef Fritzl became known, predictable and unsurprising public and professional shock and horror ensued. Fritzl's actions highlighted the endlessly ordinary cruel possibilities of violence. And once again, we are face-to-face, or so it seems in our visually saturated mediated world, with one man.

Josef Fritzl was arrested on 26 April 2008, aged seventy-three, on suspicion of serious crimes against family members, and went on trial in Sankt Pölten, Austria on 16 March 2009. He was charged with incest, rape, coercion, false imprisonment, enslavement and the negligent homicide of a baby called Michael. Consequent to a four-day trial from which the public and the media were largely excluded, Fritzl was sentenced to life imprisonment. People were horrified.

An ordinary man. His own daughter. Yet Fritzl had been convicted of 'ordinary' rape in 1967. Perhaps he is mad, he must be. No, he is deemed normal; and he surely kept his daughter Elisabeth and her children – his children/grandchildren – very secure at home.

In an interview for the international relations theory website *Theory Talks*,[19] one of the questions I was asked was this:

> You argue that . . . that destabilizing the subject of man might destabilize the whole field [of international relations]. I can already see some politicians and scholars thinking: 'but is that a good idea?' However, I'd like to ask how the masculinity of the field might be deconstructed and, more importantly, what kind of change that might bring to our approaches not only to international reality, but also to international theory.

Part of my answer was this:

> . . . masculinity is *constantly* being destabilized in the field; indeed, the persistent shoring up of masculinity(ies) defines the field in large part. To understand the depth of this, I insist we need to take gender seriously. Taking gender seriously changes how we think about what's real, what violence is, where power lies, what power is and about what's important. But what it means to take gender seriously is not well understood. For example, the UN pays a great deal of attention to rape and sexual violence in war and conflict. This certainly seems to be taking gender seriously. But we need to ask if legislation really changes anything. Perhaps not much; certainly nowhere near enough. Rape and sexual violence have so much to do with perceptions of what it means to be a 'good' soldier or a 'good' man, and what women of another country or social group represent in any given conflict . . . and indeed what counts as rape, or what counts as sex. The recent conviction of the Austrian man Josef Fritzl is interesting to consider in this context. He might be of major interest to international relations scholars engaged in research on violence, war and conflict. It was considered that Fritzl *must* be crazy – mad – insane. But provocatively, how might his acts of raping and imprisonment be linked to normal masculinity? Can his acts *really* be simply answered/dismissed though the (constructed) category of madness? Taking gender seriously might imply a reconstruction of the generic first-year undergraduate international relations course to focus on women, feminism and gender, and begin with the case study of Josef Fritzl. That might indeed be radical.

My proposition is serious: to frame the introductory theory course, the first-year international relations/IR101 with the 'case' of Josef Fritzl.

Sometimes the safe place won't help you.[20]

Betraying boundaries

*Because truths we don't suspect have a hard time
making themselves felt, as when thirteen species
of whiptail lizards composed entirely of females
stay undiscovered due to bias
against such things existing,
we have to meet the universe halfway.
Nothing will unfold for us unless we move toward what
looks to us like nothing: faith is a cascade[21]*

Alice Fulton

...feminism has always, to some extent and in some ways, been philosophical.[22]

Boundaries simultaneously offer comfort while promising violation. A boundary comes to represent the edge at which safety is supposed to end, or supposed to begin. But already that's wrong, even in its ambiguity. There simply isn't a boundary, or it's never what it seems. Like the horizon in the final scenes of the film *The Truman Show*, the clouds and sky are, for Truman, devastatingly but joyously ruptured by the bow of his escape boat.[23] Or when we look very closely at what we think is a physical edge, it materialises as a series of blurry, merging lines.[24] Yet life is full of boundaries: in rooms, bordering countries, delineating emotions, demarcating knowledge, identifying people, marking difference. We are motivated to get to know where boundaries are in order to stop on either side, or the 'right' side, or at least we get to know where we are supposed to stop and stay, and where not to go.

In this book I work with, across and against boundaries around feminism, especially as constituted within the academic field of international relations.[25] Already in the previous sentence the signs (literal and semiotic) of 'the boundary' are tangible – feminism, academic field, international relations – it's hard to avoid them as they vie for their place. I began with the idea of writing a book on 'Feminist International Relations', trying to stay within a range of academic, disciplinary and methodological boundaries. I ended up writing a book which worked to betray all those boundaries.

Betrayal is an evocative word, it's an emotive word. It's a word that demands attention even in avoidance. It also feels uncomfortable, and it feels personal. Perhaps all of these things seem inappropriate in a text putatively intended for academic communities. But impropriety is important in feminism. Being improper, to be 'unbecoming', refusing the normative and material pleasures of collaboration – 'women must tell lies if they are to succeed',[26] – have been significant political/theoretical activities within feminism. The provocative betrayal of femininity exhibited by suffragists and by refusers of Reason, blatantly insisting on the irrelevant, these all emerge as indelicate betrayals of propriety.

Betrayal is not the preserve of feminist rupture. The inventive character of philosophies and practices unfaithful to Enlightenment desires – reason, truth, innocence – regularly enacts betrayal. Think here of the figure of the rhizome offered by Deleuze and Guattari, resisting, rearranging, disorienting orders of movement, ontology, thought and inviting the invention of connections which spread beyond the covers of the text.[27] Think also of Haraway's cyborg, flouting feminist order, flaunting feminine hybridity.[28] Though institutionalised vocabularies inhibit the possibilities of 'thinking movement',[29] I offer, if tangentially and perfidiously, ruptured rhizomatic readings in this book. Working in this way implies that we will not necessarily arrive at something conventionally graspable at the end. We may arrive at nothing, or at least that's how it might seem. It's how we decide to step through the dark that matters. And which way we can turn.

As soon as you enter thought, there it is . . . the dark.[30]

Stepping through the dark

When stillness culminates, there is movement.[31]

In the work of writing, Hélène Cixous feels her way through the dark, though it is never just or only dark. And it's not that we simply 'enter' thought either; we are always in the strip-light, or 'half-light',[32] or the 'relentless brilliance'[33] of the already expressed, already written, already known, a range of critical theorists tell us this in so many ways. We aim to produce new knowledge. We feel it imperative to do so.[34] So we keep moving towards the white light of knowledge. But the white light of knowledge harbours its own violence.

The light of the methodological frames that international relations proffers is attractive, vociferously drawing attention. Emancipatory narratives in international relations, not least around gender/women, have ardently deployed epistemological and material manifestations of methodological light. The luminous energy inspires desires to produce new, active and actionable knowledge; we seem happily seduced by neoliberalism's soporific script of 'doing'. In international relations, feminism and feminist international relations, theoretical lineages and methodological mappings have been and continue to be extravagantly important, and consistently subject to robust and vigorous debates about which theory is best and which methodology is most appropriate. The energy with which these debates have been carried out is, in part, testament to the significance of the mark of the necessary boundary, at which, for example, Realism stops, feminist standpoint starts, or constructivism begins, or poststructuralism ends, or quite where we might 'fit in' 'queer theory' or the 'aesthetic turn' or something else not yet imagined, and of course the promise of the light on the other side. To be sure, there is intermittent acknowledgment of some shared epistemologies or philosophical allegiances, but the lines are persistently drawn.

Critical theory promises depth, rigour and methodologies of variable hues well illustrated by the intricate and painstaking attention paid to the work of notable philosophers and writers: Derrida and Foucault, for example. Yet the attachment to specific authors carries difficulties. Steve Fuller suggests that these philosophers are attractive because they provide *one-stop shopping for the mind* ... 'Once you've learned to think like, say, Foucault or Jürgen Habermas, you never need to think for yourself again'.[35] This does feel somewhat insulting, it clearly takes hard work and commitment to become an expert on Foucault's or Derrida's or Habermas's (or similar others') work, and the ensuing insights within international relations, for example about security or terrorism, are often profound. But Fuller insists: 'for people who dread continually having to make decisions about what to think, the prospect of one-stop shopping is quite a relief'.[36] If Fuller's aim is not simply about demeaning scholars of Foucault *et al.*, what does this tell us? And what else might one do? One can't simply make frames up. Or do we?

Moving toward *what looks to us like nothing* will surely require signposts to guide us through the inevitably circuitous routes and pathways which ensue from eclectic choices. What of the confusions and nothingnesses that will transpire, how will we cope? How will we survive the incoherence, the madness of nothing to see, nothing to show, just the dark? What ethics of unreason are there here – praying for dark?

Everything is infected with brightness, throbbing with it, and she prays for dark.[37]

Taking a detour

'Warning ... some of the images in this exhibition are disturbing'.[38] The art gallery employee on duty at the entrance to the exhibition also warns me. The photographs and images in Thomas Hirschhorn's 'The Unforgettable'[39] are disturbing: bodies torn apart, heads half blown off, ripped torsos. Hirschhorn uses an eclectic collage of materials: mutilated mannequins, some in western-style wedding dresses decorated with images of war and conflict, life-size cardboard cut-outs representing politicians, film stars and terrorists decked out in orange jumpsuits. In an ancillary exhibition called '*UR-COLLAGE*' the artist juxtaposes two images. '*UR-COLLAGE*' means 'being in agreement with the world', which for Hirschhorn means 'to look', to 'not turn away'.[40] I find it hard to look at the images which counterpose fashion models, a contemporary epitome of beauty, tall, super-slim, perfectly dressed, alongside the mutilated and shredded bodies. For me the images are deeply disturbing. I turn away.

In this book I take a distracted detour around, through and aside feminist international relations. One reason I take this detour is because I am interested in the

FIGURE 2   Thomas Hirschhorn's 'It's Burning Everywhere'

Author's photograph (© Marysia Zalewski)

brutal fecundity of violence. I am curious about the range of ways we learn about what violence is, and what it is not, and in where we think we can find violence and where we think we cannot. I am also interested in how we learn to know how to engage with and respond to violence. Violence is such a slippery concept,[41] sometimes its form seems apparent then it slips away. We think we can control it and then wonder why we can't. I choose to explore my curiosities and questions about violence through the field(s) of feminism and international relations simultaneously (as far methodological grammars and imagination allow), exploring the violences of both. Representing 'feminism and international relations' as 'one' is partly in the service of critically and imaginatively engaging questions about violence and, by default, also about knowledge and about power. My other reason for the distracted meander I take in this book is creatively to betray some of the boundaries that keep feminist international relations in place.

My choice of feminism and/in international relations is partly because both feminism and international relations are deeply indebted to and attached to violence. The bloody carnage of the First World War is conventionally defined as international relations' inaugural moment,[42] and violence remains its '*modus operandi*'.[43] The violations and degradations of gender, especially in the daily lives and deaths of women, are usually understood to have generated the birth of feminism. These violent inspirations have intuitively generated desires to produce better knowledge and to produce empowering and progressive knowledges. Yet violence remains viscerally omnipresent both on the landscapes of international politics and through contemporary practices of gender. Given this, two compelling questions recur. What kind of effect have the new knowledges, produced through the study of international politics and feminist scholarship, had on these manifestations of violence? Have they only procured and nurtured new forms and new sites of violence?[44] These are not new questions; my aim is to work to keep them open, and open them in ways that betray some of the boundaries that keep them in a cold and sterile place.

Disciplinarily, we are used to hearing compelling questions in the context of international politics; at least they are the ones that invite our attention. Serious questions are posed about a range of issues which are familiar to international relations scholars: the proliferation of nuclear weapons or other newer weapons, about terrorism, about threats to security, about new forms of warfare, about the latest war. Questions about these and other important issues are frequently asked by politicians, policy-makers, activists, journalists, scholars and students, most of whom continue look for answers. And answers are always in plentiful supply, one has only to look at government policy documents or international legislation, or listen to politicians' speeches, or consult conventional academic text books to find robust answers to a whole range of important questions about international politics. A great deal of intellectual and emotional energy is expended debating these answers, arguments about who is right, who is wrong, who should be believed, whose answers are legitimate and authoritative, whose answers will work. Getting both questions and answers right has offered, and still offers, the hope and the promise of assuaging some of the violences we appear to be so concerned about. Feminist international relations is also deeply embroiled in this mêlée of violence, knowledge and power. Yet what is 'feminist international relations'?

In the process of working on this book, selecting appropriate empirical sites and ways of thinking and writing about them has been challenging – perhaps not surprisingly, given my intention to betray boundaries, especially the boundaries that keep feminist international relations in place. But still, how might we think about feminist international relations? Is it about feminism, women or gender? Or masculinity or femininity? And what of men? Or of sexuality? And all the other cross-cutting identity formations that seem to slip off a range of political, social and theoretical agendas with persistently surprising ease, perhaps especially given their invariable positioning as afterthoughts?

Questions about whether theoretical, conceptual or empirical attention should focus on women 'in' (international relations), or women 'and' (international relations), or indeed feminism (in/and), or gender (in/and) international relations, were the subject of vigorous discussion and analysis in the academic literature published in the early 1990s. The edited volume published consequent to the 1988 conference held at the London School of Economics on 'Women and international relations' had the title *Gender and International Relations*.[45] A year later, J. Ann Tickner's book *Gender in International Relations*[46] was published, indicating a speedy move from women, to 'gender and', to 'gender in'. Currently, in the second decade of the twenty-first century, the idea that gender is discursively (in)tegrated within the theories and practices of international politics is seemingly taken for granted by many feminist international relations scholars, reflecting a more generalised turn to poststructuralism (broadly understood) in the social sciences and feminist theorising. What perhaps remains in question is the extent to which gender infiltrates, or perhaps what it really means to make claims about the (in)tegration of gender at all. If gender is discursively intertwined, what (non)sense does this make of boundaries?

Still, the question remains, what can feminist international relations be? The idea that there is a separation between feminism and international relations seems unquestionable, even if sometimes there are shared concerns – security and war are comfortable examples. How would it be possible to think the two – feminism/international relations – together, or the two at the same time? And what purpose would the obliteration of their usual boundaries serve? What might get lost? One might also be curious about why it might be useful, methodologically or otherwise, to work with the idea of feminist international relations as being 'simply' international relations: international relations here is minimally thought of as serious enquiries about international political issues. Thinking of them as the same might be taken to imply that the discipline of international relations has been successfully reworked by feminist scholarship, and thus international relations has become theoretically and empirically acceptable in regard to gender (surely not . . .). Alternatively it might imply that feminism cannot (ever) achieve an adequate reworking of international relations, and thus international relations remains an entity in its own right. In this scenario feminism simply drops down, or off, the agenda of significance (perhaps so . . .). Or it might suggest that feminist international relations stands on the same intellectual and academic platform as international relations, equal in stature (curiouser and curiouser . . .).

Rather than stabilise any of these, or position them in a place of truth, perhaps it might be possible to think, for at least some of the time and for methodologically imaginative purposes, of 'feminist international relations' as simply international relations. This is, in part, to begin to contravene the boundaries that keep 'international relations' in a place of ontological primacy and feminism/feminist 'international relations' in some 'other' place. There is nothing natural or inevitable about what international relations scholars choose to study, or about what international relations becomes, or what international politics consists of. What might international relations become?

I don't know how Thomas Hirschhorn imagines people react to the images he exhibits, or whether he wonders if some turn away from the intimacy of the ruined flesh of war. Brutal artistic images are plentiful: Goya's *Los Desastres de la Guerra* (*The Disasters of War*)[47] or Ernst Friedrich's *Krieg dem Kriege!* (*War Against War!*),[48] for example. Friedrich's album of nearly 200 photographs, mostly drawn from German military and medical archives (deemed unpublishable by government censors at the time of the First World War), offers page after page of the agony and seeping ugliness of war. The book begins with images of toy soldiers and toy cannons: 'Between the toys and the graves the reader has an excruciating photo-tour of four years of ruin, slaughter and degradation.'[49]

Dinos and Jake Chapman offer a different kind of brutal visual tour in their book *Insult to Injury*.[50] For this book they desecrated a set of Goya's etchings by drawing cartoon heads – clowns, horses, puppies – on the heads of the tortured, dead and dying. Their beautiful and painstaking blasphemy might seem childish, simultaneously viciously tampering unacceptably with the 'truth'. Some of this imagery has been reproduced into a wallpaper pattern.[51] Though the Chapman brothers' profane work makes me think again about the visual images that bombard mediated landscapes, familiar images of death, horror and pain which confirm what is already well known and with which publics become easily exhausted, beckoning forgettable repetitions.

> *Two little boys had two little toys*
> *Each had a wooden horse*
> *Gaily they played each summer day*
> *Warriors both of course* [52]

There is the pleasure of flinching.[53]

FIGURE 3   'Daddy, What did YOU do in the Great War?'

© Victoria and Albert Museum

The measure of violence

> The smirk of the now falls right into line with ideologies of modernity: perpetuating them rather than reflecting on them.[54]

I was listening to a criminal psychologist on the radio (an interesting ambiguity in the label, given the powerful regulatory role of experts). She was discussing her work with violent men who had been incarcerated for their crimes, and explaining why it was important to keep working with these men (violence is almost always still heavily associated with men) who had committed atrocious acts – usually multiple. Though she was aware that some might think it indulgent, especially if one believed such men were 'evil' (still very easy to do so), she insisted it was important to work with them to help them change, believing this was possible even for the worst offenders. She inferred that the idea that change was possible was an important one to hold onto in a civilised society. Her mediated words came across as sane and sensible, especially against a backdrop of tabloid-fuelled vengeance-seekers invoked by the reflection on 'indulgence'. Her next comment jarred. She said that violence was not very common. She did not qualify this comment or add further explanation. It was simply left to listeners to add their own meaning.

I assumed she meant that 'mad axe murderers' (as listeners we are impelled to complete the gaps) are quite rare, as are serial killers (as they are typically understood). Clearly, any critical analyst of capitalism, or of environmental pollution, or of the political and cultural economy of globalisation with its reproduction of people-trafficking and slave labour, or any feminist scholar of domestic violence or gender violence, or a social or political theorist researching 'simple' social hierarchies of people-value and the consequent rabidly different range of life chances (the photographs of the New York hotel room attendants protesting in support of the woman whom former IMF boss Dominique Strauss-Kahn allegedly sexually assaulted show few white faces)[55] – all of these people might take issue with the idea that violence is not very common. Yet how is it possible to know which measure of violence is useful, or what is required to help know violence when we (don't) see it? As a deviant category, its unwieldiness evades measure and knowing. Violence so often ends up being something else, like the violent induction of vulnerability in the IMF given media coverage of the alleged sexual assault of the hotel 'maid', alongside the potential disruption to DSK's career. Violence: a deviant category indeed.

That violence ends up being 'something else' is vividly illustrated in Lawrence Kramer's conclusion that 'sexual violence cannot be cured by making men aware of how brutal it is . . . they know how brutal it is'.[56] Or in the slick 'charm offensive' tactics of the UK's Prime Minister David Cameron.[57] Also illustrated in Žižek's remark that 'sometimes a polite smile can be more violent than a brutal outburst'.[58] This tells us something very important about the secrets and silences of violence and its intimate, fascinating, compelling ubiquity. Where will we look, and how will we look to know violence? James Dodd suggests that the phenomenological task is to explore the sense of violence.[59] The sense of violence, perhaps this might be a good measure, even if the two – sense and measure – seem incompatible. What kinds of violence might be 'sensed' in the institutional production of knowledge?

One of the compelling questions that I suggested earlier begs our attention: have the institutionalised studies of international politics and feminism procured and nurtured new forms and new sites of violence? The conventionally perceived counter-intuitive inference here is that the institutionalisation of the production of knowledge about gender through feminism, and about international politics through international relations, inhibits the possibilities of making a difference, or rather, the kinds of difference that we assume are desired; though it is more than this. The poststructurally infused implication is that these forms of knowledge have produced other/more violences. And these putatively additional violences are masked by a range of institutional mechanisms and practices which obscure and re-produce a (further) range of violent effects and practices; new violences masquerading as something else.

> The unhallowed dead of the modern project drag in the pathos of their loss and the violence of the force that made them.[60]

> *Tracking ghosts – a theoretical enterprise – tracing ungraspable thoughts and practices is accompanied by other unwelcome spectres as Avery Gordon infers – the 'slightly mad one' who keeps insisting that 'there's something in the room with us'.*

Avaricious institutions

> ... what appears to be invisible or in the shadows is announcing itself, however symptomatically.[61]

> *Alice was beginning to get very tired of sitting by her sister on the bank, and of having nothing to do: once or twice she had peeped into the book her sister was reading, but it had no pictures or conversations in it, 'and what is the use of a book', thought Alice, 'without pictures or conversations?'[62]*

'No use at all' would be Thomas Gradgrind's answer to Alice's question. Gradgrind is the teacher in Charles Dickens's *Hard Times* whose unfortunate students had to be 'in all things regulated and governed by Fact'. Before long Gradgrind hoped to have 'a board of fact, composed of commissioners of fact, who will force the people to be a people of fact, and of nothing but fact'.[63] The spectre of Gradgrind is making an increasing appearance in contemporary treatises on the malaise of the twenty-first century university, especially in the UK,[64] and the relentless resistance to the instabilities and uncertainties of learning and thinking, depressingly accompanied by an inexorable drive toward boxing knowledge tightly into sealed containers ready to ship out to the highest bidder. For Gradgrind, education is about the transmission of facts, revering measurement above everything else: 'he is to be found always with a rule and a pair of scales, and the multiplication table always in his pocket . . . ready to weigh and measure any parcel of human nature, and tell you exactly what it comes to'.[65] His pupils pay a heavy price as they sit in neat rows, all thinking and feeling from the world severed. 'Teach these boys and girls nothing but Facts'.[66] Girl number twenty (actually Sissy) is told she must not paper her walls with images of flowers, for that would be to pander to imagination; and imagination is something to be removed. Remove the imagination and we can be left with the cold beauty of pristine, atomised facts.

'Murdering the Innocents' is one of the chapter titles in *Hard Times*; Mary Evans in her book *Killing Thinking*,[67] an exposition on the contemporary university, echoes the chilling foreboding of decay. Though a sense of despondency pervades Thomas Docherty's analysis, the title and hope of his book *For the University* exhales a fine but living trail of optimism for the possibilities of thinking and learning in the contemporary university. Yet national and global financial insecurities, fiscal austerities, tightening budgets, shrinking markets, rabid competition – hard times indeed – deeply pervade the university landscape. The current remit of the institution is to produce, transmit and deliver expert knowledge on a global scale.[68] But, seemingly inevitably (as if there were no other option), the increasing demands for value for money, measured primarily through social and economic impact conventionally defined, and to deliver satisfactorily to consumers and user groups, has placed increasingly rigid ligatures on the kinds of knowledge contemporary academics can or should work with. Boundaries become clearer and tighter, asphyxiating energy.

Currently in the UK (the example with which I am most familiar), the boundaries confining what counts as knowledge have become more obvious through funding for, and accounting for, research. Eligible research must have social and economic impact which can be measured effectively. Moreover, knowledge must be properly transferrable and have quantifiable effects.[69] Though impact might be generously judged intellectually, forms of research more explicitly aligned with government policy, especially economic policy, are more likely to be successfully awarded funding, or judged appropriately useful: 'Impact is the demonstrable contribution that excellent research makes to society and the economy'.[70] An example of robust confidence in the promise and rewards of university knowledge production is Research Councils UK's commitment to addressing what it identifies as five central and interrelated global threats to security – poverty (and inequality and injustice), conflict, transnational crime, environmental stress and terrorism. To address these systematically, Research Councils UK's aim is to: 'understand, predict/detect and act'.

There is something intuitively compelling about the 'theory-to-practice' continuum implied by this triadic mantra, a persuasive sense that we can travel from being made by the world we want to change to being able to change it.[71] Its intuitive persuasiveness is held securely within the modernist charms of the idea of universities creating glittering trails of new knowledge which they benevolently deliver to the 'real world'. The model of the natural sciences still serves as the paradigmatic model in this regard: scientists are imagined to be 'discovering how things work', or coming up with 'new inventions' which will be of (real) help in the (real) world. A news report tells us that scientists in the University of California are a step closer to developing materials to make people invisible – one day this might be used in military stealth operations to help make tanks invisible to the enemy.[72] Exciting stuff! Or, more soberly, within the broad field of social science, data collated within universities, for example on the increasing violence of girls, is regularly used by government and other official bodies to make policies or introduce new legislation, or simply to locate a new group to target.[73]

In the current climate of 'hard times' there are increasing expectations that universities will and should play a significant role in helping governments to revive and keep re-energising national economies. Here the attractions and seductions of capitalism appear rock solid, especially channelled through contemporary manifestations of globalisation. As Wendy Brown articulates, 'the range of activities, philosophies and practices which are gathered under the term "globalization" evidences the penetration of capital into nearly every crevice in the globe'.[74] Though the financial crisis of late has engendered something of a revival of anti-capitalist imaginaries, capitalism continues to materialise as unassailable; voracious.

Slavoj Žižek revives Karl Marx to give a sense of this voracity: 'Marx described the mad, self-enhancing circulation of capital, whose solipsistic path of parthenogenesis reaches its apogee in today's meta-reflexive speculations on futures.'[75] Capitalism's incessant, ravenous, voracious need for 'more' (and more ... and always more) is simultaneously regenerated by its own greedy desires. Responsive to and enthusiastically engaging with such demands, the contemporary university is increasingly limiting itself to the production of knowledge which merges almost imperceptibly with the values of capital.[76] The contemporary academic, perhaps particularly but not exclusively in the UK context,[77] is increasingly seen as a unit of resource and generator of new income streams, and students as consumers, with the transmission of facts taking the place of learning and branded as 'student experience',[78] with research as simply another product in the marketplace. Gradgrind would be pleased. What place is there for wandering into the 'forest of things and signs'?[79]

★★★★★★★★★★★★★★★

Though this is not a text book, at least in the conventional sense of (re)packaging or (re)gurgitating salient gobbets of disciplinary knowledge for consumption, recirculation and reproduction,[80] this is a book which is partially inspired by students' curiosities, imaginations and passions, especially as they are articulated through their questions both inside and outside formal classes. The classroom might be thought of as a primary site of 'knowledge transfer', though I imagine that many (if not all) academics/lecturers/professors would balk at the idea that 'all' we/they are doing is 'transferring knowledge' in our lectures or seminars, or class discussions; or I hope this. But my aim is not to analyse the classroom or the arena of teaching in a quasi-sociological fashion, but rather obliquely to engage some of the questions students ask, working with them as a source of epistemological, methodological and political inspiration.

But the classroom is not isolated from the rest of what goes on in the everyday life of the university teacher/academic/professor. What importance can be attached to the everyday encounters with colleagues and the range of people we work with and encounter in the broader context of teaching/working in a university? How does the nitty-gritty of the everyday breathe life into the narratives of our work and practices? In the conventions of social science methodology, the use of first-person experience is generally regarded as an inadequate basis for social scientific analysis; personal anecdotes are usually described as a digression. 'Digression' is generally perceived to be a detour or a move away from the subject in hand, an unnecessary and unhelpful (analytically, theoretically) deviation. But, like Sara Ahmed, I wonder why we call the personal a digression. 'Why is it', she asks, 'that the personal so often enters writing as if we are being led astray from a proper course?'[81] Similarly, Judith Butler, in trying to discipline herself to stay focused on the subject she was writing about, decided that straying off course might be 'essential to the matter at hand'.[82] I wonder about my colleague's comment in a discussion about a new senior appointment: 'you do want someone who looks like you, don't you?' The new white male professor didn't look much like me, I mused, though he did look remarkably like my colleague. Robyn Wiegman is surely right when she says 'we need to attend to the epistemological practices and effects of institutionalization'.[83]

However much the contemporary academic's life is micro-managed, accounted for and accountable, the classroom can – sometimes – act as a site of something potentially radical – or at least something which might still hold the possibility of a 'political charge'.[84] The place where the 'productive crisis' which materialises (sometimes) through the combination of the 'academic and revolutionary'[85] still has a pedagogic niche. And students still ask awkward, difficult and fascinating questions. The boundaries exposed by their questions reveal a particular kind of politics at large in the site of teaching and learning; knowledge is a living thing. Perhaps this is particularly the case in the field(s) I mostly work within and across: feminism and international politics. Given their focus on violence in its many elusive forms, and given that both fields are engaged in normative relationships to and with violence, the classroom and the arena of teaching, at least for me, and I think probably for others teaching 'feminist international relations', can emerge as a potentially crucially significant political site for the diffusion and constitution of knowledge. Yet this is a site which is sorely under-theorised, though I really mean under-noticed. And this is not the only site which is vastly under-noticed in the context of the production of knowledge through the university. The university is increasingly a highly monitored site, but this is something different. The university is a deeply personal and simultaneously politicised space, to which I will I pay diffracted attention in this book.

> In some sense, we have to untrain ourselves so that we can read the struggles and debates back into questions that seem settled and resolved.[86]

How the answers got their questions

How the Answers Got Their Questions

The most difficult task of all was not
finding new questions or harder questions,
dipping your wrists into the blood of questions.

It was finding questions for the answers
Which had none, prising them out of the earth,
catching them before they burst into flames.[87]

Moniza Alvi

The blood of questions . . .

> Any force as powerful as feminism must find itself occasionally looking down as its own bloody hands.[88]

Blood is not a common topic of discussion in international politics or indeed feminist international relations, even though war, violence and death remain of central empirical concern. But blood is enticingly gendered, so often closely aligned with feminine abjectness, as menstrual extraction, wastage, seepage, excess. Menstrual blood can act as a powerful political tool and a weapon of war: think of the women's dirty protest in Armagh prison in Northern Ireland/the North of Ireland in the early 1980s. The IRA leadership (we know 'male' without noticing) refused to allow the imprisoned women to have their own dirty protest. Though the men's saliva, vomit, urine and faeces were acceptable, women's menstrual blood was not;[89] too abject.[90] Or when a US female army interrogator at Guantanamo Bay reached into her underpants to extract fake ('fake'?) menstrual blood to smear on a prisoner's face to break his spirit.[91] And as masculinely tinged, whatever the sex of the body from which it spills, consider blood on the battle-field, the blood of strength and valour. Or blood as sexualised and dangerous in its fluid transmission.

'Dipping your wrists into the blood of questions' – Alvi's poem opening this vignette invokes something suicidal. Are (feminist) questions about violence simply suicidal?

****

One might wonder about the point of feminist scholarship or the discipline of international relations if neither had any impact.

'The purpose of doing International Relations, like all social science, is to influence people, sometime, somewhere in a context which will make a difference to their actions'.[92] Much is packed into this sentence about 'what International Relations is for'. There is a clear sense that international relations, and a range of social sciences, has direction and purposive form and, further, that international relations practitioners have a measure of agency activated through their research practices enabling them to provoke changes in people's actions (which presumably might include anyone from politicians and terrorists and an assortment of other 'ordinary' people). Moreover, these changes should 'make a difference', a tautology perhaps. Though 'making a difference' has no essential content, the sense it invokes is surely one of making a difference 'for the better'. It would, perhaps, be unethical otherwise.[93] The holy grail of social justice persistently haunts the guardians of international relations theory.[94]

But it surely should be the case that the new actions consequent to the influence that international relations scholars bring to bear would produce some better actions and practices. One might particularly think, or hope, that this is the case in the context of violence, or the threat or promise of violence. This might be in the form of direct policy design, or more broadly in the context of empirically driven studies which a government or non-governmental organization (NGO) might usefully deploy; the Millennium Development Goals (MDGs)[95] are perhaps a prime example. Or philosophically oriented work might be included to help to shed light on the continuing recalcitrance of some to see reason or to act reasonably. President Obama's call in the summer of 2009[96] for a global reduction in nuclear weapons might be considered an example of how we might see some collation of these things working through in practice.[97] There seems to be something eminently reasonable, at least currently, underpinning the view that nuclear weapons are exceedingly dangerous given their increasing numbers since the end of the Second World War and the unreliability of the command and control technology upon which they rely; though the reasoned madness so excruciatingly and compellingly performed in the film *Dr Strangelove*[98] suggests something different. Arguments about the dangers of nuclear weaponry have consistently been put forward by anti-nuclear campaigners, though clearly not accepted by many powerful governments until now. Is it simply that new facts have come to light? Or that the foundations of reason have altered? Or is something other/more going on, more/other than simple political expediency?

'Influencing some of the people some of the time'... Nicholson evokes something of an ethereal vision of the potential for international relations scholars to engender change that will make a real difference. But Nicholson is clear that 'decisions can be made which actually do make a difference to how the world [*sic*] behaves...policy is possible'.[99] He suggests policy is a good place to start, even if not all international relations scholars can or want to be directly engaged in governmental policy, or any other policy-making body. Though it seems to be the case that many scholars within the British International Relations community (something of a powerful intellectual influence in IR) would like to have their work influence government policy,[100] others may be more interested in the work of NGOs, or groups engaged in actively resisting specific forms of international political practices. Examples of the latter might include the anti-globalisation movements,[101] and feminist and/or women's organisations around the world. Or, indeed, some may be interested in influencing students.

The work of feminism is perhaps more nebulously institutionally placed than the work of IR. The discipline of IR was specifically designed as an academic and pedagogic enquiry into the practices of international politics, most especially the violence of war. Feminism's relationship to and with academia is much more ambiguous. Usually understood to stem from, and be part of, grassroots social justice movements, feminism's arrival into the academy is relatively recent, around the 1970s and 1980s, at least in western countries. What, however, is taken to be strikingly clear is that feminism has an inherent mission to make a difference, and in a way importantly different from IR; certainly we see this within the precinct of feminist IR. This is rarely, if ever, in doubt. Feminism, it is regularly claimed, aims to achieve transformative change, especially in regard to the gendered violences inflicted on women; this answer appears unswerving. Work on this has appeared in a variety of institutionalised forms in the academy, most obviously through women's studies programmes, but also gender studies and feminist studies, though also through more traditional disciplines such as sociology. There may or may not be important differences between these institutional forms and their relationship with feminism, though it is not my aim in this book to debate these differences.

★★★★★★★★★★★★★★★

I think I should explain a little more how I got from writing a book on feminism and international relations to writing a book which works with betraying methodological and disciplinary boundaries. My original remit was to write a book about the (putative or hoped for) transformation of International Relations via a discussion of feminism and 'its critical others'. The 'critical others' I had in mind included masculinity studies, queer theory, critical race theory, poststructuralism and postcolonialism. Each of these nebulous bodies of thought and practice remains variably critical of and involved with both feminism and International Relations, whether the latter are imagined separately or conjoined, or indeed as merged. Moreover, each of these critical others variably materialises as 'other' both to feminism and to IR, each potentially offering (other) transformatory possibilities. But holding all these bodies of thought and practice apart (sliced into discrete chapters) as a way to appraise the (hoped for?) transformed character of International Relations via feminism seemed, to me, to enact a confirmation of, or consolidation of, particular ways of writing, thinking, doing and being. Ways that I think are too innocently violent.

Working within the frozen boundaries set by the institutionalisation of these fields of critical others, transpired as unacceptable, literally unworkable, or they kept evaporating. I kept stopping. Perhaps this is unsurprising, given that the ground I had started from was continually shifting.[102] New questions kept materialising. What routes – empirical, epistemological, methodological – might one take when thinking about the relationship between feminism, masculinity studies and International Relations, for example? What questions might be asked about this supposed triad? Perhaps about the ways in which men are constituted as warrior-soldiers? Or about how masculinity sutures diplomacy? Or how masculinity pervades power? About the violence of men in wars and conflict? Or how feminism's commitment to women makes consideration of the gendering of men difficult? I think all these questions are interesting and important. Yet they hold too firmly in place a commitment to issues of conventional empirical and political interest to mainstream IR and mainstream feminism. They gesture towards methodological frames which suggest the possibility of keeping the empirical and theoretical dependably, as in a fatherly way, separate. To be sure, working faithfully within boundaries – philosophical, theoretical, conceptual, linguistic – can help to provide comforting answers to questions asked (answers already embedded). But this is not my aim in this book. So I changed direction.

The problem comes in knowing which unanswerable questions to ask.[103]

The trail of blood

Blood on the walls?[104]

Methodology is usually understood (as I think we are led to understand it in the social/political sciences) to be about the best/most appropriate way to do research.[105] Methodologies are meant to be about helping us track our way through the maze of reality, most often to find causal chains, make the right connections and ultimately to offer potential solutions to problems identified in advance. If methodological scaffolding is carefully crafted, the idea is that this will give us the best chance of creating better knowledges and better practices. Blood, in this context, sounds an unlikely candidate for methodological use. Yet, that gender materialises as something like blood is intriguing. Both can be labelled, categorised, save lives, end lives. We can live in fear of their loss, and live in fear of having the wrong (contaminated) kind. And we cannot do without either. As blood is sticky, so is gender. And each is slippery, like violence.

The methodological choices necessary to make sense of gender and questions about violence that are of interest, however nuanced and well thought through, perhaps do not have quite the ambulatory capacity (to move through the cycle of 'theory', 'knowledge', 'policy' 'practice') imagined or hoped for. Or the agentic capacity (with the right methodological choices we can, in principle, make gender do what we want it to). Though these are both capacities strongly desired: so much promised, so much expected, and yet the spectre of profligate failure around gender continues to haunt. The red thread promised through feminism morphs into corporeal form, oxygenating both life and death.

> Red is the color of life ... every time the sign of life is brandished, the sign of death also appears, the latter at times more compelling than the former.[106]

Answers and questions

(Why does Freud giggle when the women leave the room?)[107]

"That's an excellent suggestion, Miss Triggs. Perhaps one of the men here would like to make it."

FIGURE 4 Miss Triggs

© Punch Ltd

Methodology: it's such a cold word. It harbours an icy labyrinth of blocked entrances, concealed exits, closed loops and uninviting dead ends. The coldness is numbing, slowing thinking, stifling movement.

How do you explain a revealed hoax that continues to entrance?[108]

The stupor of method perhaps makes sense of this.

Banu Subramaniam tells a story about 'Snow Brown and the Seven Detergents' in which Snow Brown travels across the seas to the 'Land of the Blue Devils' to become a scientist. On arrival she is led by the Supreme White Patriarch to the 'Department of the Pursuit of Scientific Truth'. At the end of the 'Room of Judgement' stood a mirror, 'long, erect and oh so white' to which he asks:

> 'Mirror, mirror on the wall, who is the fairest scientist of them all?' 'You are, O Supreme White Patriarch!' said the mirror. The Patriarch laughed. '. . . you should [all] aspire to . . . find Scientific Truth'.[109]

But in her pursuit of Scientific Truth, Snow Brown kept asking the 'wrong questions' and pursuing the 'wrong paths', yet her obedient desire to become a scientist impelled her to avail herself of the 'Seven Detergents' which eventually 'washed' her away and she became Snow White. Still she failed. 'How could she ever have been the fairest scientist? How could she have been anything but last when judged by a mirror that wanted to produce clones of the Supreme White Patriarch?'[110]

When I was a (post-)graduate student in the mid-1990s, the question 'what method have you adopted for your research?' made me very nervous, especially in its (still) recurrent manifestation, 'is there a distinct feminist methodology?' This was a question to which I found it very difficult to provide a definitive answer, especially when I suspected that only the answer 'yes' followed up with a robust, rationalistic and conventionally acceptable defence would suffice. I could speak at length about the absence of women and considerations of gender in traditional texts in the field of international relations, and point to the violence that this both does and masks, but this did not convince my questioners. What was it, they wanted to know, that made feminist methodology(ies) manifestly *different* from other methodologies, and was this difference sufficient to justify it as legitimate academic research in the discipline of international relations?

There seemed to be a great deal at stake if I got the answer 'wrong', which was of great concern to me, as it seemed to be the case that the only possible responses I could give were *always* (going to be) wrong or unacceptable because what ended up being left, which might be claimed as amounting to 'a distinct feminist methodology', was something relating to 'women's experiences' and/or some form of (perhaps) essentialised (messy) femininity which was clearly not conventionally acceptable in IR as a methodological tool or practice. If the label 'feminist' could not be attached to the usual tools of social science research[111] (and if it could, this tautologically seemed to imply the superfluity of feminist approaches), one was left making arguments about the validity and originality of connections between women's experiences and theorisings and claims to social scientific knowledge. The subsequent bemused look on the faces of more traditionally minded colleagues and advisors on hearing arguments prioritising new knowledge claims based on women's daily lives and bodily experiences – the 'messiness'[112] and 'mundanity'[113] of everyday life – provides a reminder of how easy it is to place feminist work at the bottom rung[114] of the ladder as far as legitimate knowledge claims in IR go.

How do we learn how to 'know', and to 'know' what kinds of knowledge will count as adequate and useful, if this is what knowledge is for? A plethora of books are available to help get students through the central part of their educational training, which is devoted to these kinds of questions. Academics spend much time teaching students and new scholars precisely 'how to study' (research methods) with the aim of making their research more, better or 'other' than ('simply') general or uniformed/uneducated knowledge. And how not to 'fail' like Snow Brown. In this quest, the 'methodology' word enters a student's lexicon at quite an early stage in their career. And it's a word and activity that, like 'theory', is regularly approached with some trepidation.

But I want to ask the question again.

How do we learn how to 'know', and to 'know' what kinds of knowledge will count as adequate and useful, especially if one is doing feminist research? Feminist scholarship has been deeply embroiled in the search for and production of better knowledges. The shameful swathes of knowledge historically produced about women: as 'deformed males',[115] as hysterics and vessels of unacceptable insanity,[116] have led feminist scholars to produce new (feminist) knowledge about women, about gender and about power and violence. Yet persistent questions remain about what 'the appropriate ingredients of a feminist politics of knowledge' are.[117] Perhaps to consider this we need to ask again why feminist knowledge is sought and how feminist knowledges are produced.

Feminists tell stories different from those that emerge from mainstream accounts, and feminists use different sources and understandings of evidence, though as Snow Brown discovered, the sway of evidence tends to hold only if it has hegemonic epistemic hues. Mary Hawkesworth tells us about a report on depression from *The New York Times* which begins with a beguilingly simple question – 'why do women suffer from depression more than men?'.[118] Feminists might suggest layers of reasons: higher levels of poverty, lower levels of confidence and self-esteem, abuse and sexism, for example. The scientific arguments in *The New York Times* differ. The claim is that women dwell more than men on petty slights and 'over think', leading to a negative demeanour and more incidence of depression. At least this is what the evidence suggests, as if evidence had such cognitive agency. Why should we care that these stories/answers are different? The answer too is ostensibly simple, but such simple answers have a way of getting ensnared in the sticky lure of common sense.

Still the desire to tell different stories about women remains strong and persistent.[119] This is especially the case given that the insights of feminism regularly seem to get lost despite the well illustrated errors of hegemonic story-telling (errors which nevertheless insist on the entitlement to represent the truth). Though we might agree with Hannah Arendt that 'an insight does not lose its validity because it has been forgotten'.[120] A disarmingly simple insight offered by feminist work is that women generally haven't had a fair societal deal, whilst men have enjoyed an overly generous one. This has been demonstrated in copious detail. The example of political representation is interesting here, particularly as the under-representation of women has provoked demands for ring-fenced quotas for women candidates in elections. This regularly engenders vigorous arguments, promptly proffered by both men and women, insisting that women should be appointed to the position in question on 'merit' and not because of their gender. Utilising feminist evidence, the case for quotas is based partially on the claim that men hold such positions in large numbers mainly because of their approved gender, which mysteriously bestows merit with some regularity. Redressing this by introducing quotas for women may be questionable for a number of reasons, but not, presumably, because gender isn't playing an active and aggressive role in consolidating the excessive numbers of men and simultaneously making this arrangement look natural. The ways in which this feminist evidence disintegrates are interesting. And repetitively damaging.

So – how do we know?

In thinking about this question, feminists have put much energy into re-thinking methodology and related issues of epistemology and ontology. Mary Hawkesworth offers good reasons for feminists to spend time on 'seemingly abstract questions about the nature of knowledge and defensible strategies of knowledge production'.[121] The two accounts of depression she uses as examples are radically different, and consequently can lead to profoundly different actions. Should women be provided with better education and welfare services? Or medically treated for illness? Or dismissed as innately weak(er) creatures; 'deformed males'? Are these importantly different truths? Or simply differences of opinion? Does this illustrate why the merits of competing theories and methodologies continually need debating? Or make us think again about the ethereality of 'feminist evidence'?

I pose the question again. What method have you adopted for this research?

> This is a persistent question. One asked within a certain tone of voice, an almost imperceptible sigh of relief that the one asking is not the one answering; the sound also of a powerful demand to know, a distanced usually firm utterance capturing in its delivery the authority of the interrogator.[122]

And the question again. What method have you adopted for this research? Luce Irigaray says this is a 'delicate question'...for isn't it the method, the path to knowledge, that has always also led us astray, by fraud and artifice, from woman's path, and to the point of consecrating its oblivion?[123]

When explaining to a colleague that that my book was about feminism and international politics, his response was, 'oh, so you'll have a chapter on Margaret Thatcher, one on Condoleezza Rice, one on Hillary Clinton – that kind of thing?' No. Sigh.

Though let me take up this thought about women in international politics, though not framed in the way my colleague (methodologically) implied, thus not a world leader or politician, but the 'unusual/un-noticed/unimportant' woman. The woman I introduce here is Miss Triggs (Figure 4, page 20).

Cartoons are methodologically mischievous. They are full of (im)mediate explanation; they offer a brief creative political opening and a simultaneous full stop. Though part of the pleasure of cartoons is that they do not (usually) require detailed explanation or deconstruction, I think it is worth thinking through this one for a moment.

The cartoon shows a group of people, it looks like five men and one woman, probably in a boardroom discussion. The caption reads, 'That's an excellent suggestion, Miss Triggs. Perhaps one of the men here would like to make it.' How would someone opposed to or unfamiliar with all things feminist read this cartoon? What explanation is there for the acceptance of the obvious (business?) worth of Miss Triggs's suggestion, yet for it to be authoritatively credible, even audible, we need to 'wait for one of the men to make it'? Who would we be if we were the ones depicted in this cartoon (a question that will place readers in very different positions)? Who might we prefer to be, if there was a choice that could be made? What *can* Miss Triggs say in response? What trails of despair lie in the pleasure of the revelatory witticism of the caption – 'perhaps one of the men would like to make it'?

The exquisite agony of this cartoon alerts us to the performative and phenomenological aspects of what happens in a room, in an institution, in a life. It begins to speak to, or rather faintly brushes by, the structures or shapes of emotions and feelings that move a conversation along, or stall it, or move it in strange directions, or in very ordinary ones. It begins to speak to the performative production of embodied legitimacy and delegitimacy. Miss Triggs's accredited sex/gender produces her own dis-authority. She really can't say anything (else) at least in that moment, though life is made up of staccato, pause-laced moments through which power drips, drips, drips. The transmission of affect is powerfully noted in the opening line of Teresa Brennan's book:

> Is there anyone who has not, at least once, walked into a room and 'felt' the atmosphere?[124]

The feminist body arrives

> When the arrival of some bodies is noticed, when an arrival is noticeable, it generates disorientation in how things are arranged.[125]

It should be hard not to notice the feminist body arriving given the exposé of violence that accompanies it. Feminist work illustrates the gendered ways people move, and though the stories of gendered lives are never simply or only horrific, it can seem that the work of feminism is only in the service of exposing and documenting violence. Although ongoing feminist embroilment in quests for social justice suggests that documenting horror and pain, especially that which exists in the quietly violent folds of life, remains a prime focus.

What of the apparently less quiet gendered arrival of feminism into IR? Perhaps the movement of ideas, the transposition of the intellect and thought have an easier passage than the movement of peoples, given that ideas, intellect and thought have apparent cerebral, asexual form. The presentation and transmission of them materialise in many diverse ways – songs, writing, art, silence, colour, speech are proffered on a range of materials: paper, plastic and celluloid, to name a few. The PowerPoint slide presentation so ubiquitous in contemporary academia to facilitate the presentation (and selling) of one's 'product' achingly fails to capture (perhaps a good thing) the multitude of ways of moving and sharing knowledge, ideas and thought. But as a body of thought feminism enters IR as an explicitly gendered figure. How might one trace the shape of this gendered arrival? As an intruder knowledge, feminism's presence seemingly naturally requires explication, justification and evaluation; an exposition which usually begins (and ends) by judging feminism within the frame of IR. We might opt to forget IR,[126] but most choose not to.

It is usual to track this intruder knowledge through the disciplinary literatures. In academic terms it is extremely important to become immersed in these literatures, and certainly (post-)graduate students and junior academics/faculty are encouraged to develop their research portfolios through this route. Weighing up feminism in this way has inexorably involved attending to both the methodological and ontological concerns of IR as well as the political commitments of the most important journals with their associated hierarchies of subject matter. Taking this heavily beaten path, familiar answers about feminism's worth (and the 'right' questions to ask to find this out) are happened across very quickly and easily, both 'judged in advance'.[127] This is the case despite the lengths to which feminist and other critical scholars have gone to depict the political, epistemological, ontological and methodological violences which are associated with judging feminism within the frame of IR. The energy suffusing these feminist forays into IR's disciplinary territory is marked by intellectual, political and emotional stamina. But the trail regularly followed is littered with expectations and demands which sap energies; perhaps this is most evident in work that attends closely to the discipline. In 'state-of-the-art' type essays it is hard to side-step disciplinary expectations. I had wanted to start a 'state-of-the-art' essay this way.

A teacher's tale

In her first post a young teacher from London took on the task of teaching the letters of the (English) alphabet to a class of four year olds in a small school in

> *a rural part of North Wales. Working on the letter* **S** *– she held up a large colour picture of a sheep and asked the class 'Now, who can tell me what this is?' No answer. Twenty blank faces looked back at her. 'Come on, who can tell me what this is?' she exclaimed, tapping the picture determinedly, unable to believe that the children were quite so ignorant. The 20 faces became apprehensive and even fearful as she continued to question them with mounting frustration. Eventually one brave soul put up a tiny, reluctant hand. 'Yes', she cried, waving the picture aloft.* '**Tell me what you think it is!**' *Please, Miss, 'said the child warily, 'Is it a three year-old Border Leicester?*[128]

One wonders how the teacher responded to the child's intrepid answer about the sheep. She clearly misjudged her small pupils. Or rather she appeared to inhabit a somewhat different epistemological place, giving rise to incomprehension on both sides, resulting in frustration, annoyance, fear and bravery. One hopes that a fruitful learning experience (especially for the teacher) emerged from this encounter. On hearing the child's (tentative) answer, one imagines the teacher breathed a sigh of relief that her small pupils were not stupid at all. Indeed, in the context of knowing about different breeds of sheep they were very knowledgeable. We might hope she became a better teacher because of that experience, less likely to make assumptions about what her pupils did and did not know, or what they should know, or what the 'right' answers were, or where to start from. Both 'sides' in this story perhaps felt relieved at the end of the encounter given that both might now understand the *cause* of the confusion, irritation and apprehension – reassured that the misunderstanding could be cleared up. At least that's the hope. But my venture into stories about sheep was judged not helpful in describing the contemporary state of British feminist IR (always something of a colonial air here, as if Britain's exclusive perspective on global matters had remained intact for centuries).

Nevertheless, it is the case that many feminist IR scholars create inventive paths through IR: one example is Catherine Eschle's and Bice Maiguascha's work.[129] Their discussion about the relationship between academia and activism reveals deep anxiety about the stranglehold of the (IR) canon, and particularly text books (while trying not to offend producers of such texts – an interesting digression).[130] They concomitantly acknowledge the difficulties of teaching large student numbers, which, combined with contemporary institutional expectations and requirements, increases the desire for, and use of, text books. They express frustration with the practices of teaching, but they deploy a variety of disruptive techniques and activities to enact their critical pedagogy. Though they offer their realisation that their 'add critical analysis and stir', and expansion of the empirical remit (which some of their colleagues call 'IR-plus'), does little to dishevel the stranglehold of the canon. But they move to suggest some other ways which might hold critical/radical potential. Catherine asks students to imagine what those from outside the canon and from different parts of the world would include as key events in world history. Bice maps the social and political context in which competing IR 'paradigms' emerge and are validated.[131] The entry of a strange body in the room is disorienting, though the requirement to adjust the body's shape to what is already there is powerful. IR-plus is suggestive of this.

The range of feminist work which has appeared in the disciplinary literatures suggests that the arrival of feminism has indeed been noticed. Though Ahmed's invocation of disorientation in the quote opening this vignette implies perplexity, confusion, disarray, at least this is one reading. Given this, the publication of work on gender in many of the discipline's key journals is curious. Currently it seems to be the case that a healthy amount of scholarly work is being published on feminism/gender in outlets that we might recognise as conventionally 'IR', including some of the more mainstream journals. In North America this includes the flagship journal of the International Studies Association, *International Studies Quarterly* (as well as the Association's newer journals *International Studies Review* and *International Political Sociology*). Other high-ranking US-based journals include *Foreign Policy*, *International Organization* and *International Security*. In the UK/Europe we might include *Review of International Studies*, *Millennium*, *The British Journal of Politics & International Relations* and the *European Journal of International Relations*. The highest academic (citation) accolade probably goes to *International Studies Quarterly*, most especially and increasingly in the context of promotion and tenure. Getting published in this journal is an ambition of many scholars, perhaps especially in North America. Though traditionally this journal has been a bastion of high-positivism and with an interest only in mainstream empirical and political agendas, it is nevertheless the case that a range of editors have indicated they would be interested in receiving more submissions relating to gender. What answer does this arrival provide to the question of what feminism's disorienting presence inspires? And what has transpired in the wake of feminism being noticed even if this presence only invokes a sense that 'there's something in the room with us?'[132]

Life is complicated. The complexities of life from the personal to the international and back again are well documented by feminist scholars of international politics. Rather than being a banal expression of the obvious,[133] recognising that life is complicated is a profound theoretical statement which begins to help us understand the ways in which power meanders through hearts, minds, bodies and imaginations. Interested in all things political, we think we can, we hope we can, and we surely aspire to measure, track, trace or map power, as if we could touch and capture power. Yet the power relations that permeate any society are never as 'transparently clear as the names we give them imply'.[134] What forms of power go forever unnamed? What forms of violence go forever unrecognised?

Avery Gordon tells a story of being on her way to a conference with 'an abstract and a promise': a promise to deliver the paper she had pledged when she submitted her abstract and furthermore to speak professionally about what kinds of methods could adequately study important issues. But on her way to the conference she got distracted, distracted 'by a photograph and had to take a detour in order to follow the traces of a woman's ghost'.[135] Gordon discovered the woman, Sabina Spielrein, by photographic evidence of her absence. At a conference on the history of psychoanalysis, Spielrein was not in the photograph taken of the conference delegates, despite her significant role in the development of the field. The invisibility of Spielrein, and the revelation of her presence by virtue of her 'not being there', started Gordon on a journey looking for the 'systematic exclusions produced by the assumptions and practices of a normalized social science'.[136]

So Gordon looked for ghosts. She took on the professional responsibility of explaining her detour, which she described as being rooted in the crisis of representation that had afflicted her academic field. One consequence of this crisis was the shattering of analytic or social scientific faith in the possibilities of achieving objective knowledge about the social world. As she puts it, writing practices, analysis and investigation are but cultural practice organising particular rituals of story-telling told by situated investigators.[137]

What has this meant in the social sciences, in IR, in feminist IR? What does it mean in a life? Michael Cunningham's domestically inflected analogy is perfect here:

> . . . recipes learned so long ago she does not experience them as knowledge at all.[138]

Intimate permissions

> Why should our bodies end at the skin?[139]

> *A part epistemological question, inevitably morphing into the corporeal as Abramović demonstrates.*

In an art installation titled *Rhythm 0*, Marina Abramović invited a randomly chosen audience and presented herself (in the street) as 'the object', offering them a choice of seventy-two objects to use on her, including flowers, lipstick, blue paint, perfume, a gun, bullets, knives, a whip, soap and honey. Abramović was stripped, cut with a razor blade, punched, a gun muzzle was thrust into her mouth and the 'whole installation culminated in a near rape'.[140] Abramović's powerful betrayal of spaces and lines of intimate permission appeared to license bloody violations of her own body. But bodies don't end at the skin. And the bodies of women enter a room differently. And the body of feminism installs a corporeally laced methodological betrayal, perhaps inviting violence, or exposing its banality.

> Daily life is not a tidy house where china ornaments are arranged in tight rows for display. In daily life, china is shattered, the shelves are knocked down, dirt is tracked across the carpet, and screams shatter the mirror.[141]

Trinh Minh-ha tells us how, during one of her forceful speeches in defence of her people, Sojourner Truth[142] had been requested by a 'threatened white doctor' to prove to those present that she 'really' was a woman. He suggested – in a tone of voice that Irigaray also notices – that she expose her breasts to provide evidence.[143]

> 'There are those among us', he began in a tone characteristic of institutional training. 'who question whether or not you are a woman. Some feel that maybe you are a man in a woman's disguise. To satisfy our curiosity, why don't you show your breasts . . .?'[144]

Tell me who you think you are!

As Trinh Minh-ha observes, 'the arrogance of such a sham of anatomical curiosity – whose needs must be satisfied'.[145] Yet does the body remain the only secure ground for women, a necessary ground upon which judgments get made? Is this what Abramović exhibits, the 'invisible contracts we make with violence?'[146] The truth, the essence of woman and, seemingly by default, also of feminism – so often seared together as one – remains archaically important.

A disciplinary imperative urges that the true (biological) essence of feminism must be sought. Like chromosomal tests for athletes and visual displays for white 'knowing' eyes, the truth of feminism must be captured and charted. Despite the institutionalised moves of feminist theorisations of women, through liberal/empiricist, standpoint/cultural–radical to postmodern/poststructural, at which point all thought of essential women had apparently been overcome, feminism, through IR's visage, re-emerges as the essentialist body of woman imagined as previously discarded. A body so ordained cannot evade the ravages of time and cultural expectations of properly gendered behaviours and attributes. A corporeal arrival offers potential for performatively exposing these.

> I am a woman. I write with who I am. Why wouldn't that be valid, unless out of contempt for the value of woman . . .?[147]

And feminism is . . .

> I had been given the course assignment of my dreams . . . feminist international relations. Five minutes into the class, an 18-year-old freshman raised her hand and asked a question, 'what is feminism? . . .'[148]

In a recent discussion while grading undergraduate dissertations, my co-marker suggested the mark I had given one student was a little too high, given the student had written something of a feminist polemic on the international organisation about which she had chosen to write, rather than a balanced account. My colleague argued that the feminist critique offered should have been set against IR perspectives. My response was that the student had not written a feminist critique, but a feminist narrative. The ensuing lively discussion over one piece of work by one student (though I imagine similar disagreements over student grades are commonplace across the academic globe) illuminates the placing/naming of feminism, as it so clearly and specifically positions feminism as 'critique' and by default as outside the prime object. Persistently classifying feminism as a particular kind of remonstrating criticiser maintains a representation of feminism as some form of eternal outsider, fated to be temporary and fleeting and to the distressing knowledge that the institutionalisation of feminist principles is destined to remain forever out of reach.[149]

> . . . what happens if we wrestle feminism from such definitional singularity?[150]

And feminism is . . .

> . . . and *I did not know how to answer the question*[151] [the question being 'what is feminism?']

Any feminist scholar, perhaps especially when teaching, will be asked what feminism is; asked for a definition. These requests are never simple, and never simply asked or simply answered (even if answers oftentimes seem easy). Asking what feminism 'is' usually carries with it expectations not only of a definition (feminism is . . . . [fill in the blanks]), but also an embedded expectation of action. This is important.

Though I do like the questions students ask about feminism (well, sometimes . . .), perhaps especially the ones that make me bury my head in my hands in pedagogic despair! After a presentation on masculinities that I gave some years ago, in which I had mentioned 'dead white European males' (DWEMs) several times, one student asked 'did these dead white men love their mothers and would god forgive them?' (I did actually bury my head in my hands at the time). But such questions are fascinating. Why were they important to the questioner? How did these questions emerge out of the talk that I gave (which did not mention mothers or god, or explicitly apportion blame or specific misdeeds in ways that suggested forgiveness might be required)? Although authorial intention is clearly speciously relevant. How could I possibly know the answers? But further, what 'answers' did my questioner have in mind in order to get to the questions he asked? Or what did he know about what I was saying that I (think) I didn't know about? The backlight of his questioning demand for definition gleams with an anticipation of 'doing'.

I imagine my questioner did not have fully formed answers in his head, but his questions indicated a clear sense of the relationship between my feminist discussion of masculinities (through the figure of 'the DWEM' in part, perhaps not one I would use so much currently, a timely strategic move perhaps) and the injustices that I was implying emerged from specific cultural configurations of gender and materialisation through institutional forms. I am not suggesting my questioner was 'wrong', or that he misunderstood me, or even that I had not articulated my arguments adequately (though always a possibility, even if this might be a too gender-inflected acknowledgment). But it inspires a rethinking about what these kinds of questions about feminism do, what they assume, what they expect. And reflection on how they keep returning us to the question – what *is* feminism (for)?

Feminism, in all its multiplicity, depth and sophistication, has regularly been viewed through quite narrow methodological, epistemological and political lenses, not least within the disciplinary boundaries of IR. This, amongst other things, has led to persistent debates about the relative success (or failure) of feminism in the context of its impact on international relations. Positioning feminism as a kind of 'handmaiden' to international relations is something of which I have generally been very critical.[152] I have also been critical of the tendency to straitjacket feminism, definitionally, temporally, politically, theoretically and methodologically, which has led me to be reluctant to offer definitions of feminism.[153] This resistant stance can often seem very confusing (irritating even), perhaps especially to students wanting to learn about 'feminism and international relations', at least initially. But I think it is important to keep deflecting the question – what is feminism?

The bloodletting of questions.

But perhaps this attempt at deflection doesn't matter, as people rarely seem to have much difficulty knowing what feminism is. I am constantly informed that feminism is about women. In this context, typical definitions are that feminism is 'a political movement organized around transforming the lives of women'.[154] Or as aiming 'to realize fundamental transformations in gender relations, [by] shifting existing power relations in favour of women'.[155] On these definitions, feminism is focused on transforming the lives of real, living, breathing, damaged women. This view appears to be confirmed by the generic reception of feminism within IR – despite geographical, cultural, institutional and pedagogical variations, the discipline of IR still largely understands feminist work to be really only concerned with women[156] and most often in regard to women's empowerment, conventionally understood.[157] As such, feminism materialises as offering reformist guidelines to a – sometimes – receptive discipline, or as offering a revolutionary agenda intent on wrenching IR from its incorrigibly masculinist moorings.

Despite the intimate relationship between the two approaches, reformist feminism is perhaps the standard way in which feminist work had been received in IR, classically reproduced in the 'week on feminism/gender' typical of most undergraduate IR programmes.[158] Although I suspect that the majority of those currently teaching the 'week on feminism' do not see themselves as providing a reformist feminist gender agenda for IR, or teach it in this way, most undergraduate students, and indeed many scholars, ultimately understand feminism to be about women, simply theorised. This always seems a little small for me, and keeping feminism small has effects. Even though feminism is, of course, about women.

The term 'feminism' . . . calls attention to women like no other term.[159]

Perhaps offering reasons for invitations to become theoretically and politically anorexic.

And feminism is . . .

I myself have never been able to find out precisely what feminism is: I only know that people call me a feminist whenever I express sentiments that differentiate me from a doormat or a prostitute.[160]

Feminism is a collection of movements aimed at defining, establishing, and defending equal political, economic, and social rights and equal opportunities for women.[161]

The UK Universities Minister David Willetts said feminism was probably the 'single biggest factor' in the lack of social mobility in Britain, because women who would otherwise have been housewives had taken university places and well paid jobs that could have gone to ambitious working-class men.[162]

Modern feminism holds that women can do exactly what they want free of responsibility for their choices.[163]

Feminism is a political movement organised around transforming the lives of women.[164]

Feminism aims to realise fundamental transformations in gender relations, [by] shifting existing power relations in favour of women.[165]

Feminism is a historically constituted, local and global, social and political movement with an emancipatory purpose and a normative content.[166]

. . . feminism is a living thing.[167]

Feminists and scholars have divided the movement's history into three 'waves'. The first wave refers mainly to women's suffrage movements of the nineteenth and early twentieth centuries (mainly concerned with women's right to vote). The second wave refers to the ideas and actions associated with the women's liberation movement beginning in the 1960s (which campaigned for legal and social equality for women). The third wave refers to a continuation of, and a reaction to, the perceived failures of second-wave feminism, beginning in the 1990s.[168]

The feminist agenda is not about equal rights for women. It is about a socialist, anti-family political movement that encourages women to leave their husbands, kill their children, practice witchcraft, destroy capitalism, and become lesbians.[169]

A decision is a terrible thing.[170]

Making feminism palatable

★Zephyrine Barbarachild, Pip Buckingham, Heather Morgan and Marysia Zalewski

What are little girls made of?

'Sugar and spice and all things nice –
that's what little girls are made of!'

This textually interwoven vignette was written by four people★ with different backgrounds, experiences, interests. One thing that connects us is our passionate engagement with feminism.

The scene of distaste

Do you think you could make feminism more palatable?

Those of us teaching feminism on first- or second-year undergraduate introductory courses know we won't have an easy ride. Student attendance at 'the gender lecture(s)' may drop and there is usually a palpable level of anxiety or opposition attached to these feminist performances. I have taught 'the gender/feminism lecture(s)' for some time now and have grown used to students sometimes walking out in disgust or disbelief, with eyes rolling upwards, sometimes making 'complaints' in tutorial sessions about the relevance of feminism to the subjects of sociology/politics/international relations. Not all students are unhappy with the inclusion of gender in the introductory course: some clearly go on to pursue further study, others are content to tolerate a certain amount of feminism or gender (not too much!), and some comment on engaging with it, but feeling defeated by it. But when, after the 'gender lecture', I was

★
Zephyrine Barbarchild
Is a radical lesbian feminist, Greenham veteran, Occupier, Quaker and independent health researcher.

Pip Buckingham
Has an MA in Gender Studies, MA (Hons) in English Literature with Gender studies and is currently an English and Sociology teacher.

Heather Morgan
Is an early-career academic with broad research interests in the concepts and practices of gender and deviance. She is currently employed as a Research Fellow at the University of Aberdeen.

asked by a student to 'make feminism more palatable', I felt disheartened, more so than usual. The idea of making feminism 'palatable' seemed to touch a raw nerve.

It turned out that it was the 'week on gender/feminism' on the introductory sociology course as well. In a tutorial discussion about gender, one of the tutors was asked by a student if she hated men. Later on in the session, when she mentioned two of her children were boys, she was asked if she hated them too.

I got a range of responses to my *Facebook* status asking for 'answers on a postcard' to the request 'to make feminism more palatable'. Some expressed anger, some amusement, annoyance, incredulity, resignation, but all with lots of ideas and food for thought. There was a simultaneous emotionally charged discussion on *Facebook* about an article on feminism. People were enraged at the way an (unnamed) author had represented feminism. An academic response to the article was being prepared and will be published. But where will all the emotion, the distaste, the scornfulness, the anger and frustration go to when the response is written?

Feminist activists/theorists of the second wave feel passionately about their work. 'No-one ever promised a rose-garden,' my mother said (she was referring to marriage – and she wasn't even a self-identified feminist). 'No-one loves a feminist' – we make others feel uncomfortable, and often feel so ourselves, to the point of guilt and despair. So this isn't palatable. The sight, thought and sense of angry feminists rancorously heckling at the educational and political margins isn't nice. The student seemed concerned not just for herself, but for the two guys sitting with her. 'I started rolling my eyes with them at one point,' she confessed. I was reminded of Sara Ahmed's comment – 'my experience of being a feminist has taught me much about rolling eyes'.[171]

Emotion, women and feminism seem always to be inextricably linked. This always seems to transpire as unpleasant. Yet another of us isn't happy.

Is it simply about emotion here? I mean, as a field of study? A methodology? A theoretical framework? Is feminism emotional? More emotional? Because we're women? Yes, there are emotions in feminism, but are other 'emotional' topics/areas met with the same distaste? Religion, conflict, race/ism – do students walk out then? Or are they more inclined to work through a difficult topic because it is interesting, shocking, challenging, or because there has been positive change/is still work to do? Why is feminism so difficult? Unpalatable? Women/sex/gender figure on 'equality' bills along with race, age, ethnicity, sexual orientation, religiosity . . . yet these each have more credence within academic discourses and teaching, and non-academic fora, don't they? I mean, do people say 'can you make the holocaust more palatable?' And apartheid: 'I'd like to leave now'. Er, no. At least not in the same way. 'People' generally want to hear about atrocity and celebrate change. Why is feminism, which, conceptually at least, could be considered similar to the range of other atrocity-acknowledging concepts, be so damned unpalatable in comparison?

But who reads academic books and articles any more? How many people ever read them anyway? How do we communicate knowledge, transfer knowledge? Measured tones and methodologically water-tight. At least that's how we teach students to write/think. That's how we are supposed to write as students and scholars. Irigaray's words are always worth remembering:

> Isn't it the method, the path to knowledge, that has always also led us astray, by fraud and artifice, from woman's path, and to the point of consecrating its oblivion?[172]

Food for thought

I'm not happy.

I was reading an article the other day celebrating a female chef, of all things – a woman who can actually cook? My GOD! Well isn't that interesting – how has the kitchen been rebranded? Also, have you seen the Gillette adverts at the moment – forget 'Cleanse, tone and moisturise': it's 'PACK, REFUEL and RELOAD!' It would seem that if we put the 'How can we make feminism palatable argument' to one side and ask 'How can we make "women's things" more important and "worthwhile?"', we could cast a glance at the crisis of masculinity happening all around us. I know it's a strange link, and I haven't cemented my thinking yet, but somehow I feel Gordon Ramsay, Heston Blumenthal and Jamie Oliver are linked to the question of feminism's palatability, and not just because of the word palatable. (Perhaps because they are men, AND have 'taken over the kitchen', traditionally women's territory – certainly in the twenty-first century – apart from superstar chefs.) I think the student who asked about 'making feminism palatable' has a rather bizarre view of what feminism is – as if she/he wants to transform 'pack, refuel and reload' into 'cleanse, tone and moisturise?' – which is awful in a million, million different ways.

Making feminism palatable. This has so much to do with 'rebranding' masculinity and femininity.

I want to ask: Who is at the dinner table sending back the feminist dish? What dish do they think they are being served? What effect does a little seasoning have? Why should we make something 'palatable' in the first place? And if we do, what are the effects of that palatability? *A propos*: revenge is indeed a dish best served cold.

Why are 'women's' razors pink? I do shave my legs and I always buy the men's blue razors. I figure they must be better (I have sensitive skin) because they are made for faces. 'I'm your Venus; I'm your fire, your desire. . .' (Gillette Venus razor) – er, no. One of the few noticeable 'benefits' of menopause – so far – is that, having all my life stalwartly refused to shave my notoriously hairy legs (on feminist grounds, 'naturally'), I now have almost smooth legs. Leg hair does not work well with tights, it actually pulls. . . and I wear a lot of tights. Who invented tights, by the way? 'They' always say it must have been a man, because they're so bloody annoying, and why do we/I wear them? Sorry, this is getting personal. Does anyone else use 'men's' products, though? And for what reason? I wear men's jeans. They fit me better. My brother wears women's deodorant (he prefers the smell). Context: ex-Navy, macho, doesn't know what feminism is. Oh, but he cooks dinner for his fiancée (love the additional e here to denote female) every night, because she's tired and too young to know how to cook (!) and he works 6 am to 5 pm and so has time. And inclination, apparently. He also does all their washing...BUT HE DOESN'T KNOW WHAT FEMINISM IS....I guess this relates to rebranding...SORRY – tangents! Maybe that's why feminism is unpalatable?

Are feminists always having to say they're sorry?

Nice girls

> It is as though the thing young women most fear is being seen as critical of men.[173]

Why do feminists have to be nice? (A question McRobbie might ask). Why do feminists *especially* have to be nice?

I was not nice this week. Last week. At a conference, some 'dude' in a leather jacket (after the dinner, and many drinks) asked me if I knew who he was. I said no and asked him whether he knew who I was. I didn't know who he was and it seemed irrelevant. When he said he didn't know who I was, he asked again whether I knew who he was. I said no, but I know that you're rude. We then talked about sheep.

I'm still not happy.

Whenever I strike a rapport with myself, I feel totally lost, I feel exhausted. I go from 'why did you put the tin of beans in the fridge' to 'is my personality one that will suffice to keep me trying in this world?' It's because of these constant questions I try and keep my self-conversation to a minimum.

I find that my mind is a total nagster and only causes me stress. To destress, I discuss my tyrannical self as much as I can with people: my friends, my partner, my family, people behind shop counters and often the postman. Don't get me wrong, I don't approach the subject in an obvious way. I don't want people to think I'm crazy. With the postman, for instance, I'll usually say something like, 'I'm sorry it took me so long to open the door, I order these books for myself and then totally forget about it, I was busy in the shower or bed, or didn't hear over the TV', you probably think that is pretty normal, but what I really mean is 'I didn't order them, I don't even want them, my other self did, the one who is trying to prevent me from letting food get stale and so I fail to see why I should answer the door'. The funny thing is the postman always laughs or gives me a nod to say 'I get it', and I feel relieved, as if at least someone is on my side.

If I go clothes shopping, I mostly can't stand anything. I don't like shopping for clothes and I suspect no woman really does. I meditate on shopping because I'm always so unhappy with the things society wants us to dress in, I think women look stupid in most clothes, they are supposed to and they do. WE look stupid in dresses because men don't wear dresses, and because of the types of dresses. Women look like they should be served on a canapé, or be unwrapped on a bed, which I feel is pretty stupid. We can't even really wear trousers whenever we want without it being a wrong statement. If you are a woman wearing trousers to a ball, you may as well be a lesbian, and if you are a lesbian wearing trousers to a ball, you are a man hater or man wannabe. I'm not sure which one I prefer being the most. I try to ignore them because I think deep down when it comes to clothes I am a woman hater, and I'm not sure if I want to unwrap women or force them all into a pair of trousers and breathe a sigh of relief, you are no longer wearing garments that are restricting you or symbolising your status as second-class citizens.

I'm sure all that would happen is everyone would think there was a lesbian convention, or men would start wearing skirts as 'they are freer' and we'd be fucked again.

The point is, I don't hate women, but I hate them because men always appear better. Better dressed with better things with better jobs with better relationships with better pubs etc., and I know it's not fair. I hate women because all I want to do when I'm shopping is buy some nice practical things for myself, like a watch that actually tells the time, or a compass that doesn't house Polly Pocket, or a pocket knife that doesn't help me adjust my make-up when I want to screw something, or a pair of slippers that are not fuzzy and pink and make me look like I've been vacuuming for hours. I want to do all of these things without abandoning women, and I find it pretty hard to choose my sides.

When I was little, I had my first bike, it had one of those low bars on it to accommodate the fact women wear skirts. I hated it. It looked like absolute shit compared with my brother's. On my first bike ride with my Dad, I stopped dead track in the road. I was furious. My pedals were worse than his, I had fewer gears, I looked absolutely ridiculous, and so my Dad conceded that I could ride my brother's bike. It was a tad higher but I had good balance, and so I rode his and he rode mine. I felt much better, but every Tom, Dick and Harry bystander had something to say. 'Isn't that the wrong way round?', 'Look at that crazy pair', and I was truly mortified. I didn't see why there was such a problem. I had to ride that hideous thing and no-one said anything so why in the hell did they have a problem with anyone else?

I'll tell you why, men are not supposed to look stupid and flimsy and a lot of women want to look stupid and flimsy because it's better than accepting that you are worse off, and that's the truth!

The student wanted to be a nice girl. 'I don't want to be (seen as) one of those angry feminists.' By whom? I wondered if my lecture has been perceived as 'angry'. I certainly did not think I had been 'angry' in my delivery – though the gender of hearing, of how one hears words, ideas, concepts, is something we don't spend too much time thinking about.

When is anger ok – righteous? ranting . . .

A day in the life of angry theory

Often it seems feminism has become a kind of private passion.[174]

Perhaps like a personal opinion or, indeed, rant.

My driving licence – I was incensed to become aware that UK drivers' licences were issued to men as JOHN DOE and to women as MRS/MISS JANE

DOE...er, WHY is marital status relevant to driving? I hounded the DVLA [Vehicle Licensing Agency] and got ANGRY like a mad customer... (well a sort of polite but argumentative one) – my driver's licence now just states my name with NO TITLE. Check yours...And the DVLA said they couldn't change the format of a driver's licence just because I asked for my title to be removed. I said: you do it for men though, and suggested I would follow up with an SDA[175] action. Who knows if I could/would have. (I discovered, quite by chance, that if you put your title as Ms on a CRB[176] check request, it will go to the bottom of the pile – because the computer doesn't have a Ms category. And this is the twenty-first century.)

Ohhohohohohohoh. Here's a comment on that from an email exchange between an ex-partner and I: 'Knowing you I'd have thought you'd have asked for Mr' on the driver's licence ...

And here's another quote I found while searching for that one:

'I'm not sure what your prerogative is or indeed, should be. I have never read any books about great women – except maybe, no, there are none. Well Joan of Arc perhaps, but that was more about a schizophrenic woman ... anyway' [his words]

I am having a 'fight' with an airline just now as I could only tick one of three 'titles' – 'Mr, Miss, Mrs' – and I HAD to tick one (compulsory field). 'But I am none of these!' I tick one – hackles rising. I email them and ask for my professional title to be used instead. They refuse. I email again asking for Ms or no title. Women have the right not to be identified by marital status ... I await a reply.

Personal development 2

How have your knowledge and understanding developed during the lectures at university from September to October? How have your knowledge and understanding developed during subject seminars? What reading have you done? Any other formative experience?

Development, Development, meant – develop, meaning to develop. An achievement; something caused through a meaning to develop. Developments aren't always good, sometimes they are recognised as progress, but sometimes they just involve a realisation that what you thought of as progress was really just a misdirection, an arrogant pitfall or (as I have come to believe recently) a loss of hope.

A couple of Fridays ago I went to a vigil in Trafalgar Square – it was in memory of a guy who was 'gay bashed'– MY, doesn't the public come up with some phrases? Anyway, I always go through the same emotions when I attend these things. There is a cocktail of embarrassment, embitterment and sadness. A tacky rainbow flag shines on my face, men weep and women look tough. I look down two corridors of stereotypes and end up immensely isolated. Then I berate myself for discriminating against the discriminated.

I also feel proud at these things. Not that 'gay pride' you hear about, but an insidious pride that I can shuffle all the cards: gender, sexuality, sex, etc....and emerge unfinished – polymorphous – open to all – yet closed to anything but UNITY.

So I am at this vigil, standing with a candle – I get slightly distracted because everyone somehow didn't have the foresight to understand that hot candles eventually drip hot wax and there is a certain amount of 'ouching', candles being dropped on the floor. I have a certain amount of annoyance at this – I brought a glass jar 'just in case', I never want to be in any situation where I have no control, but these people seem to have gone in unprepared. Something about this made me awfully sad – sadder still when the organisers began to hand out plastic cups for the tea lights to reside in temporarily, and there was a sigh of gratitude and general relief of which I was no part. In fact, my glass even started to look a little showy. I looked over at the person whom I had come with, and I felt that I had managed to isolate them too. I then snapped out of myself and berated myself even further for thinking about such things and not considering why I was actually holding a candle – even a showy one – in the first place.

The speeches start . . .

> 'WE WILL NOT TOLERATE HATE.' 'Cheer! Cheer!' I thought 'tolerate' was a funny word to use, 'tolerate' and 'gay' often go together, but usually as a result of a different aim.

> 'IT'S THE JOB OF TEACHERS TO STOP THESE HATE CRIMES.'

Ha! The thoughts that struck me when I heard this; I suddenly considered myself a king of wealth, 'There are so many ideas *I* have to offer in this position, I am about to go to school and weed out the snake in the grass, the tabloid in the newspaper, the beastly heart of corruption . . .' I must have forgotten the stinging sensitivity of the earlier candle scenario and the way my cheeks went crimson and I felt the whole world shuffle away from me . . . nope – now I concentrated on my plans to educate the world!

I wrapped my scarf around me and licked the air with a determination. At this point in my story, I haven't yet learnt to be better, to think quieter, subtler thoughts. At this moment I haven't learnt to prefer the crimson girl, I haven't learnt that my ambition is flawed.

I listen to the radio a lot, watch TV, surf the web and watch a good few films. Apparently, the 'average Briton' spends half their waking hours using technology, especially media technology.[177] There's a discussion about homosexuality, one woman expressed distaste at the way a head teacher is 'flaunting' her lesbianism by being 'out' to the children. 'I don't mind what people do in their own homes but it shouldn't be publicly flaunted in this way, especially in front of children.' The 'flaunter' responds beautifully, explaining that she isn't flaunting her sexuality any more than heterosexual women who wear wedding rings or call themselves Mrs. The 'other' woman splutters incredulously, unable to comprehend this rational, reasonable response. Homophobia runs deep. I'm fed up of it.

I'm in a meeting, mostly men around me. One of the men mentions the new configuration of his subcommittee – and we've managed a 50–50 gender split, he exclaims, big grin on his face. Giggles all round. Giggles? I suppose Freud might know why. Later on I complain (nag?) about the use of the word 'chairman'. But there isn't time for the 'niceties of language'. I decide, after a momentary pause, not to say anything. Perhaps I am being 'unreasonable'. Though perhaps not as de Beauvoir infers:

> If the 'woman question' seems trivial, it is because masculine arrogance has made of it a 'quarrel'; and when quarrelling, one no longer reasons well.[178]

Getting gender right

> But wait! A place and time beyond sex and gender – wasn't this the revolutionary feminist dream?[179]

Was it just a dream? Nevertheless, a dream that inspired some clever conceptual choreography to capture the movement of gender; necessarily so, given that gender's insistent (if periodic) invisibility (once only sex seemed visible) suggests a sneaky capacity to evade theoretical detection. Yet gender has become a word, and by implication a concept, with significant intellectual and institutional currency. Anyone involved in a publicly funded institution, certainly in western contexts, or in an NGO, or in numerous government departments across the globe will be aware that gender is regarded as something deserving of serious and careful attention. At least this conclusion can be convincingly reached, given the hefty range of policies and legislation in place to make sure gender is attended to properly. Millennium Development Goal (MDG) 3 (to promote gender equality and empower women) represents the tip of the iceberg in the context of gender policy initiatives worldwide. Given the global commitment to gender, it clearly matters that we get the story about gender right. To do this, a definition is usually required: here is one example.

> The term 'gender' refers to the socially constructed (as opposed to bio-logically determined) identities of men and women. Gender is not the same as 'sex', and gender differences are not the same as sex differences. For instance, the ability of women to bear children is a sex, or biologically determined, difference from men; that women, in many societies, are responsible for food preparation and household chores is a gender, or socially constructed, difference.
>
> Early socialization assigns gender roles to men and women. These roles cut across public and private spheres; are specific to a given culture at a given time; are affected by other forms of differentiation such as race, ethnicity, and class; and can change in different sociopolitical and economic contexts within a society. World Bank literature notes that in any given society, gender

shapes the definitions of acceptable responsibilities and functions for men and women in terms of 'social and economic activities, access to resources and decision making authority'.[180]

This comprehensively encapsulates what gender 'is', and is particularly clear about the ways gender is different from sex. It also holds an implicit but profound assumption that gender is both malleable and amenable to targeted intervention. Its positioning at the beginning of a document on *Sustaining Women's Gains in Rwanda* is ostensibly an indication of great success for a country scarred by a not-so-distant mass violence. Rwanda now stands as the first country in the world where women outnumber men in parliament,[181] a statistic that led Professor Silas Lwakabamba (Rector of the National University of Rwanda) to claim that MDG 3 had been achieved.[182] Though the document and definition relates to Rwanda, the theoretical archives from which definitions like this (and this is a very familiar one) are taken are informed largely by western-based feminist scholarship, which follows distinct temporal lines: the progressivist tenor promising an incremental unfolding of gender's secrets across the centuries.

The first phase of this story about gender began by releasing gender from sex, potentially offering women respite from the normative demands of sexed minds and bodies beckoning toward untold emancipatory possibilities. Mary Wollstonecraft in *A Vindication of the Rights of Woman*[183] gestured toward this, not least through her choice of title for her book. Simone de Beauvoir articulated the idea of something deeply powerful constituting woman's difference from man in *The Second Sex*,[184] and countless feminist writers since have launched copious arguments suggesting the necessity of, and the potential for, remodelling how gender is practised most regularly when sited in the bodies, minds and practices of women. Things need not be the way they have always been. At least, this seems to be the hope.

A further iteration in this phase began to uncover the ways in which gender, perceived to be constituted as a hierarchical binary predicated on sexual difference, nourishes political agency and subjectivity but with consequent differential rewards and punishments, hinted at in the definition above. This story considers more deeply the idea that women are different, focusing on the ways these differences have been relentlessly authorised through the (allegedly) rigorous and objective practices of a broad range of distinguished disciplines and professions, including biology, craniology, medical science, political theory and psychoanalysis, as Wollstonecraft and de Beauvoir prophetically suspected.[185] Or as Trinh T. Minh-ha puts it, 'authorized voices authorize themselves to be heard'.[186]

Almost without exception, so the story goes, these differences have been presented hierarchically in that 'female difference' has been positioned as inferior to the 'male norm'; this arrangement not very conspicuous in the definition above. The deleterious effects of these differences have consistently sparked feminist anger and resistance; poignantly reflected in the frame of unreason in which such passions become entrapped. A classic feminist response, one often attached to liberal traditions, has been to ignore or downplay such differences as they have been consistently used to determine and (de)limit the spheres to which women had access.[187] The ensuing demand for inclusion into these recognised realms (paid employment, political representation, professional rewards) philosophically centred on the idea that women are essentially the same as men (the mind has no sex in this phase) with any biological/physiological differences deemed irrelevant in the context of claims to equality, rights and justice. Demand for entry into these privileged realms has been an unremitting feminist rallying cry.[188]

Rethinking the shape of gender's difference as time moved on inspired a second story, at least in the temporal grammar of western feminist theory,[189] one that suggested women's difference from men, real or constructed, still a dichotomy between the latter two here, might be the place to recover. This time, a retrieval of woman's femininity was called for, rescuing it from derision and salvaging the feminine from its inappropriate place of vilification. In the context of second-wave feminism, the reclamation of sex/gender difference owes much to radically inspired feminism which fully endorsed the binary opposition between male and female, woman and man, while simultaneously seeking to transform and revalue the meanings of 'female' and 'woman'.[190] Consequently, the female body, especially through its reproductive and sexual capacities, became a central focus of recuperation and adulation. But more than this, also included was a move to transform this reclamation into an epistemological device which might more viscerally and effectively provoke transformative political action. This philosophical move – a profound one – continues to permeate questions about what difference women might make.

A further move energised the epistemological implications of assertions of ontological difference, in all its physical, psychological and philosophical manifestations. The idea that women are, or, crucially, become different suggested the potential for far-reaching changes in the realm of the construction of knowledge and its myriad enactment in everyday life. This is not inevitably attached to essential traits; and indeed most feminist scholars distance themselves from any hint of the charge of essentialism so despised within feminism and contemporary social and political theory.[191] These ideas about 'special' difference were nurtured and developed in the generic context of feminist standpoint theory, and more specifically in the body of work associated with the ethic of care and maternal thinking.[192] What does this look like?

Girls' and women's more scattered (even with its feminised lingering attachment) thinking on morality became reinterpreted as more complex (masculinely inflected), suggesting the possibility of more sophisticated and better theories and practices of justice.[193] The seemingly universal practice of mothering (or rather mothering's imagined potential) offered the prospect of utilising the best of this in the service of theories and practices of peace.[194] All of this suggested that feminist politics that ignored or downplayed sex/gender differences injudiciously assumed women's sameness, thereby potentially condemning women to a life of constant struggle in order to compete with men on their (unequal) terms.[195] But further, in their eschewal of female difference, equality/sameness feminists missed the political opportunity to capitalise fruitfully on alternative ways of thinking and acting that this 'different voice'[196] offered. But, given increasing knowledge about the intricate, intimate, subterranean, slippery and silent ways gender weaves into minds, practices, bodies and senses, its evisceration began to appear more and more unlikely.

A third story in this temporal narrative suggests that using the feminist subject (regularly taken to be woman) for emancipatory purposes has proved to be deeply problematic, given this subject is constituted by the institutions and discourses that are deployed in the service of her liberation. If 'the feminist subject turns out to be discursively constituted by the very political system that is supposed to facilitate its emancipation',[197] politico-epistemological claims made on behalf of woman were potentially damaging rather than being beneficial, given the performative reconstitution of woman's inferior ('othered') status. A deep sense of binary inflected temporality pervades this triadic narrative: reject differences, use differences, challenge the constitutive character of the binary subject.

Is this a straight line? Is there a line which we can draw on/through from sex to gender to theory to legislation to policy to practice? Does this temporal narrative of gender slide easily through to practice, or does something else intervene? Does it help to get gender right? Perhaps not quite the right question.

The definition again

The term 'gender' refers to the socially constructed (as opposed to biologically determined [*note an almost silent inference of real sex here*]) identities of men and women. Gender is not the same as 'sex', and gender differences are not the same as sex differences. For instance, the ability of women to bear children is a sex, or biologically determined, difference from men [*still always from . . .*]; that women, in many societies, are responsible for food preparation and household chores is a gender, or socially constructed [*hints of imagined agency and subsequent movement*], difference.

Early socialization assigns gender roles [*quiet gesture of agency embedded in a 'role' and the animated if unlocated idea of 'early socialization'*] to men and women. These roles cut across public and private spheres; are specific to a given culture at a given time; are affected by other forms of differentiation such as race, ethnicity, and class [*the afterthoughts*]; and can change in different sociopolitical and economic contexts within a society. World Bank literature notes [*notes – such an empty word, especially so narratively close to the life-and-death potential inhabiting the words that follow*] that in any given society, gender shapes the definitions of acceptable responsibilities and functions for men and women in terms of 'social and economic activities, access to resources and decision making authority'.[198]

Everyone has a theory of gender.[199]

Morphing, transforming, transmuting, simultaneously common-sense, personal opinion.

Theory

> Knowledge (a certain knowledge) cannot merely be rejected (in a contaminated world where every gesture reverberates endlessly on others).[200]

> *Rejection is never quite it.*

On receipt of a complimentary copy of a textbook on IR theory, one of my colleagues expressed exasperation about the number of theories the book covered. 'Why so many?' my colleague wanted to know. 'How many do you think would be reasonable?' I asked. 'About five', he replied – though he suggested feminist theory should be one of them. Given my identification as a scholar of feminist IR, my colleague's suggestion may well have been because he was talking to me . . . as an ardent scholar of feminism, a robust discussion might follow any suggestion that IR theory should not necessarily include feminism on its list of 'main' theories. I am, of course, not implying that my colleague was disingenuous in his suggestion about the significance of feminism in teaching international politics, but I do want to linger on his vexation about the plethora of IR theories, particularly in the teaching context.

When repeating this story to colleagues, it invokes a mix of amusement, bemusement and exasperation. Only five theories! But how *do* we know which theory is the right one? Or the wrong one? And why might five seem like a reasonable number, if we agree there has to be more than one? Why not fifty-five? Or 300? How many ways of knowing or understanding do we imagine there might be, if this is what theory works with? Textbooks on international politics, especially those designed for core courses (presumably considered to cover the most significant and important aspects of international politics, otherwise optional or indeed unimaginable), would surely be impossibly cumbersome if there was an expectation of covering the 300 central theories deemed necessary to engage in order to be deemed as having properly taken a core course in international relations theory. If five is not everyone's personal 'limit', I suspect 300 might appear radically superfluous to most. Though the proliferation of theoretical approaches within the field of IR has been lengthily debated, the sense of 'too many theories' – simultaneously welcomed and bemoaned – remains palpable.

Reaching a manageable number is surely not the best criterion with regard to theory selection, though space and time often figure in books and articles that offer fleeting gestures toward significant topics, but for which 'space and time' prevent adequate attention. Which five theories would my irritated colleague choose to teach on the core undergraduate course in international politics? Queer theory? Radical feminism? Poststructuralism? Which theories might my exasperated colleague argue are potentially optional? Realism? Idealism? Constructivism? What subjects or issues might we all agree are crucial to the study of international politics? Will we assume this is self-evident, and simply begin? Or will we spend the whole course wondering what might be an appropriate subject to study, or theory to study our chosen issue with? Where might this anarchic route lead (us)?

Of course, decisions about what to include are made all the time in teaching, research and writing; the ability to make such choices is one of the skills we are impelled to acquire and impart. There is a general institutional acceptance that these choices are necessary, as the world is a pretty complex and messy place, and as scholars and students we tend to see part of our job as making some sense of this mess. And to be sure it is currently the case that when students arrive at university to study contemporary international politics, they are faced with a dizzying array of significant topics they might study. Climate change, incessant wars, gender-inspired violence, terrorism, inter-state aggression, globalised poverty, climate change, voracious capitalism, bioterrorism, sexualised cruelty, belligerent militarism: the list that might appear in contemporary teaching texts seems endless. 'Theory' becomes the crux upon which sense is made, becoming a central and necessary part of a student's career even though it consistently transpires as the thing that students mostly hate. We might wonder why this is so, given theory's important role in making sense.

Most recently I have taught courses on 'gender, sex and international politics' through the auspices of gender studies. The students on these courses come from different disciplinary backgrounds, some from 'gender studies', some from 'IR', but also sociology, anthropology, law, history and literature. The different expectations of these students and the different questions and understandings they have are immensely fascinating, revealing and challenging. As they do not share the same disciplinary 'training', they tend to ask very different questions and expect very different things. The 'IR' students, for example, often bring conversations back to the conventional theoretical anchors of IR. Though mentions of 'Realism' leave the 'non-IR' students with blank faces; they ask what it is. The explanations always sound banal and odd, nothing to do with student 'inadequacy', I think. The interdisciplinary background of my students does make teaching my courses challenging. I don't start with IR. I don't start with typologies of feminist theory. I begin with confusion (sometimes), as I don't see my role as leading 'obedient [students] out of the darkness and into the light'.[201] I bring in Socrates to help.

> 'I'm thoroughly confused; I don't know what to think!' To which Socrates replied: 'Now that you know you're confused, we can begin to progress.'[202]

The return to theory seems inevitable; but not any theory will suffice. Not any theory will fit the demands of disciplinary desires. 'High theory' is usually deemed best, perhaps especially that attached to heroic philosophers. But 'low theory' perhaps offers more, or something other that beckons a way of exceeding 'a certain knowledge' that Trinh T. Minh Ha mentions in the quotation opening this vignette. The kind of theory that inspires Stuart Hall[203] and the kind that Judith Halberstam[204] works with. Theory that hovers below and aside the radar of disciplined knowledges and that is assembled from eccentric texts. Low theory that works at many levels at once, and seeks not so much to explain or instruct, but to involve. I invite readers to become involved. I invite readers to lose their way and find their way. I invite readers to be cautious of institutional demands to order knowledge in ways already packaged to confirm the 'hierarchies of knowing that maintain the *high* in high theory';[205] a tightly catalogued world.

But IR theory is a strange beast, oftentimes presenting as beleaguered, like Truman in his escape boat. The search for truth, or 'something', keeps beckoning a heroic resolution. The attraction to and desire for grand theory remains viscerally present; grand, high theory written and presented by individual theorists of importance and canonical significance: from Waltz to Wendt. Much gets written about the flaws and failures of such authors, yet like a Scott 'of' the Antarctic, a Bear Grylls, a Ranulph Fiennes or a James Cameron, these theoretical explorers keep valiantly materialising, replete with heroic endeavours to keep striving to reach . . . though what is it they are searching for? What are they looking for? Perhaps it is a life or death situation

To unravel the riddle of a text is . . . to commit some kind of 'murder'.[206]

Crossing disciplines

The promise of interdisciplinary scholarship is that the failure to return texts to their histories will do something.[207]

Though failing to return may be problematic given . . .

. . . disciplines surely discipline. Disciplines discipline ways of producing knowledge, forms of knowledge and what counts as relevant and irrelevant knowledge, and as legitimate and illegitimate knowers. Certain things count. Lots of things don't. Some readily attain the label of expert, others will readily fail. More strongly put, 'disciplines . . . reward and punish, they statically reproduce themselves and inhibit dissent'.[208]

Interdisciplinary research promises rebellion, generously offered as a way to explore the areas within, outside and across disciplinary structures – the 'betwixt and between'.[209] Interdisciplinary research is not a new idea in the social sciences; in 1931 Margaret Mead called for 'co-operation, for cross-fertilization in our disciplines'. And earlier, in the 1920s, the United States Social Science Research Council had endorsed the idea of fostering and supporting research which involved more than one discipline.[210] More recently, the idea of interdisciplinarity has been rabidly re-energised, fast becoming the epitome of what counts as the best kind of research (particularly that produced in the university) promising more useful insights and thus deemed most important to support. Currently, certainly in the UK, interdisciplinarity has become almost a precondition for securing any research funding, at least from the Research Councils.[211]

What might be achieved with interdisciplinary research? Sara Ahmed gestures towards 'failure' in the opening quote – the failure to return . . . will 'do something'. Sliding through the ramparts which weld knowledge into a piece with a view to dishevelling the knowledge there – this might 'do something'. Yet what might it do? The synthesising of disciplinary expertise to return more 'useful insights' veers solidly toward universalist thinking which is inevitably accompanied by a host of difference-obliterating epistemologies and ontologies. And the requirement that this work advance specific social, economic, political and cultural agendas set by governments of all persuasions suggests that an instrumental, economistic rationale buttresses contemporary calls for interdisciplinary work. Though 'suggest' is a trepid word here.

There is something deeply disheartening about this. But then it is not difficult to feel disheartened by the contemporary university; I speak in the context of the UK, though it is the case that the entrenchment of neoliberal managerialism, perhaps at the icy heart of current desires for interdisciplinarity, has global import. At its worst, the university is a place where 'everyone mistrusts everyone',[212] where knowledge has morphed into information collation, a place that has become a breeding ground for 'killing thinking',[213] where academics have become gripped by discursive practices to which many are so vehemently opposed, and where compliant policing has become the norm.[214] It's hard not to despair, perhaps especially given the rebellious inferences that 'crossing disciplines' promised: feminist anti-disciplinary imaginations is one example.

Moving from the justice projects of the streets in the 1960s and 1970s,[215] feminist-inspired knowledge entered western universities offering experimental ideas about teaching: opening up curriculum design (more participatory), disturbing pedagogical principles (disrupting traditional hierarchies of power), encouraging team-teaching (moving away from the idea of the sole academic imparting/professing their individualised expertise), and radically expanding course content (working from and with the idea that the 'personal is political').[216] Perhaps weighted down by the force of conventional disciplinary authority and expectations – 'discipline based pedagogy demands the presence of a master'[217] – what has disappointingly tended to transpire is less a 'crossing' of disciplines but rather a working 'side-by-side'.[218] An additive model of knowledge (multidisciplinarity perhaps) emerges from this which has not delivered the kinds of transformative or innovative knowledges hoped for by feminists.[219] Though perhaps interdisciplinarity necessarily remains elusive in practice, given its 'betwixt and between-ness'. There is an ethereality to this that speaks to the luminosity of disciplinary boundaries, offering a tremulous promise of prising apart concepts and exposing thoughts, ideas and desires which may not mean the same thing at all. But comfort beckons as Stuart Hall astutely suggests that 'one of the main functions of a concept is that they give us a good night's sleep'.[220]

There's a scene in the film *Lost in Translation*[221] which imparts a sense of the shaky spaces across and within meanings. The main female character Charlotte and her husband John (who are not getting on) are in the hotel lobby when a woman appears (Kelly) who seems to be very well acquainted with John. What follows is an animated and warm conversation between Kelly and John. At the end of the conversation, Kelly infers that Evelyn Waugh is a woman. Kelly then leaves.

> CHARLOTTE Evelyn Waugh?
>
> JOHN What?
>
> CHARLOTTE Evelyn Waugh was a man.
>
> [John shrugs.]
>
> JOHN Oh, c'mon, she's nice. Not everyone went to Yale.
>
> Charlotte shoots him a look.[222]

Creatively, Avery Gordon suggests that interdisciplinarity moves us towards creating a new object that belongs to no-one. Working with Roland Barthes' insights, she suggests it is not enough to choose a subject and gather around it two or three disciplines. Or, for Karl Popper, 'we are not students of some subject matter, but students of problems, and problems may cut right across the borders of any subject matter or discipline'.[223] Yet isn't collecting a 'subject' and gathering around two or three (social) sciences exactly one of the primary ways interdisciplinarity is currently institutionally imagined?

Perhaps the merging of IR and feminism qualifies as interdisciplinary work. Though if I hold IR in a place and weave and knit the insights of feminism into it, what will I have done? What will the 'something' be that is meant to emerge? The disciplinary authority of IR perhaps holds 'something' at bay. If I hold feminism in a place and offer analyses of international politics, what will this do? Will 'something' other emerge? Here the different hues and tones of feminism might materialise. Will I know what international political issues to focus on? Will I take for granted the people and events that the discipline of IR foregrounds? Will I, instead, focus on events, people and issues that seem removed from what we know IR to be interested in? Is this the choice I have to make? No happy endings, perhaps.

Much of the film *Lost in Translation* focuses on the relationship between a young woman (Charlotte, played by Scarlett Johansson) and a middle-aged man (Bob, played by Bill Murray), each lost and looking, yearning for 'something'. A format that might easily slide into a clichéd sexual liaison between the two, in this film it does not. Instead, the focus of the film strays from the phallogocentric gaze and we see what Charlotte sees as she meanders through the streets of Tokyo. And nothing much really happens, some talking, drinking, dancing, laughing and being lonely. Pretty ordinary.

> The impure subject cannot but challenge hegemonic divisions and boundaries.[224]

Transformation

> Not only does the future not necessarily follow from the past, the past could be other than it was.[225]

The temporal gesture here offers potential for thinking transformation otherwise.

Transformation has a revolutionary, masculinist feel to it; taking hold of something, as if by the scruff of the neck, and reworking, reshaping it into something recognisably and radically different. If the model of effective resistance is coded masculine, Sandra Harding wonders if we 're-code ourselves as the great feminist resisters'[226] sneaking heroic individualism in the through the back door of theory?

It's quite easy to miss the stop for Memento Park[227] a few miles outside Budapest, though the driver of the local bus, aware that a motley range of tourists are on this bus route, loudly announces our destination –'Memento Park!' As we get off the bus, Stalin's boots on the roof-top catch my eye (Figure 5).

Inside the park – though more of a piece of waste land, no heroic grand landscaping here – there are an assorted range of statues and plaques from Hungary's

FIGURE 5   Cast of Stalin's boots

Author's photograph (© Marysia Zalewski)

FIGURE 6 'Soviet Man'

Author's photograph (© Marysia Zalewski)

Communist past. The one regularly used to advertise the park to draw tourists is 'Soviet Man' (Figure 6).

It is gargantuan. It surely evokes stories of revolution, of masculinity, of vigour and imagined glory. No visible trace of femininity here, I think, except though oppositional imagination, though mothers of men usually figure somewhere. I attach a postcard of this statue to my office door, next to a picture of Michelangelo's sculpture *David* from a film still from *The Children of Men*.[228] Both are, if differently, impressive, but in the settings in which they are presented, they are both 'out of place'. The inspirational if gloatingly conventional terrorising stance of a generic idea of 'Soviet Man' becomes almost enchantingly quaint in his new setting, one ripe for tourist photo opportunities. The intense, spirited masculinity of David, in what Žižek enthuses is an 'elegant scene' in *The Children of Men*, also metamorphoses into something else.[229] Perhaps into nothing, or into more apparent emptiness, given that the world in which its context is secured is no more.

When I ask people what IR might look like if it was transformed by feminism, or what a (feminist) transformed set of international political practices would look like, my questions remain unanswered. My questions are too gargantuan, too demanding, too impossible. And it's not as if I could answer them either, though I am not expecting (or wanting) an 'answer' as such. The difficulty of thinking about the question and its lingering emotive touch is interesting and helpful in itself. Though it would, perhaps, as Judith Butler suggests,[230] be easier if we could spell out very clearly what the ideal relations between genders should be, or what gender should really be like, and consequently we could tell when justice or equality had been reached, or when transformation had been completed.

Butler's suggestion might be perceived as a little odd given that feminists *have* laboriously spelled out what is wanted, even provided specific 'shopping lists'. Liberal feminists, for example, are understood to have demanded that, minimally, women should not be treated worse than men, and have provided copious examples of inequities in this regard. Policy or legislatively oriented scholarship or practice usually presents a clear view of what is wrong and what results are expected or desired to achieve change. Think about this United Nations announcement relating to women and gender: the UN Secretary-General Ban Ki-moon stated with much clarity that: 'I have made gender equality and the empowerment of women one of my top priorities – from working to end the scourge of violence against women, to appointing more women to senior positions, to efforts to reduce maternal mortality rates.'[231] Three very clearly spelled out end results here. As such, it should be exceedingly obvious what feminist transformation means or what it would look like.[232]

Clarity is also on offer in the field of international relations. The transformational intentions of feminist international relations are well detailed by Kimberly Hutchings in her 2008 essay.[233] Commenting on the commemoration of twenty years of scholarship on gender and international relations, she describes the transformational project of feminist international relations as being directed toward the hegemonic powers that have dominated both the academy and the practices of international politics. Specifically, she temporally and spatially places these intentions in this way.

> When the project of bringing feminist insights to bear on international politics was formulated it had a clear-cut set of goals: to demonstrate how gendered relations of power sustain contemporary world politics and political economy; to deconstruct dominant masculinist conceptual frameworks; and to work to transform both the academy and political practice in the light of feminist values.[234]

This is a very ambitious set of aims, though with hindsight transforming the academy and political practice armed only with 'insights' and 'values' appears, perhaps, excessively ambitious. Yet Hutchings's narrative about feminist IR of the late 1980s is very well confirmed in the disciplinary literatures (which is where feminist IR is usually tracked). However, by 1998 Hutchings suggests that the feminist project, mirroring movements within feminist theory more generally,[235] had changed. 'There is less sense of the project of reconstructing a social science and more of the difficulty of treating gender as a straightforward way in which to understand social and political phenomena.'[236] The change over the decade suggests that 'reconstruct-ing social science' (the social science being IR in this instance) came to be seen as unrealistic, indeed unrealisable. (Had we got something wrong? Missed some-thing?) For one reason, gender transpired to be much more complex than initially perceived by those working in IR, functioning in much more labyrinthine ways than imagined, persistently evading detection and capture.

Though I understand very well the temporal narrative that Hutchings describes about feminist movement through IR, and the change in tempo, focus and strate-gies it indicates, I am curious about its consolidation and ready acceptance. And even more curious about what it tells us about how we think about transformative change and the place and pace of feminism (in IR). For some the place of feminism has transpired as overly significant and the pace of feminist change too swift, turn-ing to the military (specifically western militaries) for evidence of this. This should be a good example, given that militaries both reflect and produce gendered/sexed divisions and figure highly on feminist/IR theoretical and empirical agendas. Has feminism transformed the military?

Francis Fukuyama begins his article on 'Women and the evolution of world politics' with a story about a 'Machiavellian' struggle for power by an 'ageing alpha male' chimpanzee.[237] Moving to discuss what he anthropomorphically describes as 'murders' of another group of chimpanzees, Fukuyama concludes, after some 300 words or so, that 'female chimps have relationships; male chimps practice realpoli-tik'.[238] Another move takes Fukuyama to argue that men will not become (much) less violent than they ever have been (regardless of what feminists want) because violence is in men's nature. His overall conclusion is that (western) feminists do the world of international politics a disservice, particularly in regard to the military. Given women's less violent nature (and the visceral expectation that hot-blooded 'other' men in more masculinised militaries are waiting to pounce – the swooping pose of the gargantuan Memento Park statue gives a sense of this imagination), western militaries will appear weak and vulnerable especially in those 'other' areas of the world 'run by young, ambitious, unconstrained men'.[239] An intriguing analysis, though one that offers no evidence of any change in gender regimes, much less transformation to standard heteronormative gendered attachments and imaginations, or to other violent markers of difference.

In the 2011 film *Rise of the Planet of the Apes*, the origin of the metamorphos-ing of apes into speaking, thinking, acting ('human') beings[240] is revealed. In com-mon with many early twenty-first-century 'blockbuster' movies, a sense of impending apocalyptic futures if humans do not change their ways in regard to people, animal and planetary exploitation is offered as a less-than-subtle warning. Though one perhaps easily forgotten in the mesmerising mire of CGI and motion-capture technology. The central chimpanzee character (named Caesar) in *Rise of the Planet of the Apes* enacts a touching and recognisable range of emotions and human behaviours, feelings and struggles, as do his fellow apes. Compassion, hate, bitterness, loyalty, love, cunning, intelligence: just like 'us'. Interestingly, if not surprisingly, gender seems irrelevant and the gender regime of this new form of 'humanity' is cinematically unremarkable and unquestionable. Action and agency are masculine marked, with females (re)presenting as love/sex interest and reproducers. That apes might be perceived as 'human', yet female agency and activity are consistently subsumed into the quagmire of invisible gender is telling; telling of the 'ongoing manic project of the renaturalization of heterosexuality and the stabilization of relations between men and women'.[241]

There is a touching scene and something of a Lacanian 'mirror moment' when Caesar catches his own reflection. Having just rescued one of his 'human owners' from attack by another man, the ensuing *fracas* raises questions about Caesar's place in the world of humans. He looks at himself in a full-size mirror. He exudes disgust at his nonhuman-ness. He does not look like the others (the other humans). The pretend human heart of the film is exposed in this false moment. In our 'looking at primates we know they look back'.[242] In this scene the 'looking back' seems, as it so often is, stolen by white hu(man)ity. The image of the 'dominant white male' is viscerally *not* reflected back. The racial inflection is stark. The murder of whom are tellers of authorised knowledges afraid?

Transformation: it's a word and idea with significant aspirational and bold ambitions. It has magical connotations, inspiring hope that something ugly will be transformed into something beautiful.

The struggle is also between one fiction and another.[243]

The morning after

Time and direction are both forces that work together to crush willpower.[244]

In her book *The Morning After: Sexual Politics at the End of the Cold War*, Cynthia Enloe begins with a story about a woman, Esmeralda, who has taken her IUD out 'now that the war is over'.[245] A pregnancy in wartime seemed to Esmeralda to be politically irresponsible (the personal as always political), yet in the postwar period she 'was being urged by men in the political leadership to imagine her post-war life as one devoted to being a good mother'.[246] Things, it seems, are always 'different' for women, not least at the endings, beginnings and middles of wars. The political/national needs change Esmeralda's mind, body and heart with some speed. Enloe uses the sexually imbued metaphor of 'the morning after' to invite a (re) imagining of how wars, both hot and cold, 'like love affairs, don't simply end'.[247] This imagery conjures up a cocktail of mixed feelings, perhaps regret and confusion, but also potentially hope and possibility. 'Mornings after' emerge as times 'for puzzling, for sorting things out, for trying to assess whether one is starting a new day or continuing an old regime'.[248] What happened the morning after feminism? Did something new begin, or just the continuation of the same old regime? Or something else entirely?

I eventually persuaded my colleague in regard to the disputed 'IR' undergraduate dissertation.[249] The student had written a feminist analysis of the United Nations and, although my colleague's initial reaction was that it was a feminist critique/ polemic and therefore not properly set against 'IR perspectives', we eventually agreed it was appropriate to award a first-class mark. The view that robustly argued feminist scholarship might be perceived as polemical is not, I think, best understood as simply being about individual idiosyncratic evaluation or institutional anachronism. The heat and passion of feminist arguments, which frequently draw explicit and stark attention to pain and violence, especially where pain and violence are not otherwise seen, readily conjure emotive readings and readings of emotion. However measured and controlled the writing, the emotion cannot fail to be read, or felt. 'Feeling one's work'[250] perhaps remains institutionally suspect, surprising given this is not limited to feminist work – it only appears this way. But still, given the length of time feminist scholarship has been part of the IR theory lexicon (one can't now really imagine a generic IR theory text without a chapter on feminism/gender), what stops feminism becoming an 'IR perspective' in its own right? To address this question, the story of feminism is once again hurled back to 'beginning'.

★★★★★★★★★★★★★★★★

FIGURE 7   Cheshire Cat

http://en.wikipedia.org/wiki/File:Cheshire_Cat_Tenniel.jpg

'Would you tell me, please, which way I ought to go from here?'

'That depends a good deal on where you want to get to' said the Cat.[251]

It seems that the main thing most people remember about the Cheshire Cat in *Alice in Wonderland* is its peculiar vanishing act: 'vanishing quite slowly, beginning with the end of the tail, and ending with the grin which remained some time after the rest of it had gone'.[252] This was probably unnerving enough for Alice, added to which was the rather inscrutable reply to her very polite question, making her rather ordinary question sound slightly irrational.

★★★★★★★★★★★★★★★★

Feminism arrived into IR with enthusiasm. Despite mounting dismay at incremental revelations about the gender secrets of the discipline, the sense that IR was ready, intellectually and empirically, for feminist work was palpable. Conventionally dated back to the late 1980s,[253] subsequent publications exuded animated belief in the possibility of change.[254] As radical insights began to flood out of feminist work which insisted that women mattered, one wonders what IR scholars imagined might happen consequently to the discipline with such a redesignated focus. The appearance centre stage of the ostensible epitome of femaleness in a discipline usually fixated on masculinely saturated images of presidents and prime ministers, wars and violence, and leaders being 'eyeball to eyeball' was/is intriguing.

The gender secrets proliferated: love, sex and death were not simply intimately related, but were intertwined in and through the theories and practices of international politics. Housewives, fishwives, film stars, mothers and sex workers all began to make an explicit appearance on the IR scene. Women, it seemed, really mattered.[255] An extraordinary claim in fact, though the power of it often diminished given repeated simplifications of the complexities knitting this gendered construction into a piece. The philosophical and theoretical archives upon which feminists construct their work was shrewdly (re)packaged for a recalcitrant audience. In a popular teaching text, V. Spike Peterson and Anne Sisson Runyan developed an innovative conceptual tool for IR students and scholars unconvinced of the worth of gender.[256]

Using the metaphor of a lens, Peterson and Sisson Runyan demonstrated that seeing the world of international politics through an alternative (gendered) focus facilitated the 'seeing' of depictions of international politics alternative to those conventionally offered. In the first and second editions of their book, they included a picture to illustrate how the gender-lens metaphor works. It shows two giant-like (in size) white men (with miserable expressions) each wearing a western-style man's suit, shirt and tie, and both wearing spectacles with blacked-out lenses. In front of one of the men is a 'normal' size white woman (not giant-size) standing on a ladder, wearing an apron, a scarf on her head and carrying a bucket (one is led to assume she is a 'cleaning lady'). She is shown on top of the ladder reaching up to clean the spectacles the two men are wearing and working on the second lens of the first man's glasses, having, we assume, wiped the first lens clean. The second man's spectacles are still completely darkened. The attached caption explains this is a 'graphic depiction of how lenses affect fields of vision and how women at the bottom of the world politics hierarchy are struggling to make elite men see the world more clearly'.[257] Is this how feminist IR looks?

The idea of gender as a lens is such an interesting example of feminist work in IR, epistemologically, methodologically, politically and temporally. In all these ways, the link with what we might, and do, call radical feminism[258] is clear. We can see this in the persistent insistence that it is crucially important to centralise women's lives, particularly given women's ongoing place on many of the 'bottom rungs'[259] of significance or international care. And women's lives for their own sakes, not for the benefit of the economy (a 'good' which runs like a steel rod through UN legislation and rhetoric), or some other more generalised 'larger' benefits (such as democracy). But the feminist claim is that without this concentrated focus on women we will not see these 'other' worlds of international politics, as they are methodologically and politically obscured when we fail to look through gender(ed) lenses.

What does feminist IR look like now? Like this?

FIGURE 8 'Corporate ladders'

Liberation, when? The abolition of gender, when? Perhaps things will improve eventually, but what accounts for the delay?[260]

The current positioning of 'feminist IR' is multiply represented. There are romanticised tales of how everything has changed.[261] Other stories suggest that feminism remains on the margins of IR, and dispute remains as to whether this is negative or positive, or indeed something other.[262] Some suggest feminism was truly never fully formed or robust enough for IR, or too theoretically immature, or too minimal, implied by feminism's overt empirical and theoretical concern with women.[263] Other versions avert the issue of whether or not feminism has made a difference to IR.[264] And still other stories imply that feminist work on the injury of gender both reinstates the injury through a persistent attachment and attention to that injury, as well as hoisting gendered injury onto others, specifically men and transgender people. Subsequently, some infer that a deep sadness, even a kind of pathological melancholia, is attached to feminism.[265] As such, feminism's time is arguably over, though it might have been that feminism could never be enough. Still other versions imply the ongoing and still real possibility and necessity of achieving change within IR.[266] And further still, other narratives within the discipline imply that there has been a dissipation of feminist scholarship suggestive of postfeminist incorporation or, conversely, indicative of feminist embeddedness within IR.[267] What a picture: melancholic attachment to the injury of gender, a vibrant and energetic force, an ineffective set of theories and politics, a necessary force for change, a disappearing entity, a marginalised discourse, an irrelevant discourse, an indispensible set of theories and practices. A wonderful, evasive concoction. Perhaps 'something' else entirely transpired the morning after; though I think Irigaray is on to something when she counsels women to 'stop trying'.[268]

The subtitle of this book references a Surrealist thematic – *Exquisite Corpse* – which I write about in the second vignette and work with tangentially throughout. My choice of cover image also draws on Surrealist imaginations and subjectivities, specifically through the work of artist Dorothea Tanning.[269] Tanning oftentimes works with domestic imagery, kinds of 'homeliness', the consequent imagery in her paintings showing an acute awareness of what is visible along with an attentiveness to the unconscious and barely traceable forces that animate our worlds.[270] Fascinated by the clarity of words and the elusiveness of memory, Tanning works at the juncture of 'visible reality and a convulsive emotionalism that is less easily defined'.[271] Drawing on her own ordinary worlds – 'my dreams are bristling with objects which relate to nothing in the dictionary' – she described her home town as a place where 'nothing happens but the wallpaper'. To recall the lines of Alice Fulton's poem

Nothing will unfold for us unless we move toward what looks to us like nothing:[272]

FIGURE 9 *Eine Kleine Nachtmusik*
© ADAGP, Paris and DACS, London 2012

But the wallpaper is not without life or secrets, at least this is how Tanning depicts it in her 1942 painting *Jeux d'enfants*.[273] In this, 'terrible little girls' are violently tearing the wallpaper off the walls – 'tearing a porthole in the bourgeois domestic order'– revealing the house as a feminine body beneath the wallpaper. Breathing life into the sense that 'bodies don't end at the skin', the body behind the wallpaper is intimately conjoined to the bodies of the girls, the imagery is suggestive of umbilical cords. Visceral corporeal connections are on show here. A bloody image, even violently suicidal, as the painting infers the expiration of at least one of the girls. At least this is one reading.

It is Tanning's *Eine Kleine Nachtmusik* (1943) that I choose as the cover image and part methodological inspiration for this book. There is a different kind of beautiful dissidence and dissonance in this painting. Toying with conventional Surrealist fascination with Lewis Carroll's *Alice*, Tanning's discordant artistry appropriates the idea of Alice in subversive ways. *Eine Kleine Nachtmusik* is serene and disturbing, uncertain and nonchalant, quietly violent, yet avoiding the emotional excess of irrationality and chaos that surrounds the Alice of *Wonderland*. And then there's the enticing light through the open door. Tanning's thoughts are disturbing.

Behind every appearance lie violent winds.[274]

Feminism's time

> ... the very nature of human memory lies beyond scientific objectivity.[275]

Despite its abstract character, invisibility and relativity, time offers heavyweight measures to help shape feminism's way through IR. From feminism's timely arrival in the midst of social and intellectual commotion in the early 1980s, arriving to dishevel the adequacy of IR theories to make pedagogical space for the injection of gender theory, through to intermittent demonstrations of the changes feminism scholarship has (or has not) brought to IR, ideas about time and its accompanying tools help feminism to measure up. But there seems to be, paradoxically perhaps, some distance between the cool objectivity of measuring and calculating through and with time's tools and the emotion engendered by the idea of time's passing.

Images of emotion are not in short supply in international politics. In the various iterations of this work, news reports have persistently brought to attention images of the dead, the diseased and the dying. Some instances: the anguished survivors and agonised rescuers in the aftermath of the earthquake in China's Sichaun Province (May 2008); the suffering of the neglected victims of Cyclone Nargis in Burma (May 2008) accompanied by numerous expressions of righteous (western) horror at the initial reluctance of the Burmese Junta to allow foreign aid into the country. Time moves on, and more recent images in 2010 show the devastations caused by the earthquake in Haiti and the floods in Pakistan saturating our plasma screens. In 2011 the earthquake and consequent tsunami in Japan; the revolutions in the streets of Tunisia, Egypt and Libya – 'the Arab Spring'; the 'Occupy' protests in the wake and presence of the global financial crisis and ongoing corporate greed; the bloody violence in Syria in 2012 – all matters of international political significance assailing our ocular senses.

But who or what notices the passing of time? Clocks? Buildings? Wars? These answers don't really make sense. Though wars may end and start and start and end, or, of course, simply merge until we don't notice the difference any more, but wars don't feel time. Clocks surely measure time, at least we make clocks to serve this purpose, but they too, we assume, don't feel or know time. Buildings exhibit the passage of time which we can see and feel and make judgments about: 'sheared-off buildings are almost as eloquent as bodies in the street'.[276] But it is the subjective experience of time, or rather the way time constitutes subjectivity, which perhaps makes most sense. This constitution of time makes its most obvious mark on the bodies of people, and bodies of theory.

Things change with time, yet there is a constant bombardment of seemingly endless, relentless, inexorable stories of brutal rapes and sexual violence in conflict and war zones. Drastic events continue to rupture the flow of lives, and since the shattering actions in September 2001 the western study of international politics has been indulgently and parochially immersed in the politico/emotive reverberations of those attacks on the USA, most especially on the World Trade Center: images of the fragile burning towers, the 'falling man', and the ultimate devastating crashing of these gargantuan monuments of western capitalism to the ground – to dust – these images continue ethereally to haunt and fuel political/personal imaginations and fears. Responses to all these events are acceptably and unsurprisingly emotional. Yet the ensuing political actions, and supporting theories, have to be rational, practical and effective. Time, reason and theory meet, but they are not alone in this relationship: emotion sutures the narratives.

Time, and how it is used in everyday lives, has become increasingly important in twenty-first-century, fast-paced, westernised lifestyles. The ubiquitous phrase '24/7' indicates how time has speeded up. More can now get done in smaller and smaller amounts of time; this is the idea, at least. Multi-tasking (once masquerading as a natural feminine gift) has taken violent hold on lives. I try and get students to think about time, and I sometimes use film to help me do this. I ask, if feminist IR were a film, which one do they think it would it be? Their answers are varied, though they usually involve some 'obvious' IR agenda. Each film choice oozes gender imagery and allusion, each film is suggestive of movement, and imagined futures and pasts. And possibilities of the present.

G.I. Jane is a film feminist IR scholars have often used, as it seems to raise important issues for feminist IR. Its release in the 1990s temporally aligns it with some of what have come to be regarded as the early developments of feminist IR. Furthermore, it sits nicely within a conventional international political frame, given a storyline which revolves around the US military and ultimately threats to national (US) security. It can be a great film for teaching feminist IR, as it surely does drip with gender imagery and allusion, strong women acting 'just like' men (whether as a successful US Navy Seal or as a corrupt politician), though illustrating the significance of the relationship between these enactments of gender and the 'real world' is consistently pedagogically difficult. The narrative of equal rights in the film (always for women to be treated the same as men) dovetails well with the public perception of feminism, particularly in a US/western context. And as the film draws to its finale, the ultimate displacement of gender in light of the need to rescue courageous US soldiers in a 'Middle-Eastern' country neatly (re) positions gender into an apparent non-place; as watchers we are comfortably drawn back to the 'bigger picture'.[277] The (gender-equality) battle has (seemingly) been won. Now it's time for the real thing, the real battle, at least in the film's narrative. Just like (IR) life.

G.I. Jane is a late 1990s film; time has moved on. Has the feminist battle in IR been won? If such a transformed IR were a contemporary film, which one would it be?

There is no shortage of women leaders in post-9/11 US/western/Hollywood films and in popular television programmes: Meryl Streep as CIA boss Corrine Whitman in the film *Rendition*,[278] President Allison Taylor in the series *24*, the German Chancellor in the film *2012*.[279] The all-encompassing disaster movie *2012* (and cinema-goers dearly love disaster movies)[280] is one of several post-apocalyptic films which marked the filmic transition from the first to the second decade of the twenty-first century; others include *The Road*[281] and *The Book of Eli*.[282] Each of these post-apocalyptic films dabbles with many of the more visible international political concerns of twenty-first-century western publics (as filtered through the hegemonic cinematic lens of the USA), in something of a post-post-9/11 atmosphere. These and earlier films such as *The Day After Tomorrow*,[283] *The Day the Earth Stood Still*,[284] *War of the Worlds*,[285] *I Am Legend*,[286] *The Invasion*,[287] *Children of Men*,[288] *Rise of the Planet of the Apes*[289] all invoke and deploy (if variably) neoliberalism's hypnotic narrative about the necessity of action – now![290] They all invoke some of the consequences of not taking seriously the mistakes of now, imagining for us a future which might be unforgiving and unlivable; as if this was not already a reality for many.

The 'end-of-the-world' scenarios, consumed eagerly by publics, either from some 'outer world' invasion or an 'inner world' catastrophe, are not new stories in literature, art, film or poetry. But we can look to the populist revival of these kinds of imaginings, and the hopes and fears they portray, to (re)imagine feminism's time-bound aspirations of a transformed IR. How does gender figure in these post-apocalyptic films? The gender of state leaders seems to transpire as irrelevant. Even if the numbers of women political leaders have increased exponentially in some examples, as has been hoped for by some liberal feminists, also by some standpoint-inspired feminists, the difference they make seems ungendered, or perhaps unfeminist. Imagine that Sara Ruddick's philosophical analysis of the work of mothering[291] had been as seriously positioned as Samuel Huntingdon's 'The clash of civilizations?'[292] or Francis Fukuyama's *The End of History and the Last Man*.[293] It isn't that Huntingdon's or Fukuyama's work has avoided criticism, far from it, but what might be the possibilities for international political practices around war, peace and post-conflict/peace-building scenarios if work drawing on feminist standpoint theory and radical imaginations about ethics had been (truly) transformatory – repositioning thought and emotion?

Ruddick's philosophical ruminations about the possibilities for peace led her to theorise about 'mothering'. Her work has a very important place in the archives of feminist theory, yet there remains something of a deeply transient and peripheral character to it. Though Huntingdon's 'clash of civilizations' thesis seems more eas-ily to accrue timeless significance, regardless of uncompromising and violent ideo-logical disagreements surrounding it (perhaps especially as this work taps easily into popular imaginations about 'us' and 'them'), Ruddick's meditations on mothering and peace materialise as spatially bound through and in time. Temporally attached to an earlier grammar of feminism, the work is easily displaced within the confines of hegemonic knowledges. That her feminist thinking becomes temporally and spatially frozen in frigid time slices is the interesting point here, the cold, petrifying movement of such ideas.

Perhaps my discussion assumes too little about feminism, as both liberal feminism and elements of standpoint and radical feminism surely *have* been taken seriously. Gender equality legislation abounds, if varied across the globe, but mostly has the aim of ensuring, for instance, that women have equal opportunities in employment or political representation. International legislation and initiatives have become increasingly robust, from the Beijing Platform for Action in 1995[294] to the range of UN Security Council Resolutions.[295] In 2009, Mme Irina Bokova became the first female Director-General of UNESCO in sixty-three years. One of her first acts as Director-General elect was to make the opening comments on a roundtable on gender, convened to mark the fifteenth anniversary of the Beijing Platform for Action.[296] The (female) chairperson noted with some pleasure that this was the first time the room had been full. Perhaps the time for feminism has come (and gone). An arrival and a departure.

In the films *The Book of Eli*, *The Road*, *The Day After Tomorrow* and *2012*, the actions of individuals are paramount. These films are saturated with narratives of heroic rescue/sacrifice in the face of horrific circumstances. In *The Road*, dignified, masculinely inflected heroism stands side by side with relentless instances of violation, greed, exploitation, the pinnacle of human violence, perhaps culminating in the 'cellar scene' where living, if barely, human beings are being stored as food, some partially devoured while still 'alive'. As in the Nazi death camps, gender here, perhaps, ceases to matter. There is always a point in time, it seems, at which gender will stop, where attention to gender seems not just trivial, but obscene. Surely we have heard enough about gender? But yet

> Are there still untold stories about feminist scholarship in International Relations?[297]

Do you like women?

> My brother used to tell me that the place for a woman is either at home or in the grave. He said: 'If you leave the house, I'll cut off your head and put it on your chest.'[298]

Politics

> *Mid-afternoon, just in from lunch,*
> *he will stop ostentatiously*
> *in front of your desk*
> *and say, to no-one in particular,*
> *What have I got to do*
> *to get that on the end of my prick?*

That evening, over a drink or two
with your steady boyfriend,
you won't know who he thinks he is . . .
when another will sit down, grip your haunch
behind everybody's back
and suggest that you two meet later that week, for dinner, and some fun afterwards –
in those, or in so many words.
Your boyfriend will agree that it's grotesque.
He'll wonder where it will end.
It ends in a room with a single naked bulb,
your naked body they will stretch
between electrode
and switch.
On it they will etch
a map of desire.
And will you be the more betrayed
by whimpers, shouts, the steady trick-
ling of yourself onto the floor,
or – when one of them, sucking ostentatiously
on the remains of a joint and extinguishing the rest
just below your left breast,
slams back the bolt
of a hand gun he has slid
cold inch by inch, half-way inside –
by your involuntary spasm of diarrohea?[299]

Alan Jenkins

The poem brings violence up close. The violence is like a crescendo, unexpected, shocking. Does it have any bearing on readers' lives? Do we simply want to turn away?

'Do you like women?'

This is a question that one of my colleagues asks her students in her feminist IR class. The range and tone of answers (and the silences) must be fascinating. Why does she ask this question? Would asking, 'do you like men?' seem appropriate in any other ('regular') IR theory class? And how different either question would seem if asked in a regular IR theory class. It surely is the case that oftentimes feminism is about caring for women, and caring for the pain women suffer because of gender. Feminists mourn women, they mourn the continuum of their gender-induced loss and pain, and the loss of liveable female lives. These losses are extraordinarily and exhaustingly well documented by feminists both within the discipline of IR and in the everyday world of international politics. And to invoke the timelessness of these violent losses, feminists have persistently drawn attention to the relentless tradition of violating women. Breathing life into the long dead, hoping to provoke change.

At the Ohio Women's Rights Convention in 1851, Sojourner Truth, a woman who had been born into slavery, made a speech which has accrued something of iconic status in feminist theory. Truth's speech and her life have regularly been used to impart a sense of the historic legacy and depth of violences done to women and the ongoing fight for women's rights. I have spoken about Sojourner Truth in class many times. Truth's words, at least as they have been represented, resonate powerfully. They (usually) do make us feel something. Here is an extract from her speech.

> That man over there says that women need to be helped into carriages, and lifted over ditches, and to have the best place everywhere. Nobody ever helps me into carriages, or over mud-puddles, or gives me any best place! And ain't I a woman? Look at me! Look at my arm! I have ploughed and planted, and gathered into barns, and no man could head me! And ain't I a woman? I could work as much and eat as much as a man – when I could get it – and bear the lash as well! And ain't I a woman? I have borne thirteen children, and seen most all sold off to slavery, and when I cried out with my mother's grief, none but Jesus heard me! And ain't I a woman?[300]

Reading Truth's words, we could say she describes herself as both man and woman, but simultaneously neither, or not perceived as either. She emotively, passionately demonstrates the fragile, fluid nature of sexed and raced identity, and the embedded violence committed through and with these identities. On this reading, we might think of 'ain't I a woman' as an exercise in, or an example of, deconstruction, though it has more typically been used as a modernist feminist plea for the rights of women. The spirit of the Enlightenment has oxygenated Truth's prose down the centuries. Her ardent enragement at the life meted out to her as a black/slave/ woman engenders the sense that her life did not have to be so hard, it *could* have been different, it could have been better if only more had been known.

Sojourner Truth's speech has become an important part of the feminist archive regularly used to demonstrate the constitutive and damaging power of gender and race and to make retrospective sense of the making of this woman's life, and of the lives of black women born in the centuries after her. Read through the legislative and philosophical prism of modernist politics, a powerful sense of agency emerges, strongly accompanied by vivid expectations of change. How could anyone fail to be moved, intellectually, politically, by Truth's words? Though it might be prudent to ask if (all?) women's lives been transformed as a consequence of words like Truth's, or rather through ensuing theoretical– political usage of them? Something profound was surely meant to transpire consequent to such usage.

Speeding through the centuries since Truth's speech, it has become a truism that there have been many changes for women. Measured legislatively, women have gained many rights, at least in westernised countries, rights possibly unimaginable to Sojourner Truth, if we can imagine her life/thoughts at all.[301] In the study of international politics there is a wide range of work on women, and there are robust international policies promoting women's equality and in the service of preventing gender-induced violence.[302] Here are US Secretary of State Clinton's remarks on women, peace, and security, made in December 2011.

> Today, I want to focus on one aspect of peacemaking that too often goes overlooked – the role of women in ending conflict and building lasting security. Some of you may have watched a week ago Saturday as three remarkable women – two from Liberia, one from Yemen [no names] – accepted the Nobel Peace Prize in Oslo. For years, many of us have tried to show the world that women are not just victims of war; they are agents of peace. And that was the wisdom behind the historic UN Security Council Resolution 1325, which was adopted a decade ago but whose promise remains largely unfulfilled. So it was deeply heartening to see those three women command the global spotlight and urge the international community to adopt an approach to making peace that includes women as full and equal partners.[303]

Though many insist that feminism manifests in a range of different ways, persistent and focused attention on women remains, as well as on the traditional invisibility and triviality of female pain and degradation. The new knowledges that materialise through centralising the conventionally trivial and unimportant have been epistemologically strikingly illuminating. Yet the focus on pain and emergent knowledge through injury has inflections of religious revelation, or martyred affection for pain. The desire for progressive change is disfigured by the attachment to the injury of gender, the latter becoming indelible and indispensible. Etched in pain, women's gendered suffering continues.

And women still suffer. Or at least the claim is vigorously that women are still suffering gendered violence, if in metamorphosing forms. Why? My students ask. Why? I'd like to be able to tell them. But I don't know why, not really. Potentially there are numerous reasons: legislative failures, misogyny, political lethargy, female inadequacy, structural discriminations writ large, male inadequacy, evil, female provocation, feminist failure. Each of these reasons may be right, at least in part, so remedies might be sought and implemented. More strenuous legislation might be put in place to bolster UN Security Council Resolution 1325 and subsequent Resolutions relating to gender. Or in the UK, the Equality Act of 2010, introduced to bolster the equality legislations of the previous forty years to secure equality more fully and effectively. Or more evidence might be gathered together illustrating how misogynistic attitudes still suture everyday practices, personally, locally, globally, with a fine but intensely durable thread.

Do you like women? Many of my students want to analyse the prevalence of rape, and though they tend not to use the word or concept of misogyny (not one that I use with any frequency – too temporally tainted), they seem to sense an air of woman-despising in the sites they choose to study: in a range of contemporary films (the easy and very ordinary slide to sexual assault in *Hollow Man*),[304] in wars, in the high street, in language, in the home, in the courts, in the everyday. And female inadequacy? Women don't make the grade, though it surely depends where in the world this question is asked. In the UK, girls seem to be doing very well in school and university. Though women still earn less than men, and only 22 per cent of MPs in the UK parliament are women; the comparable figure in Rwanda is 56.3 per cent and in Timor Leste 29.2 per cent.[305] 20 per cent of UK companies in the FTSE 100 index had no women in their boardroom and just 5 per cent of executive positions were held by women.[306] Though elsewhere, Angela Merkel won her second term of office as German Chancellor in late 2009, and in 2011 Jóhanna Sigurðardóttir became Prime Minister of Iceland. And, of course, women can be soldiers and suicide bombers. Yet the military acknowledges that 'our gender is soldier',[307] this knowledge should be significant.

In her class presentation on gender and human rights, one of my students drew on an article by Moya Lloyd.[308] The student was struggling with the idea that distributing rights to *women as women* does not always liberate women from being designated and subordinated by gender. I ask the other students in the class what they think this means. One student says that men need to be more involved for women's human rights to be more successfully implemented. The students look expectantly back at me for a response. There is a lot of empirical detail which they can access on human rights; it's a 'safe' gender and IR topic to teach. They are, unsurprisingly, appalled at the human rights abuses that women suffer; though Joel Oestreich, teaching at a 'technology-oriented' university, is constantly surprised by the lack of sympathy shown by the students in his classes. And perhaps expecting some kind of 'gender symmetry', he is especially surprised by women's disinterest.[309]

My class is disciplinarily mixed as is usual in the fourth-year undergraduate gender studies module. I am trying to get the students to think a little bit more creatively and intensively about the work that gender does. I think this is hard for them. Most of them have jobs outside university; some have dependent children or parents. Most are very keen to get good grades, some just to get a pass grade. The IR students struggle with the idea that I am not offering an IR course, and that I don't pay attention to the traditional IR agenda. The sociology students know that gender is important (usually as a role), but are variably resistant to a relentless focus on it. The anthropology students wait patiently for more details from 'the field'. The legal studies students enjoy the respite from the reams of case law they are wading through. All start wanting more answers, more definitions, more empirical evidence. They struggle with the idea of 'militarisation'.

As mostly 'non-IR' (trained) students, they largely self-identify as 'not that interested, or know nothing about international politics, or politics at all'. They struggle with the distance there is between their own lives and interests and 'militarisation', or the distance they assume there is. Though all of them had seen or heard about the news reports the weekend before, '15,000 bikers roared through the Wiltshire market town [Wootton Bassett] on Mothering Sunday to honour troops killed in Afghanistan'.[310] They all knew about Wootton Bassett (now Royal Wootton Bassett), a town which became the mediated focus for mourning British soldiers who died in Afghanistan.

Feminism, part progenitor of modernity, has been deeply involved in the struggle to achieve cultural, social and political changes for women. Yet despite the depth, breadth and impact of the documentation around harms that is so readily proffered, there is something ethereal and transient attached to the detail. What happens to the acknowledgement of gender-induced pain? How do the stories of harm to women appear? How do they manifest through and within contemporary IR? Do they move us? And what of the slippery elision of race as women merge into one?

Enacting liberal forms of political changes has proved painfully elusive, impossible: a promise perhaps predictably unfulfilled, as Secretary Clinton acknowledges in the excerpt of her speech quoted earlier. Pain and injury return, but this time attached to feminist work which both relies on the injury of gender to eradicate gender violence and simultaneously re-creates the violence that gender becomes. The feminist deployment of woman *en route* to alleviating pain works, paradoxically, frustratingly, terrifyingly, to reinstate that pain. Frozen in the pain, gender fuels its own injured identity. Wendy Brown puts it pithily, 'well intentioned contemporary political projects and theoretical postures inadvertently redraw the very configurations and effects of power they seek to vanquish'.[311] Or for Moya Lloyd, 'the feminist subject turns out to be discursively constituted by the very political system that is supposed to facilitate its emancipation'.[312] Or for Žižek, this implies that culturally constituted inferiors 'secretly consider themselves inferior'.[313] A persistent idea, as Franz Fanon articulated in *Black Skin, White Masks*,[314] and an idea that is certain to provoke anxiety.

One might wonder, then, if there is anything left that is politically or philosophically attractive about feminism, and especially the subject so traditionally dear to feminism's theoretical heart. Yet if woman is a fiction and it has proved impossible, actually *undesirable*, to claim that women as a group have something in common that we can all agree on, the question remains — what is attractive about the category, the one that keeps drawing attention despite attached unsightliness?

The dearth of women in high office in the academy is down in part to a perceived lack of 'likeability' among strong female candidates.[315]

Sick and mad

Certain diseases become a woman.[316]

As a pathological category, women have persistently been labelled as sick, though possibly more often as mad. Does it matter what this pathologising does; or how it feels? Feminism's ailing form is also interesting in this context, though in theory feelings are usually considered unimportant, though rancour around subjects, agency and political action continues to flicker heatedly. This is not surprising, given that lives are at stake. Yet the sorry history of medicalising the feminine ignores conventional representations of theory as disembodied. Academic feminist theory is thoroughly enmeshed in familiar indictments of feminised malaise. Here performative analyses of the (re)production of the injury of gender have become compelling. Moreover, the charge of feminist melancholic attachment to the wound of gender (identity), unsurprisingly, has severely dented the theoretical and political pride of those who insist on clinging (with all its feminised traces) to the category of gender and its promises. By hailing oneself as woman, and thus by theoretical inference a subordinated gender, the injury is persistently reaffirmed, destroying the hope of a future free from the shackles of gender.

Failing to reach a future that once warmly beckoned ushers in a certain amount of regret and atonement. With a grinning Žižek, and probably Freud hovering, Wendy Brown asks, 'what conservative political impulses result from a lost sense of futurity attendant upon the break-down of progressive narratives of history?'.[317] Failure to admit that the body of feminism, birthed in weakness, has perished, Brown suggests that the capacity to imagine ourselves in power has been lost, relegated instead to the 'rancorous margins in which we are at best a permanent heckle to power'.[318] Quite embarrassing; it can be hard to know where to look when your best friend is terminally diagnosed.

But perhaps there is something in this. Contemporary social theory remains destabilised by its failures and the impossibility of reaching some 'noncomplicitous place of knowing'.[319] The sense of unexpected violation, a 'cruel optimism when something you desire is actually an obstacle to your flourishing'.[320]

I am sick therefore I am.[321]

The dead body

Even while dead the female still engenders her sexual punishment.[322]

The symbol of red lies not simply in the image, but in the radical plurality of meanings.[323]

In its passage through IR, feminism materialises as (a) body replete with many of the conventional pathologies of the feminine. With its bloody excesses, leaky boundaries and haunting insistent presence, feminism's corporeality is visceral. Injuries to this body regularly show up in generationally inspired crises – echoing conventional female maladies – repeatedly invoking the consequent need for diagnosis and treatment. Mary Hawkesworth recognises the absurdity: 'a strange phenomenon has accompanied the unprecedented growth of feminist activism around the globe: the recurrent pronouncement of feminism's death'.[324] It is strange to speak of feminism as a body, and one that might (will) die. Yet might we invite or welcome feminism's death?

In *Three Guineas*,[325] Virginia Woolf imagined a future funeral pyre for feminism, suggestive of a time beyond or outside of feminism, or a time when feminism would no longer be necessary. Tales of distressful decay seem unnecessary if feminism is no longer required. A timely and dignified demise would seem more elegant, more fitting. Yet the death of feminism is not marked by quietude for some recent storytellers of feminism; instead it is marked by rape and bloody murder. These stories of feminism's corporeal demise are tantalisingly conjoined by a trail of blood.

For Hester Eisenstein, the seduced body of feminism has been left for dead.[326] Persistently captivated by the promised pleasures of liberation, the credulous body of feminism materialises as easy prey. Victim to the vicissitudes of the freedoms proffered by the economic and political power of the market and seduced by the more radical and sophisticated postmodern turn, feminism has become, for Eisenstein, minimally, very sick; a damaged and diseased body resulting from violated theories and practices. In sum, feminism has been ravaged by the powerful forces of neoliberal capital as well as by the masculine signature of contemporary social theory and philosophy. In this story, men have rematerialised as sexual terrorists in competition both for women and for hegemonic masculinity status, with corporate elites vying with socialist men for alpha male status. But it is not only ('real') women who end up bloodied and raped, but also feminism in its materialisation as an innocent 'feminine body' ravished by the (wrong) masculine forces, messily bleeding out her radical potential.

Yet perhaps not all is lost, as the gift of gender which feminism bequeathed has sturdily remained; though, for Eisenstein, the present memory of the seduced/raped body has eviscerated the force of gender, emptying it of political power. Gender had been offered by feminists in the hope of delivering social justice in the realm of sexual politics, but its feminist politics have posthumously imploded, with the ensuing gender debris picked up and warmly embraced by the establishments feminists (used to) spurn. The state, governments, international institutions all speak with and own the language of gender. Now all that is left of a once vital and energetic feminist body, for Eisenstein, is a bloodied, vacuous shell.

The trail of feminised blood violently extracted that Eisenstein follows is exceedingly well worn, as lists of bloodied women and girls consistently assault our mediated senses. 'A Turkish teenager found dead in a hole next to her house was probably buried alive, a post-mortem examination has revealed.'[327]

Blood features differently for Janet Halley,[328] with feminists emerging as sticky culprits with blood on our hands. The violent theoretical and conceptual structures of feminism, along with its logically inevitable empirical manifestations favouring women (white, middle-class, western, straight), have given rise to its own practical brutalities. This time, the gift of gender has transmogrified into an arsenal of powerful regulatory tools indelibly but falsely emblazoned with the mark of feminism. But this is a gift that promises pleasure and power to those who wield it. Halley's trail of blood infers feminism is its own cause of its bloodlust and ensuring violent actions.

Anaemia marks contemporary feminism for Angela McRobbie,[329] its oxygenating life blood drained. In a fate after death, feminism has become 'undone'. It has lost its political efficacy through its popular culture makeover as simply an assertion of sexual allure, rendering it trivial and non-threatening. In the journey(s) from/to thought/concept/passion, to/from institutionalisation, feminism has undergone a governance makeover, and as a consequence feminism has become palatable for contemporary use, perhaps explaining its mainstream acceptance and even its cultural appeal.

Feminism dead or dying, or indeed vampiric; yet with gender vital and alive. These three contemporary feminist investigators find forensic evidence of the violence that is now egregiously meted out in gender's name, in part because of the very ambiguity, slipperiness and elasticity that the (feminist) use of gender has entailed. This unexpected uncontrollability of gender potentially makes feminism culpable for the violence done in its name, providing the motive for its attempted murder/suicide.

> Red defies all literal, male-centred elucidation.[330]

> ... when the over and done with comes alive ...[331]

I am

> You call one of us a slut, we're all sluts.

The spring of 2011 was a fascinating time for anyone interested in international politics. The speed of global information flows has had a profound impact on when and how we (as viewers/listeners) get to know 'what is happening'. When one lone Canadian police officer advised a group of female college students to avoid dressing like sluts to protect themselves from sexual assault, a feminist-inspired global riot ensured. Gender trafficking of a different kind, global 'Slut Walks' began first in Canada then the USA, Britain, Australia, Argentina, the Netherlands, India and more.[332]

'You call one of us a slut, we're all sluts': this comment was made by the organiser of the Glasgow Slut Walk.[333] A lovely response to the round of dreary, predictable

FIGURE 10   Glasgow Slut Walk

© Getty Images

FIGURE 11   New Delhi Slut Walk

© Shelendra Kumar

questions raised by those concerned about the word 'slut' and whether such a tainted word can be reclaimed, or whether women, especially young, attractive women (or so it is persistently inferred) can really expect men to be unmoved by the sight of 'provocative' flesh.

The International Monetary Fund (IMF), perhaps a more recognisably important feature of the international political scene, also hit the global media-scape in the spring of 2011. The newspaper headline that caught my eye was this: 'The lawyers were "surprised" at how unattractive the maid was'.[334] Had she 'dressed up as a sex object', as journalist Melanie Phillips described the women and girls on the Slut Walks? Though how can one tell, given the deviancy of gender?

Out alone wearing a deviant gender.[335]

The slut walkers know very well that what women wear is irrelevant.

Knowing gender

I don't even know what gender is.[336]

I don't even know what gender is – this was Milena Vilanova's first thought when she arrived in post-conflict Timor Leste, perhaps a surprising comment, given her official remit was to work on sexual and gender-based violence.[337] Though perhaps even more surprising, given we all seem to know a great deal about gender: from policy-makers, to film-makers and viewers, to journalists, to cartoon producers and consumers, to advertising executives, to the Pope, and the person next to you, now or later.

The series of images that littered the early website materials advertising the UK's Gender Equality Duty legislation (now no longer used in this context) depicted relatively young people, some seemingly not (quite) white (presumably a nod toward racial awareness), but most in recognisably heteronormative poses/relationships, if slightly skewed to make a specific point about gender. The 'thought bubble' with the second image above is this: 'Doctor! I . . . I thought I'd never see you again!' The caption underneath reads, 'With most public services open 9–5 only, he'd almost given up hope of making an appointment . . .'

There is a nice, if relatively undemanding (as we all know so much about gender) play on still typical (we are led to presume) assumptions about gender here, the doctor turns out to be the woman in the picture, which we might not automatically assume or see, despite the stethoscope round her neck. The 'serious' gender message is that men find it harder to get an appointment with the doctor, given their conventional gendered work commitments in western settings. This is surely a welcome theoretical and practical acceptance that masculinity can be as

Gender Equality Index

Send an e-Card

Downloads

Useful links

FIGURE 12 'Gender Equality Duty' images

pathological as femininity, given the acknowledgment that men can also suffer as a consequence of gendered expectations.

Colourful gendered images also play a part in reconstruction efforts in post-tsunami Aceh, Indonesia. As Marjaana Jauhola observes, the two stick figures are readily identifiable as male and female appearing in modern Muslim dress (man's hat, woman's long dress and jilbāb). Moreover, this idealised picture portrays not only an ideal religious identity, but also an ideal character of a citizen (Acehnese/Indonesian). The dress suggests an economically stable, urban, middle-class couple and a monogamous, nuclear, heterosexual relationship, overall reinforcing the idea of uniform and uniformed citizens, an image, as Jauhola explains, which erases religious, social, economic and ethnic differences.[338]

FIGURE 13 'Apa Itu Gender', Women's Empowerment Office, Indonesia

From Jauhola, M., 'Building back better? – negotiating normative boundaries of gender mainstreaming and post-tsunami reconstruction in Nanggroe Aceh Darussalam, Indonesia', *Review of International Studies*, 2010, 36, 29–50

Oh! So that explains the difference in our pay?

FIGURE 14 Leeds postcard

FIGURE 15 Girls' school in Rwanda

Author's photograph (© Marysia Zalewski)

Here are more images that (im)mediately tell a story of the very familiar narrative of the relationship between gender and sexual difference. The first is produced by Leeds Postcards with the caption 'Oh! So that explains the difference in our pay?' (The child on the left is wearing blue, the child on the right is wearing dark pink.) The second is a photograph taken in a girls' school in Rwanda which has the (we assume girl child on the right, wearing pink) commenting to the (we assume boy child on the left, wearing blue) 'So that's why you have more opportunities'. There are clearly different inflections in these images, one being the focus on 'pay' in the Leeds postcard[339] as opposed to 'opportunities' in the image from the Rwandan school. Yet the predominant message in both is one that illustrates the profound impact of the discovery of the cultural character of gender. And that we all know gender so well.

Popular culture is saturated with gender knowledge too. In Ridley Scott's film *G.I. Jane*, there's a scene in which the central female character Jordan O'Neil (played by Demi Moore) complains to her boyfriend that, though they are the same age and entered the Navy at the same time, 'he was the one with the stripes'. His reply was that 'I just got lucky'. Though the film's feminist credentials have been consistently contested,[340] I think his answer articulates, at least for a moment, the problem for which gender was introduced as a solution. To put this another way, a feminist reading of that line is that he did not simply 'get lucky', but rather that his ascribed gender accounted for his better career success, at least in comparison with hers.

It is so interesting when seemingly fleeting and simple references to the social construction of gender crop up in popular culture and everyday life. Though we might imagine the film's director, Ridley Scott, was making a (feminist?) point, the possibility that such a comment might be unreflectively received (even if simultaneously 'getting it') by a viewing audience is strong. In making this comment my aim is not to patronise the viewing public, but rather to suggest that gestures toward the socially constituted character of gender are replete in the everyday. Indeed there is something of a popular industry with global reach[341] which constantly gestures toward and reminds us about the social construction of gender.

Even the Pope knows about gender, perhaps too well.

> Its Congregation for the Doctrine of the Faith, presided over by Joseph Cardinal Ratzinger (since installed as Pope Benedict XVI), has issued an important dogmatic letter specifically to refute feminism, complete with a concentrated attack on the ideas that biological sex and cultural gender are distinct and independently variable . . . that is to say, the current pope has devoted a substantial portion of his time to refuting feminism.[342]

Vatican scholars may not be poring over what academics (and/or activists) might consider feminist texts, though they might and certainly did at the Fourth World Conference on Women in Beijing.[343] Rather this demonstrates how deeply the feminist conceptual separation of 'biological sex' from 'cultural gender' has infiltrated, how it has become something of a conventional idea, not least in the context of gender mainstreaming in an international setting.[344] UN documentation and rhetoric, for example, is bursting to the seams with commitments to change gender practices, especially the ones that are understood to harm women. There is a long line of legislation in this regard from CEDAW[345] to, at the last count, Security Council Resolution 1889,[346] which mandates peacekeeping missions to protect women and girls from sexual violence in armed conflict. It was unanimously adopted and much praised by Secretary of State Hillary Clinton and UN Secretary-General Ban Ki-moon.

> The Security Council decided this morning to specifically mandate peacekeeping missions to protect women and children from rampant sexual violence during armed conflict, as it requested the Secretary-General to appoint a special representative to coordinate a range of mechanisms to fight the crime. Among other measures, the resolution called on the Secretary-General to rapidly deploy a team of experts to situations of particular concern in terms of sexual violence, to work with United Nations personnel on the ground and national Governments on strengthening the rule of law.[347]

Deploying teams of experts in situation of gender emergency? It sounds quite exciting, and excitement seems to be a regular emotion attached to activities around gender in the realm of national and international legislation. Spontaneous applause greeted the UN General Assembly's unanimous vote in July 2010 to create a 'single, powerful body to promote equality for women round the world' with a $500 million drive to end global inequality at last. Interestingly, the same amount that the Jimmy Choo conglomerate has been sold for.[348] An oblique reminder of the very different manifestations of 'feminine gender' that is 'woman' across the globe. Money may not be able to buy you love (even if a great deal is necessary to buy those much admired shoes), but it seems it can buy you the end of gender, or, and this is important, the parts of gender we don't like. The reasons generally given for the sluggishness of gender change consequent to CEDAW, the Declaration on the Elimination of Violence Against Women (DEVAW) and the Security Council Resolutions are manifold, ranging from patriarchal governments, lack of serious resources, inadequate implementation and institutional apparatus.[349] Yet with a profound rap of the Assembly president's gavel, there was, once again, a view that 'the world's hitherto unreachable corners of prejudice' may be, at last, exposed and defeated.[350] Given that we know so much about gender, and that at last it has become politically visible and institutionally important, the hope is conspicuous.

Learning often takes place completely independently of teaching.[351]

I was at a training day on 'gender and development' at which one of the trainers lamented the failure of gender mainstreaming. She asked me why I thought it had failed. I, though suspecting my answer would not be comprehensible to most of the people in the room (a disparate group of academics including scientists, humanities and legal studies scholars, and social scientists, who were all keen to know how to tick the 'gender boxes' on their research funding applications), said that gender mainstreaming fails because gender is already mainstreamed. To be sure, the people in the room had, by and large, no (formal) 'gender training' up until that point, so it was probably a little too much to expect them to understand what I meant straight away; perhaps they simply needed more 'training'. But 'more training' isn't quite right, I think, partly because they all seemed to know very well what gender is. Certainly they were content with the idea that gender is socially constructed, but they also had very strong opinions about gender, especially in regard to when, where and how much it mattered. It turned out that 'development' mattered significantly more than 'gender', and my persistence in returning to gender in the discussions (after all, the theme of the day) began to irritate some a little I think. Though there was consensus that social construction offered profound analyses of gender, there was a sense that something new (and exciting) was required, as social constructionism had not delivered satisfactorily. Or at least, it didn't help with ticking those boxes.

Of course it might be the case that the participants held erroneous views about gender, what it is, how it works, how it might be enacted more positively, and thus their incomprehension was understandable, and crucially therefore (even if 'only' in principle) correctable. But incomprehension around the conclusion that gender is already mainstreamed seems commonplace; at least this conclusion might be reached given the insistence that more legislation and initiatives are the answer. Yet there seems to be an extravagant failure around gender; at least, we have not witnessed the changes in gender that are assumed to be necessary for equality to be convincingly reached, or for gender-based violence to be a rare or an unusual occurrence. I wonder, despite our overabundance of knowledge about gender, have we got gender very wrong, and perhaps wrong in very serious ways?

> The compulsion to 'help' the needy ultimately leads to 'bombing people into the acceptance of gifts'.[352]

Looking awry

> There is not a great amount of fluidity between disciplines and styles of writing these days.[353]

In the film *The Day After Tomorrow* there are no bad women. This is a film that is ostensibly about contemporary concerns about climate change as the story involves large parts of the Northern Hemisphere freezing over in a matter of days, indeed minutes in parts (though the main action takes place largely in Manhattan, New York). On its release it created some consternation in regard to its 'scientific accuracy'.

> On Memorial Day weekend 2004, Twentieth Century Fox released *The Day After Tomorrow*, a disaster movie depicting an abrupt and catastrophic climate change. In the movie, a global warming-induced shutdown of the North Atlantic thermohaline circulation system triggers extreme weather events worldwide and subsequently a new ice age, with wrenching global consequences. Before it even hit the theaters, however, the movie generated an intense storm of media controversy as scientists, politicians, advocacy groups, and political pundits debated the scientific accuracy and . . . [354]

As a post-9/11 blockbuster Hollywood movie, it is replete with themes of redemption, recuperation and rescue. But I keep noticing there are no bad women. There aren't many bad men either, perhaps some misguided, such as the US Vice President (his physical similarity to Dick Cheney noted by many) who initially mocks the scientist's (the central male character in the film, played by Dennis Quaid) dire warnings about climate change.

> . . . our economy is every bit as fragile
>
> as the environment.
>
> Perhaps you should keep that in mind
> before making sensationalist claims.

Yet, at the end of the film and speaking from the safe haven of Mexico, where the fleeing Americans have sought safety, he sees the error of his ways.

> People have abandoned their cars,
> grabbed their belongings . . .
>
> . . . and they are wading across the river
> illegally into Mexico.

He speaks as the new Commander in Chief following the death of the President, who (unlike ex-President George W. Bush on the day of 9/11) had stayed 'too long' on the site of the disaster, thus too late to survive . . .

> Mr President.
>
> All right.
>
> I'm sorry, sir, we can't wait any longer.
>
> We're the last ones.

Acting as an embodied metaphor for a nation's apology, the new President renounces the error of his/the US's ways.

> These past few weeks have left us all
> with a profound sense of humility . . .
>
> . . . in the face of nature's
> destructive power.
>
> For years, we operated under the belief
> that we could continue . . .
>
> . . . consuming our planet's natural resources
> without consequence.
>
> We were wrong.
>
> I was wrong.

> The fact that my first address to you
> comes from a consulate on foreign soil . . .
> . . . is a testament to our changed reality.
>
> Not only Americans . . .
> . . . but people all around the globe
> are now guests in the nations . . .
> . . . we once called The Third World.
>
> In our time of need,
> they have taken us in and sheltered us.
>
> And I am deeply grateful
> for their hospitality.

As a 'father and son combo', Dennis Quaid and Jake Gyllenhaal perform appropriately heroic masculine rescues. The women are sacrificial and feminine. Though, while burning books to keep warm enough to stay alive (burning books is always a matter of life or death), there is a feminist moment.

> Friedrich Nietzsche?
>
> We can't burn Nietzsche.
>
> He was the most important thinker
> of the nineteenth century.
>
> Please. He was a chauvinist pig
> in love with his sister.
>
> He was not a chauvinist pig.
>
> But he was in love with his sister.

The impropriety of potential incest stops feminism in its tracks.

The feminine heart of the film and Gyllenhaal's love interest, Laura (played by Emmy Rossum) evokes a filmic memory of Bernadette in the Oscar-winning *Song of Bernadette*.[355] As a novice nun Bernadette seems never to be good enough despite her abject feminine submissiveness and religious devotion and servitude. Not until she physically exposes her cancerous knee, revealing her obvious constant excruciating pain which she has suffered in silence for a lengthy time, not until this point can her true worth as a paradigm of sacrificial womanhood finally be acknowledged. As they shelter in the New York Public Library on Fifth Avenue, Laura won't wake up.

> I told you that she has a fever and her . . .
>
> She's got a really cold sweat.
>
> How's her pulse?
>
> It's really fast.
>
> Does she have any injuries?
>
> Like a cut that might have
> gotten infected?
>
> She was complaining about a cut
> on her leg a few days ago.[356]

I went to see this film when it was first released in the UK, with me were my partner, sister and two daughters. We had an animated discussion about the film afterwards, or perhaps it was me who rather animatedly responded to my sister's opening post-film comments about the problems of global climate change, expressing her concern that something climatically catastrophic might indeed happen in the not-too-distant future. I, having watched the film totally absorbed by the catastrophic CGI'd drama of it all, but at the same time (almost) totally aware of the straight lines the film was taking me down, said 'but that's not what it was about!' – subsequently proceeding to explain at length the subtle but obvious (to me) gendered and heteronormative frame of the film. Perhaps it's easier just to be normal . . .

> Normal people get to just enjoy a flick.[357]

It's been quite some time since Judith Butler's exposé of the intimately heteronormative binds of gender. Yet the curving, bending fluidity of (hetero)gender, and the capacity of gender to be one thing, then another thing, then nothing at all, are all, often unexpectedly, very effectively herded up (as if by magic). The jagged alchemy of gender obediently straightens up into rows of neat-looking lines. Noticing this remains difficult. Knowing where to position oneself to keep this gender sorcery in sight is evasive. We know that it's hard to change tradition, or too quickly to disturb the usual order of things, but sometimes, perhaps when things or practices shatter, the time and space of transition offers new starting places. Though . . .

> To create is not so much to make something new as to shift.[358]

What would Valerie Solanos think?

In her vituperative polemic *The SCUM Manifesto* – 'an indefensible text'[359] – Valerie Solanos has this to say:

> Eaten up with guilt, shame, fears and insecurities and obtaining, if he's lucky, a barely perceptible physical feeling, the male is, nonetheless, obsessed with screwing; he'll swim through a river of snot, wade nostril-deep through a mile of vomit, if he thinks there'll be a friendly pussy awaiting him. He'll screw a woman he despises, any snaggle-toothed hag, and furthermore, pay for the opportunity. Why? Relieving physical tension isn't the answer, as masturbation suffices for that. It's not ego satisfaction; that doesn't explain screwing corpses and babies.[360]

I imagine, for a nanosecond, reading this out in the undergraduate second-year IR theory lecture (a very sanitised lecture on feminism and IR, though the one in which a student asked me to make feminism more palatable). It's even problematic reading the book on the train, as it seems like pornography. The cover boldly states *SCUM Manifesto*, and even though the 2004 edition is attractively designed in black and pink, on closer inspection the image on the dust jacket is a discreet knife. Perhaps *SCUM* is a feminist snuff pornography of sorts; though there is solidity and substance to it. When she wrote it in 1968, was Solanos really speaking about men? Suggesting there should be a Society For Cutting Up Men? Can we forgive her for knowing that words can make you bleed, and cry in pain? Forgive her for the pleasure she took in foisting linguistic injury, firing insults on every page?

> ...the male is an incomplete female, a walking abortion[361]

> ...the male has one glaring area of superiority over the female – public relations[362]

> ...the male has a negative Midas touch – everything he touches turns to shit[363]

> ...the male has a vested interest in ignorance[364]

Monique Wittig suggested that what was necessary was a 'political genocide ... once the class "men" disappears, "women" as a class will disappear as well'.[365] A more reasonable annihilation, perhaps.

Men have consistently been the target of feminist anxiety. It is men who perpetrate the most crimes, or so it is consistently argued. It is men who are primarily responsible for wars and violent acts, or so it is consistently claimed. In *Against Our Will: Men, Women and Rape*,[366] Susan Brownmiller marshalled a wealth of feminist 'evidence'– for some an oxymoronic idea[367] – on rape, culminating with the claim that 'for some men rape provides a sufficient threat to keep all women in a constant state of intimidation'.[368] In a 2010 television documentary programme on feminism and its contemporary impact, Susan Brownmiller was interviewed about her 1975 book.[369] She spoke about her surprise (and hurt) that, at the time, despite the book's relative commercial and feminist success, it did not make her more popular, or had made her less popular. 'What did you expect, writing about rape?' was the response. Perhaps feminists keep forgetting that feminism is received as violent in its doing violence to oppressive epistemological, ontological and social orders through their obliteration of barriers, blurring of boundaries and confronting power.

But the view that men are 'the problem' (for feminism? for women? for gender? for violence?) is currently theoretically untenable, at least within western theory. The 'problem' relates to the enactment and discursive entanglement of masculinities, which have increasingly become a key target for theorists, policymakers and activists. A central aim of much of the work on masculinities has been to try and wean men off masculinity, or to weed out inappropriate and harmful masculinities. This theoretical shift complicated a number of things, not least who we think can be harmed by gender. Even men close to hegemonic ideals suffer, given that the nearness to 'perfection' makes masculinity's impossibility viscerally hard to bear. The exquisitely painful business card scene in the film *American Psycho* imparts this well.[370]

. . . New card.

What do you think ?

Whoa-ho. Very nice.

Look at that. Picked them up from the printer's yesterday.

Good coloring. That's bone.

And the lettering is something called Silian Rail.

It's very cool, Bateman, but that's nothing. Look at this.

That is really nice.

Eggshell with Romalian type. What do you think ?

Nice.

Jesus. That is really super. How'da nitwit like you get so tasteful?

I can't believe that Bryce . . .

prefers Van Patten's card to mine.

But wait. You ain't seen nothin' yet.

Raised lettering, pale nimbus . . . white.

Impressive. Very nice.

Hmm.

Let's see Paul Allen's card.

Look at that subtle off-white coloring.

The tasteful thickness of it.

Oh, my God. It even has a watermark.[371]

Bateman loves the idea of 'murder'. Michael Kimmel notes that

It is from that gendered shame that mass murderers are made.[372]

Perhaps all men, even particularly men mired in subordinated masculinities (poor, ethnically dis-privileged, sexually suspect) suffer their gender. To be sure, women too (always?) also suffer via men's own gendered injury. Failures to achieve appropriate masculine subject positions (to be a real man) regularly wreak havoc on women.[373] Domestic violence perhaps. Rape perhaps. Warmongering perhaps: 'the action heroes of death machines'.[374] When more visibly intertwined or discursively shot through with lived discourses of race, class, sexuality and colonialism, the task of effectively wielding a gendered epistemological scalpel – to slice out masculinity's worst – appears harder and harder. Rape, particularly in war and conflict, has been demonstrated to have less (nothing) to do with individual men's 'natures' and a great deal to do with ethnic rivalries, globalised power struggles and nationalist resentments. Procedures to successfully carve out masculinity's worst impotently scatter.

Yet masculinity consistently rematerialises attached to the bodies and practices of men, certainly in the shape of societal rewards and punishments. This is intriguing, frustrating, horrifying, especially consequent to the seemingly successful filleting of masculinity from the bodies and minds of men through critical, poststructural and postcolonial theorising. Raewyn Connell's description of the overwhelming preponderance of men at the top of business (97 per cent of the top executives in Australia are men), politics (men make up 82.5 per cent of members of national parliaments worldwide), religion (no women popes, archbishops, patriarchs, ayatollahs, muftis or chief monks), militaries (generals and admirals are overwhelmingly men) leads her to claim that 'patriarchy seems decidedly resilient'.[375] Masculinity doesn't belong to men;[376] doesn't belong to anyone. It seems an error has been made; though a dangerous one 'given the desire to keep proving the mistake'.[377]

What would Valerie Solanos think about contemporary sophisticated, calm and reasonable attempts to carve out unacceptable fragments of masculinity? Or about the therapeutic aims to wean men off the seductive charms of their gender? Would she concede our epistemological scalpels are now honed enough to do the job? Or would she still demand that we take our theoretical courage to its limits?[378] Can we think of IR without men?

So. Sometimes you have to scream to be heard.[379]

Violence

> We just stood in line and screwed her.[380]

Feminism and violence are intimate. For many, feminism is borne out of anger at the violent stranglehold of gender and the piles of dead women in gender's vicious wake. Feminist work has consistently exposed the violent choreography of gender practices, offering copiously detailed information about the abuse and degradation that has been, and remains, well documented, and continues to be meted out to women. These violences have so often remained quietly unseen, silenced, forgotten, mis-recognised. Feminists have persistently raised their voices, often in anger and rage, to give names, light and vision to this abundance of discarded and disregarded pain.

The domestic violence of love.

> Your neighbors hear you screaming. They do nothing. The next day they look through you. If you scream for years they will look through you for years.[381]

The paternal violence of medical science.

Gena Corea and Robyn Rowland theoretically scream warnings to other women and tell stories about violated women in the search for masculinely inspired reproductive virility; 'within the reproductive brothel, women would be totally reduced to Matter'.[382]

The natural violence of sex.

Stories of rape have ravaged for centuries, in war, in literature, in memorials, in art. Some examples include Sierra Leone, Kosovo, the Darfur region of the Sudan, the Democratic Republic of Congo (DRC), Rwanda, the former Yugoslavia, Helen of Troy, women in the Scottish Highlands in the eighteenth century, Belgian women in the First World War.[383] News reports about rape seem more frequent than before, perhaps since rape became categorised as a war crime. Perhaps because of feminist activism. Perhaps because of the success of governance feminism. Perhaps there is more rape than before. Sometimes media reports about sexual violence come with a warning: viewers may find some of the images in this report upsetting.

> The Chamber found that four girls were taken to the accused's [. . .] apartment in October 1992 and were 'constantly raped and humiliated and degraded'. One girl, who was just 12 years old, was eventually sold off by the accused and never seen again.[384]

Feminism sometimes also comes with a warning. Andrea Dworkin's and Gena Corea's work, for example, perhaps marking a less shock-absorbed stage of feminism, has been held to account for portraying women as victims, denying women's agency, and feeding patriarchal narratives about women's essential passivity and psychological and physical vulnerability. But more, perhaps a worse fate than this, the bombardment of tales of horrendous bloody violences done to women seeps into epistemological spheres and imaginations such that it becomes the only, or primary, way that we can imagine women – as sites of bloody injury. Sheila Jeffreys' abrasively titled *Industrial Vagina*[385] relies on an arsenal of evidence to detail depredations of the contemporary global sex economy: the globalisation of prostitution, pornography, strip clubs and sex tourism. Jeffreys is relentless, women *as* always victims and men as always aggressive perpetrators. Woman always as wound. A vicious bloody circle as feminism emerges as violator with hands stained red.

But my students still insist that these stories of injury simply have to be told. Stories of trafficking in women and girls, of women's lives used and discarded, though these are never simple stories and they are never simply gendered. They like the film *Taken*, a conventionally packaged contemporary 'trafficking tale'.[386] The 'good girl' is saved in the end, though they absorb without noticing blatant reinscriptions of the rightful place of 'real fathers'. As a beleaguered ex-husband, with income and professional status (and ability to 'buy stuff') paling in comparison to the new husband (step-dad), Liam Neeson's valiant rescue of his virginal daughter successfully re-secures his rightful fatherly place.

They are moved by the film *Lilya 4ever*.[387] In this, Lilya's mother makes a partially gendered decision to leave the country with her husband, not Lilya's father we learn (no Liam Neeson-style 'real' father heroism here), leaving the young teenage girl to fend for herself in the harsh post-Cold War environment of, we imagine, a former Soviet satellite state. The reverberations of globalisation and the end(s) of the Cold War have made life hard for Lilya and her family. In the film, we can trace a faint and erratic line from *perestroika* to the trafficking of Lilya into sex slavery and to her eventual suicide, still in her teenage years.

Narrating stories about gender violence has been seen as necessary to facilitate the political power and strength of feminism. Women's stories of violence, 'are not trivial . . . they are radical, they are threatening, they would mean revolution'.[388] And is revolution not a form of violence? Violating conventional boundaries of personal and public, insisting on and fighting for legislative changes to accommodate the truth of gender, and methodically planning and arranging these intentionally transformative alterations, is a deep part of feminism's remit – a very bloody remit for some. There is a confusing sense of power and strength in all of this, and so a place where violence might easily remain hidden.

The violence that women do is perhaps less than rigorously documented, though sometimes it seems that feminists do not speak, write or think about violent women, or believe that women can be violent. There are, of course, many instances of women who are violent, though there is often a peculiarly gendered price for women's violence for which many pay. Slavenka Drakulić notices this, detailing the price paid for Biljana Plavšić being the only woman among 'macho Balkan politicians' on trial for war crimes committed in the former Yugoslavia between 1991 and 1995.

A woman in such a position had to be far better than the men, and under the circumstances, for Biljana Plavšić, that meant she had to be more radical . . . and she was . . . when this woman ruled Bosnia, it was pure hell.[389]

Yet, though the idea that women carry a metaphorical gene for peace is consistently denounced by feminist scholars, it lingers very strongly. There are a number of reasons that might account for this. Women's internationalised and transnational actions for peace are strong.[390] Culturally engineered femininity oftentimes seems to translate into less aggressive scenarios and perhaps more 'complementary' styles of leadership. But also perhaps because people still want to believe it, though for different reasons. Francis Fukuyama's curiously theorised article published in the journal *Foreign Affairs* exudes socio-biological beliefs about the natural violence of men: his story necessarily relies on a simple and dangerous gender binary which inevitably invokes the oppositional sense that women would, for one reason or another, be more peaceful. A poorly concealed racial fear trembles through his essay, with the spectre of western democratic countries becoming overpopulated by the mid-twenty-first century and led by the older and feminised (men or women), counterposed by 'other' nations' (Africa, the Middle East, South Asia) growing populations led by younger men.[391]

Or, perhaps serving a different function, the UN's drive to include more women in post-conflict peace talks is heavily suggestive of undiminished faith in the equation of women with peace: 'We all know that women count for peace' (Under-Secretary-General for UN Women, Michelle Bachelet).[392] It seems to feel more comfortable to orient oneself to the idea that women are (the) different and (essentially) nicer, the comfort here shimmering enticingly through the boundaries keeping gender apart.

This is compounded by the sense that there is something 'different' about violent women. Such women are often treated and imagined very differently. Women are seemingly always imagined as potential mothers, even those who never intend or want to have children, or who never have. This morphing of woman–mother stalks women who kill: Myra Hindley, Rosemary West, Aileen Wuornos.[393] Women–'mothers' who sexually abuse children also figure strongly in the area of gender taboo, viciously tampering with boundary rules. A woman who admitted abusing children and taking photos of the abuse in the nursery at which she was employed was asked by a police officer (in an interview, part of which was broadcast on a UK news programme on BBC Radio 4) to reveal the names of the children she abused. On her refusal he said; 'surely as a mother you understand the parents want to know'.

Feminists plan and arrange violence, though perhaps not violence as it is immediately imagined. That feminists commit violence is all the more intriguing in the context of feminism's positioning as vulnerable and beleaguered; Janet Halley suggests this. In her book *Split Decisions*, she claims that feminists think they are powerless when they are, in fact, powerful. They think they are innocent, when they/we have 'blood on their hands'.[394] To be sure, Halley's 'feminists' are largely governance feminists – possibly the most easily recognisable and acceptable set of internationalised feminists. This usually includes those in the 'velvet triangle' of NGOs, some respected academics and activists – who work together to create the most effective theoretical, practical and policy environment to deliver successfully on gender aims.[395] But shifting benefits in favour of women has costs; others will suffer.[396] People suffer because of apparent feminist success, but perhaps especially men.

At the last of four conferences marking twenty years' scholarship on 'British Gender and International Relations', we had constructed a 'wall' made of paper for delegates to write comments on. Whilst most delegates were in panel sessions, the male caterer wrote on the wall 'if it wasn't for men you wouldn't have had any coffee this morning'. That a conference hosting a variety of panels relating to gender, feminism and (international) politics inferred that an ultimate goal was to 'get rid of men' is disturbing I think; though an interesting reversal of injured domesticity.

Yet it is the case that the idea that men have more than their fair share of the societal 'cake' has elicited violent responses from feminism, insistently violating boundaries and borders, ideologically, epistemologically, pedagogically, physically, politically and personally (simultaneously creating new ones). These shifts have implications for how we think about the violence that insistently permeates the international realm and what violences feminism is involved in. This seems egregiously simplistic, yet arguments regarding feminist intention, impact and effect powerfully invoke the metaphor and feeling of balance. One way that has emerged in 'feminist IR' is as a range of anxieties about the injustices of feminism and the damage this does to men, explicitly invoking the idea and practice of balance,[397] repositioning men at the centre of the feminist (IR) agenda. We might think of this as a phenomenologically efficient move. Thus from the violated bodies, hearts and minds of women – feminism moves us to violate the bodies, hearts and minds of men. There is something unthinkable about this.

> When things go astray, other things can happen.[398]

Going through the day

> Memory is itself a disciplinary mechanism.[399]

Of the many *YouTube* clips featuring Slavoj Žižek, the one in which he enthuses about the film *Children of Men* is interesting.[400] For Žižek, the most important thing in this film is what is happening in the background. Looking awry,[401] or taking a 'sideways reflection',[402] are characteristic of Žižek's work. As he implies, it is exceedingly easy, comfortable and often dangerous to remain focused on the centre, or what insistently materialises as the centre. Though it remains a challenge to keep consistently, persistently and seemingly illogically side-stepping this seductive heart.

★★★★★★★★★★★★★★★

Jack Bauer never charges his cell phone because it is powered by testosterone.[403]

In the US television series 24, Kiefer Sutherland plays the iconic Jack Bauer.[404] 24 is about the fictional 'Counter Terrorist Unit' (CTU) which fights all kinds of 'terrorist evils' that befall (largely) the USA.[405] CTU's key agent is Jack Bauer, who voraciously performs his role. Jack Bauer is, without doubt, (represented as) a 'real man', a twenty-first-century western man, one fit to protect and serve in a post-9/11 era.[406] And a real man, a bleeding, emotional, sometimes frightened man, not an outer-worldly super-hero. His public popularity is evident, many websites are devoted to the series and to Jack Bauer in particular, including a 'Jack Bauer for President' site,[407] and numerous 'Jack Bauer jokes' sites.

> Jack Bauer once saw two gay men making out. They immediately turned straight.[408]

Jack's twenty-first-century (hegemonic/heteronormative) masculinity is not in doubt.[409] His heroism, inflected with all the frailties and fragilities of contemporary western manhood, is also not in doubt. A lone Rambo-esque character updated for the threats of the twenty-first century: cyberterrorism, bioterrorism, the ubiquitous newly 'other(ed)', this time too often masquerading as 'one of us'. And he spends a lot of time worrying about his grown-up daughter Kim, who is the only female figure who remains a (living) constant in his life (even if tangentially) throughout the series. Jack portrays a beleaguered but ultimately triumphal father; a theme that has become emblematic of early twenty-first-century western popular cinematic culture, Tom Cruise in *War of the Worlds* being just one example.

> Kim Bauer once brought her father to school for a parent/teacher conference . . . and got expelled for bringing a weapon onto school grounds.[410]

Heteronormative familial relationships constantly ripple through contemporary media narratives about war. It's hard to avoid them, especially the apparently peripheral ones. The grieving girlfriends and young wives of the dead soldiers making their casketed journeys through the streets of (Royal) Wootton Bassett are interlaced with images of 'old soldiers'. Dressed in military paraphernalia with medals of honour pinned to jackets, their 'fatherly' distress is visceral and moving. The mostly young heroes killed 'in action' in Afghanistan (usually, at least recently) have their lives and deaths remembered in a number of public/private ways. In the drama of international politics, the deaths of men have always been of primary concern, this seems unsurprising. Though all suffer and die in war, the deaths of so many men, and usually very young men, in the service of their country has been and remains a major motivating factor for the study of international politics.

Paul Hardcastle's song *19*[411] was a number one in the UK pop music charts for five weeks in 1985 and was simultaneously in the top twenty in the USA. In 2010, the album *Coming Home* by 'The Soldiers' (three men who have served in Afghanistan and Iraq) reached number four in the UK album charts.[412] It is surely the case that 'the gender drama is never absent'.[413]

I took the photographs of a terracotta panel in Figure 16 on a visit to the Old Parliament House in Canberra, Australia. The panel is entitled 'The Greek Mother', which, as the caption states, tells a stark tale of a 'Spartan mother giving her son a shield. She commands him to come back from battle carrying the shield with honour, or on it – dead'. The gift had been described by the curator of the exhibit as having 'little obvious connection to the world of politics'. For a feminist scholar this seems a bizarre comment to make, though our tour guide enthusiastically endorsed the idea of its irrelevance to matters of high politics. Feminist scholars would tell a different story, pointing out that this gift is intensely political. It illustrates the intimate connections between gender and politics, especially international politics, given that the example involves one of its archetypal concerns: war. The panel depicts formidable expectations of dutiful masculinity (combined in the figure of a good son/Spartan warrior) alongside a powerful demonstration of civic motherly duty, to the extent of preferring her son's death to his return from battle without honour.

Honour in a battle of sorts is central in the film *World Trade Center*.[414] Its two central characters are unlikely, unexpected heroes, as they are just 'normal' guys, ordinary family men replete with financial and personal anxieties. The story of their ultimate heroic survival and rescue from the suffocating ruins of the twin towers is splintered with flashback images of their normal American lives. One has a wife and children, the other a pregnant girlfriend and small daughter, all of whom are shown anxiously waiting with their families, friends and neighbours for the safe return of their men. The men's rescue is ultimately made possible by the arrival of a US Marine, visually and symbolically presenting as the embodiment of contemporary western militarised masculinity; strong, single-minded, committed and proactive. I ask my students if they think the story would work cinematically if the two central characters were lesbians.

There is an elegant moment for Žižek in the film *Children of Men*,[415] a dystopian film in which human beings can no longer procreate and where violence, degradation, filth and fear pervade the London streets, where most of the action takes place. The central character is Theo, a depressed former social justice activist; in one scene he visits his cousin (a government minister) for transit papers he needs to help transport a miraculously pregnant woman (an extraordinary

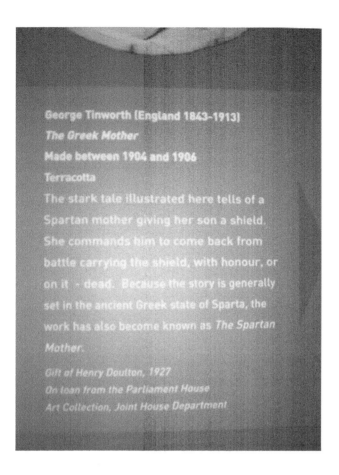

FIGURE 16 A Greek gift

Author's photograph (© Marysia Zalewski)

conception, given the last child to be born in the world was now eighteen years old) to a sanctuary at sea. As Theo enters the classy 'penthouse' apartment (ministerial corruption inferred), the clean lines and smart furniture in stark contrast to the abject dirt and devastation of the outside, his cousin greets him dwarfed by what we assume is the original Michelangelo's seventeen-foot-tall 'masculine masterpiece', *David*. But *David*, as Žižek argues, has become meaningless, as he no longer signals a certain type of world and value, its commodified power emasculated. For me this evinces a powerful sense of meaninglessness and offers a beautiful insight into the political value of unmooring epistemological anchors.

> . . . forgetting becomes a way of resisting . . . heroic and grand logics.[416]

Securing men

> We argue that men's political violence has been accepted and normalised: global political actors try to curtail or minimise it, but are not shocked by its existence or befuddled by its implication.[417]

Are we not shocked or befuddled? On 24 November 2009, UN Secretary-General Ban Ki-moon marked the tenth anniversary of the International Day for the Elimination of Violence against Women by launching a Network of Men Leaders. This he introduced as a major new initiative bringing together current and former politicians, activists, religious and community figures in order to combat the global pandemic of violence against women.[418] Emotive rhetoric and promises of extra resources bolstered his words, and he called upon men and boys not to ignore or condone acts of sexual violence against women. He announced new grants for projects on the ground to be awarded by the UN Trust Fund in Support of Actions to Eliminate Violence against Women, managed by the UN Development Fund for Women, amounting to $10.5 million for thirteen initiatives in eighteen countries and territories. He stressed that his commitment to this issue stemmed not just from his role as UN Secretary-General, but also from his role as a son, husband, father and grandfather. 'Men' he claimed 'have a crucial role to play in ending such violence – as fathers, friends, decision makers, and community and opinion leaders'.

We, especially in a westernised milieu, think we are shocked by sexual violence, and we surely are. Sexually violent atrocities, such as those frequently reported in the DRC,[419] receive a great deal of media, political, legislative and academic attention. Much effort is put into trying to do something about sexual violence – curtailing it, rooting out the causes, finding the perpetrators, treating the victims – and this is the case on a global scale. The incidence of sexual violence, particularly in war and conflict, but not only then, are matters of great concern for individuals, communities, local and national legislative and political machineries *and* international legislative and political machineries. The 'scourge' of sexual violence remains viscerally part of everyday lives. Why is it so ubiquitous? Why does sexual violence keep on material-ising as simply part of the soft fabric of everyday life?

> Shedla Abedi's age was no protection when the rapists came to her village. 'Imagine – a young boy of twenty, and me aged sixty-two, old enough to be his grandmother', she said. She pointed to a frail, older woman walking with a stick. 'Her too', she said, 'And she's over eighty.'[420]

It is shocking. The UN representative was crying on the television report I viewed: the young woman, born in the DRC but raised in London, was distraught and wretchedly surprised on learning that a four-year-old girl had been raped. Visiting a hospital for women in the DRC, it was clear she had never imagined that a girl so young would be subject to rape. How could a man rape a four-year-old girl? Or an eighty-year-old woman? Though why age matters, if rape isn't sex, is curi-ous. The eighty-year-old woman wasn't dressed up as a 'sex object', one imagines. Nor the four-year-old. As if this mattered at all, when . . .

> 'Woman' in the abstract is young, and, we assume, charming.[421]

Men or boys raping women or girls hurls us back to thinking about men, about masculinities. Of course it isn't (simply) one or the other – though what is the question that precedes 'men or masculinities?' Is there something about men, or about particular men, which prevents all the efforts to stem sexual violence from being successful? Is it still particular cultural manifestations and expressions of masculinity that sustain unacceptable understandings of sex, rape, women and violence? And in what complicated ways do race, class, ethnicity weave through? Is Kramer right when he says that

> The tendency to sexual violence seems lodged in the very core of ordinary subjectivity like a bone in the throat.[422]

We know some men are brutal (though some women are, too). We might deploy traditional sociological or psychological or even religious explanations which con-clude that some men (and some women) are 'evil/bad' (even if through cultural training). Their violence can be explained. Various cures for violent individuals have persistently been sought – medical, therapeutic, retributive, retraining, care, education, love – all in the pursuit of changing men's violent actions by getting at something that will prevent future violent actions occurring; the 'something' relat-ing primarily to masculinity. Like the *Facebook group* 'Real Men Don't Rape'.[423] Though is this what UN Secretary-General Ban Ki-moon thinks he's doing when he asks men to 'unite' to stop violence against women – changing something in men; making men think differently about the ways cultural masculinity shapes their actions and feelings? Kramer makes sense again:

> Guilt, no matter how sincere, cannot break the cycle.[424]

Despite the richness of contemporary theory, which reveals and details in extraordinary depth how the simplistic category of 'men' is a profoundly poor one on which to base any serious analysis or policy, the category retains astonishing depth, power and reach. Classic unity is stickily attached. Solanos's unreason returns via Ronnel:

> No matter how you cut it, universal – whether common or communist – meant 'man'. It is hard to kill a generality, a genre or gender.[425]

The academic search for the light of theory promises so much. Not just explanation, but crucially also action. Though 'the facts' never speak for themselves, they do tell stories, not ones that can simply be 'read off' as if they had objective, transparent meaning, but stories that we can look at to see how theory weaves through. Here are (some of) the 'theory-facts' in Ban Ki-moon's speech launching his Network of Men Leaders initiative

- These men will add their voices to the growing global chorus for action.
- 70 per cent of women experience in their lifetime some form of physical or sexual violence from men, the majority from husbands, intimate partners or someone they know.
- Break the silence.
- When you witness violence against women and girls, do not sit back. Act.
- Violence against women and girls will not be eradicated until all of us – men and boys – refuse to tolerate it.
- By 2015, the UNiTE campaign aims to achieve the following five goals worldwide: adopt and enforce national laws to address and punish all forms of violence against women and girls; adopt and implement multi-sectoral national action plans; strengthen data collection on the prevalence of violence against women and girls; increase public awareness and social mobilization; and address sexual violence in conflict.
- My commitment to this issue stems not just from my position as UN Secretary-General, but also as a son, husband, father and grandfather.
- Men have a crucial role to play in ending such violence – as fathers, friends, decision makers, and community and opinion leaders.[426]

I want to take some sideways glances at the stories that weave through these (sometimes) innocuous, (sometimes) powerful statements, oftentimes both.

These men will add their voices to the growing global chorus for action.

There is a mellifluous charm to this simple but evocative statement, woven through with and by a rich and embedded array of dangerous theory. For example: binary gender theory (with its attendant hierarchies and essentialist seductions), a simple logic of numeracy (with accompanying weight of additive progression), the authority of voice (never ungendered), and, of course, action. The treacherous hopeful beauty of linear progression.

> 70 per cent of women experience in their lifetime some form of physical or sexual violence from men, the majority from husbands, intimate partners or someone they know.

Seventy per cent – globally? How many women is this? The world population is 7 billion, half of these must be female (if not a little more). This means around 2.45 billion women will (eventually) be violated by men over their lifetime. Percentages carry with them a weight of authority; numbers (allegorically) count. Men are the main perpetrators (theory of gender binary sutured with/by heteronormativity). If 70 per cent of women suffer in this way, what percentage of men are responsible: 70 per cent? In any room, will 70 per cent of the women be a 'victim' and 70 per cent of the men a perpetrator? Though the equality of percentages does not necessarily follow, the heteronormative, familial set up of narratives around sexual violence suggests this 70/70 'equality' would be the case. Should we not then ask a question about the fourteen male leaders Ban Ki-moon names: will 70 per cent of them be (potential?) perpetrators of sexual violence? Or, minimally, 70 per cent of their wives, mothers, daughters and sisters would have (or will) experience sexual violence? Isn't this how statistical averages work? Or is it always going to be 'other' men? What (theoretical) story is being told here, almost without our noticing? Or by accident?

> Break the silence.

This is an odd mixing of metaphors and senses – how is (a) silence to be broken? Can silence be grasped hold of and fractured, smashed, splintered? And what might transpire from such a violation of a quiet void? Can this violent grasping and shattering be controlled such that the rupture has only 'intended' consequences? But silence is clearly *something* – Ban Ki-moon does not indicate that violence is empty, or a vacuum. So what inhabits the silence?

> When you witness violence against women and girls, do not sit back. Act.

This makes some (more) sense of the mismatched idea of breaking silence. The silence is actually a kind of unproductive blindness. It refers not to what is heard (or not), but to what is (not) seen. A visual silence, though this also seems odd. There is a cruel spectre here of complicity, of knowing and 'seeing' but not saying or acting to stop, or even acknowledge, the violence. The image(ry); the acknowledgment, the confession is stark, shocking. 'I' witness (but do not 'see') a woman or a girl being violated. I sit back and watch, or pretend not to see. Or I cannot see any more, even though it is in front of my eyes. Or 'I' see, but it's not what it is. It is something else.

> Violence against women and girls will not be eradicated until all of us – men and boys – refuse to tolerate it

Women never seem to be enough, here they are not enough to eradicate violence (against women and girls). Men and boys are needed because they need not to stop being perpetrators (here), but to refuse to tolerate sexual violence. A striking admission perhaps. Toleration is such an interesting word, idea, practice, theory.[427] It often carries with a weight of disgust – 'I will tolerate you' (even though I despise you, find you despicable, unacceptable). Thus I wonder how the idea of toleration works in this context. If sexual violence is currently tolerated by innumerable men and boys (though a number is surely reachable given the statistical information available . . .) what is it that they despise?

> By 2015, the UNiTE campaign aims to achieve the following five goals worldwide: adopt and enforce national laws to address and punish all forms of violence against women and girls; adopt and implement multi-sectoral national action plans; strengthen data collection on the prevalence of violence against women and girls; increase public awareness and social mobilization; and address sexual violence in conflict.[428]

Are these not already well established?

> My commitment to this issue stems not just from my position as UN Secretary-General, but also as a son, husband, father and grandfather.

Given the information provided by Ban Ki-moon in narrative on the launch of UNiTE, what conclusions might we draw from this inclusion of a range of male familial roles? That Ban Ki-moon has witnessed violations of female family members but has not spoken out or failed to act? This seems potentially libellous. Instead, one is theoretically–emotionally drawn to imagine love, care and compassion incurred by being a son, a husband, a father, a grandfather. Yet there is something profoundly contradictory here – theoretically and empirically. Who metes out the violence to 2.45 billion women worldwide according to Ban Ki-moon?

> Men have a crucial role to play in ending such violence – as fathers, friends, decision-makers, and community and opinion leaders

There is something enticingly obvious here, men have a crucial role in ending such violence. But as Ban Ki-moon has noted, such violence is 'largely perpetrated by husbands, intimate partners or someone they know'. The messages in UNiTE seem confusing, even, or perhaps especially, because of their simplistically read theoretical clarity.

There are a wide range of theories available with which to deal with the 'scourge of sexual violence'. Biologically determinist arguments, though largely theoretically discredited, still hold much public credibility – some men are just evil, or men are naturally aggressive/violent, psychological explanations utilising a variety of sources and ideas around early trauma, repressed emotions, inadequate moral development, failure to resolve the vestiges of oedipal conflict, sociological explanations which work across and between a wide range of culturally constituted identities and societal arrangements to demonstrate the production of violent consequences acted out by individuals and collectives. What is being secured? Though an answer is elusive and indeed illusive given that ...

The thinking field is not level.[429]

IR without men

> And if the thinking field is not level, then ...

> Only within the genre of the fantastic is it possible to imagine completely new social orders and ways of being that differ radically from human existence as we know it.[430]

A provocative idea, of course: IR without men. The absence of women conjures a different kind of imagined world, a more familiar one.

Kenneth Waltz's canonical book *Man, the State and War*[431] remains important in the study of International Relations. It perhaps does not currently figure as the core text on most introductory or foundational IR courses, though the book, and Waltz's influence on the development of IR theory, are strong. More recently, a double special issue of the British-based journal *International Relations* was devoted to Waltz's work.[432] It inspired an animated discussion on *Facebook*: 'wow – I have been out of official "IR" for quite some time – I am more astounded that we are still talking about Waltz!'[433] Another post indicated that Waltz is most certainly still being taught, 'Yeah, I just (unfortunately) read with my class an entire book that would only have been half as long if the author had stopped trying to save Waltz from himself.'[434] The e-discussion became even more animated over the article in the special issue that engaged feminism in relation to Waltz's *Man, the State and War*. The gist of the comments coalesced around the almost total lack of attention paid by the author to feminist IR literature, despite writing with robust clarity in the article on the claims of 'feminist international relations' scholarship. The speedy theoretical evaporation of feminist work is very familiar.

If a book with the title *Woman, the State and War* had been published in the same year as Waltz's *Man, the State and War*, what are the chances of it having the potential of claiming canonical status in IR theory half a century later? After all, there is only one word difference. But a book on *Woman, the State and War* does not feel the same as a book on *Man, the State and War*. The difference is not about the traditional intellectual and political exclusion of women (at least explicitly), or the preponderance of men in the mindsets, agendas and imaginations of academics and politicians, though both of these remain profoundly important. The gender of Waltz's book should not be absent-mindedly ignored (minds are not absent) because of the era in which the book was written. Though we might now assume or accept that Waltz's 'man' was meant to be an inclusive term for 'human', or attempts might be made in this corrective direction. When Mitchell B. Reiss, Director of Policy, Planning Staff at the US Department of State gave a talk on George W. Bush's approach to foreign policy at the Fletcher School of Law and Diplomacy at Tufts University, he began with a reference to Waltz's *Man, the State and War*. 'As many of you know, Waltz began his study with a timeless question – "why do humans go to war?".'[435] Reiss's updating from 'man' to 'human' was presumably meant to overcome the gender-deficient knowledge of 1959 and to be attuned to the more gender-aware student population of the twenty-first century. Though I don't think this works: human is still something of a singular force which 'man' is secured by – a certain genre of this category at least: 'The enlightenment's man turns out, indeed, to be a man'.[436]

Pursuing the idea of International Relations without men seems counter-intuitive, impossible and inadvisable. Jean Bethke Elshtain recoils at putative pleas for the reduction of the number of males in the population.[437] Laura Sjoberg wonders about the veracity of this plea, given she could not find a source for it,[438] though Elshtain has probably read Solanos's *SCUM Manifesto* but may have misimagined some of its meanings.

IR without men? The collective discursive imaginations of millennia which forces men seamlessly, though not effortlessly, to the surface emerges as natural. Hierarchies of race, sexuality and gender all line up comfortably as if by magic. Cynthia Enloe used a photo of Margaret Thatcher – one white woman in morass of white men – to help us see this.[439] So too Andy Warhol's Campbell's soup cans: just another row of what we become inured to. For Roland Bleiker, 'such undistorted representation of external realities can be subversive insofar as it draws attention to what is taken for granted and would otherwise go unnoticed';[440] an 'ironic mimesis' for Bleiker. Irony and subversion were not lost on Solanos, 'her texts were loaded with irony and pointed at the real'.[441] And like Derrida, Solanos was less interested in annihilating men and more interested in the steadfast assurance of the concept of man. And similar to the ways in which science fiction writers creatively work with imagination, as well as things not yet imagined, the radical feminist energy exhibited by Solanos (if we might momentarily think of Solanos as working with radical feminist ideas) helps propel us toward strange thinking with all the attendant severe tests of believability which accompany this.

Yet that a book with the title *Woman, the State and War* would surely be different, perhaps (always) radically, from a book with the title *Man, the State and War* is theoretically and philosophically fascinating, as well as being empirically and politically significant. But that a book with the title *Woman, the State and War* might keep emerging as trivial, at least in the grand scheme of international political activity, whether in theory or practice, is something to think again and again about. Though that 'Women' might make the titular grade suggests that perhaps 'woman', unlike 'man', continues to evade the capture of the trapped subject position. Yet recall the fear of unravelling the riddle of a text.

The more power you hold, the more power holds you.[442]

Rape

Words are bodies which can be hurled at the other.[443]

I think there is more tension than usual in the undergraduate class. The student presenter has read about rape in war and conflict, and is speaking about men's sexual desires and needs as potential explanation. Detail emerges about the 'unimaginable' amount of rapes in the Rwandan genocide and the ubiquity of rape in the DRC. The students in the class, mostly female, are not very used to theorising about gender. What can they be thinking or feeling as we try to discuss the apparent inevitability of rape in war? Or about Susan Brownmiller's inference that all men are potential rapists? The tension merges with disinterest.

The Code

We have discovered the secrets of life.
Francis Crick

How each thing gathers to a whole,
the leaven in its heart
holding a pattern before it shows
capacity —

the tree inside the feathered stamen
the egg inside the bird
are infolded, not unthought –
like something heard.

As if intention stored itself
in the unspeaking world,
or creation longed to speak
one secret word –

Who failed to crack the egg?
I-I-I cries the lark.
Who missed the mystery of birth?
The nodding larch.

Alone in our unceasing day
we press against the curve
that presence makes of land – and sky –
and hear the beat

of what can never come to term
but stopless grows:
the public secret of a code
the whole world knows.[444]

Fiona Sampson

Where is rape?

Rape begins in the rapist's mind.[445]

The quote comes from Susan Brownmiller's book on rape, *Against Our Will*, which is positioned as something of a classic in feminist literature.[446] Written for women, as the 'our' implies, though such explicit gendered identification of audience is unusual, if not surreptitiously commonplace. Women casually appear in Kenneth Waltz's book as whores[447] or potential peacemakers,[448] suggesting Waltz was writing to and for men. Brownmiller's book, published in 1975 and written in an accessible, pacy style, was chosen by *The New York Times* as one of the outstanding books of the year. It is a *tour de force*, working with materials drawn from history, psychology, sociology and the law. In a chapter on war, Brownmiller trawls through very familiar horrendous tales of mass rape, casual rape and murderous rape that still appear inevitable in contemporary sadistic practices of war.[449] Fascination with these rape stories remains high.

I attended a talk on 'rape in war' a couple of years ago. Like Brownmiller's work, the talk was based on detailed historical research. Someone in the audience asked about the men who rape in war but who subsequently say they had no choice. The example was given of the many Serbian men who ended up (as if by mistake?) raping their former friends and neighbours in the war in the former Yugoslavia in the early 1990s.[450] They raped, some of them explained, *against their will*, usually because they would be killed if they had not joined in the ritual of raping 'enemy women'. In response, the speaker suggested that the man – the new (surprised) rapist – still had some kind of benefit from the rape, though he left the precise nature of the benefit unstated. This left me wondering about the legacy of radically inspired feminism, as it seemed the speaker was suggesting, like Browmiller had, that all men are always potential rapists. And more than this – that all men in the act of rape would ultimately experience some measure of benefit or pleasure.[451] Do only men who rape know if this is true? Did the speaker wonder about how women in the room felt?

Feminist moves to refocus attention on 'perpetrators' rather than 'victims' has generated a great deal of recent work, much of which pays serious and nuanced attention to men who rape. Borislav Herak, as Cynthia Enloe puts it, was an 'ordinary man'.[452] He also did not appear to be a violent man; this is the usual definition of 'ordinary', perhaps. In 1993 he was charged with murder and mass rape. Perhaps he became brutalised in the short time since the war came to his home town of Sarajevo. Enloe suspects that his training to be a man, or the specific cocktail of expectations of what it meant to be a man in the post-World War II multi-ethnic Communist state in which Borislav Herak grew up, had something to do with his eventual acts of rape. Herak was convicted and sentenced to death.

The case of Borislav Herak is used by Enloe, in part, to demonstrate the inadequacy of understandings of wars, nationalisms and associated violences if attention is not paid to masculinity. Similarly inspired by horror at the egregious persistence of sexualised violence in war and conflict, Maria Erikson Baas and Maria Stern's curiosity focused on the question – why do soldiers rape?[453] They are interested in feminist (and other) deployments of gender, and how these deployments are discursively embroiled in fuelling failures to stem sexual violence, or to even begin understanding why rape, especially in war and conflict, seems so intractable. To investigate this, they pay attention to what soldiers say about why they rape (methodologically intriguing). The men they interviewed were not incarcerated soldiers, but free men. They found the soldiers were troubled by the raping they do. Yet the men explained that there was a difference between 'lust rapes' and 'evil rapes'. Lust rapes were about relieving sexual tension, the men explained, especially when 'their woman' was not available. Does 'lust rape', as Susan Brownmiller suggested in 1975, begin in the rapist's mind? Or, as inferred by the rapists, in the needy body? The distinction that emerges is meaningless here with men rematerialising as actors.

Exhaustively analysed in recent years, there has been an increasingly broad range of explanations for its incidence, and particularly for why men rape. It is the case that women participate in assisting men to rape, and that some women rape women and men and children (of both/all sexes); however, legal definitions of what counts as rape (popularly ingrained) have traditionally worked on the principle that rape involves the penetration of a (woman's or girl's) vagina with a (man's or boy's) penis. More recent legislation works with the reality that any bodily orifice ('natural' or 'unnatural') can be penetrated, and with a range of objects, though it is the case that the generic public understanding of what counts as rape is the 'traditional' version. It is also still overwhelmingly the case that men rape. If there were no men, would rape disappear? Solanos tangentially implies this: eliminate men and women will shape up.[454]

Eliminating is a serious theoretical idea though not a serious empirical one, though Solanos's usurpation of the hegemonic domain of violence remains a violating surprise. By comparison, Brownmiller's tame invocation of the 'rapist's mind' as the cause of rape is partially suggestive of psychological explanations. Some men are, or just become, bad. Or some men just don't have the right upbringing, or something outrageous happened to them (war, abuse) which assembles the worst in them. Dr Jekyll metamorphoses into Mr Hyde, and Mr Hyde was surely the literal personification of masculinised evil (with racial and class inflections always suturing the disgust, stunningly represented in the 1931 film).[455] And yet, for a radically modulated feminism, the rapist, however his identity has been constituted, still benefits. His positioning on a continuum of competing yet always unequal masculinities suggests the strong influence of structural explanations. But still the actions, words and deeds always end up being done by someone, or some people, or some men. So I ask the question again, without men, would there be no rape?

The *SCUM Manifesto*, first published in 1968, is surely obscene in parts, and it can easily be presented as having no contemporary theoretical/artistic merit or depth, paradoxically laughable in its absurdity. Resurrecting Valerie Solanos seems unwise. Though, in the tradition of polemical writers whom we now think of as related to feminism (or sex and gender in some way), Solanos despaired at women's collaboration and complicity in their own violations; recall that she wants women to 'shape up'. Mary Wollstonecraft, who, like Solanos, worked on developing, reshaping and radically usurping philosophical thinking of the time, railed against women's feminine manners.[456] But unlike Wollstonecraft, Solanos wanted women to 'fuck-up' rather than 'grade up'.[457] Even 'dropping out' of the system wasn't enough for Solanos, as this, she argued, was a form of passive complicity which simply kept the system operating as normal.

I don't know if I was the only person in the room at the talk on 'rape in war' I mentioned earlier who felt discomfited by the answer to the question about men who rape by 'accident'. I would be surprised if I was the only one, given the answer seemed to, once again, conjure the idea of woman as always rapeable.[458] It also injected a shadow of masculinised pride putting rape in its usual place. The shape of rape was present. Though care is always necessary here, given that . . .

> A powerful subject like rape can be a trap . . . we can be seduced into thinking the material itself is so strong . . . we don't have to engage with it very deeply – an outpouring of emotion or an emphasis on graphic detail will suffice.[459]

Why can't a woman be more like a man?

> Don't go all Jodie Foster on me.

The 'would-be rapist' in the 2011 film *Horrible Bosses* is a woman.[460] Given that this is what Judith Halberstam might call a 'stupid white male film', the attempted rape scenes are meant to be funny.[461] The 'stupid white male' resists his boss's seduction techniques, recasting them as attempted rape. 'Don't go all Jodie Foster on me' she shouts.[462] One imagines this is a reference to the character that Jodie Foster plays in the film *The Accused*,[463] an allusion perhaps with a touch of heteronormative correctiveness to it, given Foster's sexuality.

Horrific images of sexual violence have become commonplace, partly because of feminist insistence that people must see the truth to know it. Describing some of this work as using 'shock and awe' tactics, Kristin Bumiller[464] takes a look at one specific image: Sue Coe's artistic depiction of rape in her 1984 painting *Romance in the Age of Raygun*,[465] a painting showing a gang-raped woman. In it we see a skeletal figure with her arms outstretched, almost in Christ-like pose, blood seeping from wounds which are spread all over her body. Her bloody crotch is exposed and she is surrounded by a 'predatory landscape' of dark, ghostly and, by implication, inhuman male tormentors and onlookers.[466]

The actual case on which Sue Coe's *Romance in the Age of Raygun* was based is the New Bedford, Massachusetts gang rape in which six Portuguese immigrant men were accused of gang raping a young Portuguese–American woman on a pool table in a bar surrounded by cheering onlookers. The case was popularised in the Hollywood film *The Accused*, in which Jodie Foster plays Sarah Tobias, the fictional woman materialising on screen as white.[467] On its release the film attracted much attention and box office revenue given the very explicit rape scene. Also of feminist significance in this film: in the court proceedings that followed this real/fictional rape, it was the woman's body which became the truth, or 'the terrain of verifiability' upon which the prosecution rested its case.[468] To prove that rape took place, intricate, intimate and constant inspection of the woman's body emerged as the necessary source of confirmation. Not the woman's voice. In the film, Tobias's voice was reduced to muffled screams during the attack and muted testimony during the trial. As Bumiller notes, 'without the victim's voice, the power of interpretation belongs both to the law's vision of sexual crime'[469] and to one of the male onlookers (white, middle-class) whose testimony alone gave the truth.[470]

The juridical strength of voice given to raped women in courtrooms was not present here. Yet unwelcome consequences transpire from attaching the potency of juridical authority to the figure of the 'raped woman'. Becoming vocally powerful in the courtroom scene of rape invites an evaporation of the weakness that is the condition of the strength of her testimony: 'her not counting makes her words count'.[471] It is strange that gaining one's voice should metamorphose into such violent silence. A timely reminder of Kramer's analysis.

> Sexual violence cannot be cured by making men aware of how brutal it is. They know how brutal it is.[472]

Looking again at images of sexual violence and rape, not least those presented with feminist intentions, Kristin Bumiller suggests that such persistent forays into the pathologised feminised sphere invites further violence. Drawing on the imagery in *Romance in the Age of Raygun*, Bumiller argues that such images play readily into time-worn scripts of 'racialised perpetrators', further criminalising men of colour, whether perpetrators or not. These images also reproduce the typical script of 'feminised victims' by eliciting therapeutic and legislative interventions by experts to both con-firm and ameliorate the trauma that victims of sexual violence are expected to express if they are to be believed by the courts.[473] And believability is structured in particular ways, with hierarchies of rape victims holding a solid place in courts and popular, media-fuelled imaginations:[474] an eighty-year-old, a four-year-old, a slut.

> Yet there are always those who wish to speak on behalf of those who seem-ingly cannot.

> The United States has repeatedly condemned the epidemic of sexual violence in conflict zones round the world, and we will continue to speak for those who cannot speak for themselves.[475]

Clear, confrontational, confident: the United States remains insistent on ventrilo-quising those who they claim cannot speak for themselves,[476] especially the raped women in conflict zones round the world. Feminist activists, scholars and legislators have insisted there are effective ways to remind people that rape is wrong *en route* to securing successful actions to stem the scourge.

United Nations Secretary-General Ban Ki-moon's **UNiTE to End Violence against Women** campaign aims to prevent and eliminate violence against women and girls in all parts of the world.

UNiTE brings together a host of UN agencies and offices to galvanize action across the UN system to prevent and punish violence against women. Through UNiTE, the UN is joining forces with individuals, civil society and governments to put an end to violence against women in all its forms.[477]

In Toni Morrison's *The Bluest Eye*,[478] Cholly rapes his eleven-year-old daughter Pecola.

> Removing himself from her was so painful to him he cut it short and snatched his genitals out of the dry harbor of her vagina. She appeared to have fainted. Cholly stood up and could see only her grayish panties, so sad and limp around her ankles. The hatred would not let him pick her up; the tenderness forced him to cover her.[479]

In the film *Gone with the Wind*[480] there are two 'rape scenes'. In the first, Scarlett O'Hara is carried, under protest, by her husband Rhett Butler to the bedroom. In the context of her refusing his sexual advances and, by inference, his sexual needs for some time, the implication of the scene is cinematically clear. The following morning, we see Scarlett sitting coquettishly and happily in the marital bed. It seems that what might have been a forced act of sex (a rape?) had become an enjoyable successful seduction for both Rhett and Scarlett. In the second 'rape' scene, a black enslaved man happens across an unconscious Scarlett in her over-turned horse-drawn carriage. She wakes to see him looming over her and she begins to scream. He runs away and Scarlett is rescued. Subsequent to this a lynch-ing party is sent in pursuit of the black man.

Rape, race and romance; a heady mix in this scene of violence. Also a precarious and easy subject, yet

> Rape shows the victim that the world is not as it seems.[481]

An ordinary man

> . . . the apparently wrongful infliction of sexual violence actually serves to uphold a purely conventional order.[482]

> *Kramer's use of 'apparently' is telling.*

In Terrell Carver's concluding chapter to Laura Shepherd's edited collection *Gender Matters in Global Politics*, he advises readers, 'not to go home'.[483] The 'home' he infers is IR (and Realist IR at that), and is the home to which (feminist readers/novices) might be persuaded not to return once they have read Shepherd's book and taken in its meanings and messages. Home is, perhaps, as Carver claims, where the heart is. He urges we may not wish to 'go back there'; though we may not be able to, 'leaving home can only happen because there is a home to leave'.[484] What if (Realist) IR has never been a real home at all, especially given the violence there? What might we make of such an allegory in contemporary feminist international relations? Recall *Rancière* from earlier:

> Everywhere there are starting points, intersections and junctions if we refuse . . . the boundaries between territories.[485]

Framing the first-year International Relations course or module around an 'ordinary man', Josef Fritzl perhaps might, naturally enough, end up looking typically 'IR Realist' – power, sovereign control, masculinity, violence. Being face-to-face with one man. Nothing new there. As an ordinary man, public desire for Fritzl to be a monster is strong. And, naturally enough, questions recur about how women like Elisabeth, his daughter, might be protected, given the security already on offer.

Austrian author Elfride Jelenik won the Nobel Prize for Literature in 2004. This was shocking for some given her work has been described as 'whining, unenjoyable public pornography'.[486] Her novels slice into post-World War II Austrian family life, giving a picture of bitterness, resentment and 'vicious incestuous love in the wake of fascism'.[487] She offers ugly depictions of small-town family life. In her novel *The Piano Teacher*,[488] the central character Erika, like Marina Abramović perhaps, invites bloody violation. This seems like a patriarchal narration of female masochism, another opportunity for Freudian amusement. The cutting and slicing, the dishevelling of sense and reason, bodies and gender. There is a refusal here which we might linger on, given that

> . . . violence against women, always feels legitimate to the man who enacts it. That is why it is so readily excused, even by its victims; that is why it is so easily repeated.[489]

Woman's place

> What makes a woman is a specific social relation to a man.[490]

> *Always relational . . .*

'My book? Well it's about feminist International Relations.'

FIGURE 17 Sarkozy and Rice

'So – you'll be writing about Hillary Clinton, Margaret Thatcher and Condoleezza Rice, then?'

'No. Sigh.'

A woman standing for high office still sparks special interest. In May 2007, conservative Nicolas Sarkozy won the French presidential election; the opposition candidate in the final vote was the socialist candidate Segolene Royale. This 'right-wing/left-wing' battle provoked much national and international interest. Royale's last-ditch attempt to gain more votes by suggesting it was time for a woman to be elected to this powerful position was not successful. Simultaneously, Sarkozy promised 'equality of the sexes' in his cabinet, allegedly provoking a battle for posts amongst a group of women dubbed 'Les Sarkozettes',[491] a feminised diminutive readily reminiscent of 'Blair's Babes' *circa* 1997.[492] Time marches on, yet more than ten years after 'Blair's Babes', the likelihood of a female successor to him (and subsequently Gordon Brown and Ed Miliband) remains low.

Comfortably assuming we know why it is important to ask questions about women, to keep noticing women is precarious,

> As long as there is no women's struggle, there is no conflict between men and women.[493]

When foreign policy-makers and feminist academics meet

> ... the world needs women's perspectives and particular talents in top positions.[494]

I was invited to a workshop to discuss the role of women in US foreign policy. We were a 'cross-community' gathering (academics and policy-makers) so the day promised much in the way of generating constructive dialogue. Clearly, we imagined the women who were actively involved in US foreign policy could speak about their experiences 'as women' in that arena; it was going to be interesting to hear their views on how much they thought (their) gender mattered. I also wondered what the policy-makers imagined the academics would say. Here's a comment that taps into some of the muddied heart of the day.

> 'That was a lot of fun.'

This comment was made with some measure of relief by one of the policy-makers after a presentation on Condoleezza Rice given by Nicola Pratt, an academic from the University of Warwick. The presentation was indeed a lot of fun. It was intellectually stimulating and full of interesting insights about the intertwined role of gender and race in US foreign policy-making. And it had great potential for illustrating – in profound ways – precisely why it matters to think seriously about how gender weaves through race in the conduct of US foreign policy. But profundity and seriousness appeared a little out of place in light of the received levity of this presentation.

V. Spike Peterson used the word 'seriously' with much precision and intention in an early chapter on gender.[495] More recently, Laura Sjoberg reminds us why it matters to take gender seriously.[496] Their use of the idea and practice of 'seriously' indicate they are acutely aware that work on gender is so easily considered lightly, something which has a double effect. One is that the 'results' (of gender(ed) knowledge) are not taken adequate notice of, intellectually, conceptually, practically. A second, and integrally intertwined, effect is that the complex work necessary to probe the work that gender does is habitually and effortlessly disregarded. Discussions about gender regularly and easily disintegrate into (sometimes defensive) debates deploying 'everyday logic', unreflectively dismissing the theoretical, philosophical and methodological work necessary to speak seriously about gender.

Nicola Pratt showed us a PowerPoint image of Condoleezza Rice resplendently attired in a high-fashion long, black coat and high-heeled black patent knee-high boots, alongside another showing Rice languidly propping up a piano, this time dressed in a floor-length, off-the-shoulder evening dress.[497] Given she is a skilled pianist, one is led to imagine Rice is about to play. Pratt was motivated to think about Rice's raced/gendered identity in relation to Pratt's work on the Middle East, but also consequent to reading a popular magazine article about Rice. The piece focused on Rice's 'girly shopping' trips and love of clothes. Here's an extract: [OW = Oprah Winfrey].

CR: 'I also love to shop. I can get lost in a store for hours'.

OW: 'What do you like shopping for?'

CR: 'Clothes – and shoes. Love the shoes!'

OW: 'Do you have girly-girl moments with your friends?'

CR: 'Oh, sure'.

In her conclusion to her paper, Pratt suggested that Rice's 'girly femininity' was deeply significant in the enactment of US foreign policy, especially around the time of the Iraq war and the invasion of Afghanistan in the early 2000s. For Rice to be able to 'own' and enact such a modern western form of femininity against a deeply racist backdrop of excluding black women from the realm of womanhood/humanity positioned Condoleezza Rice as representing what Pratt described as 'a new feminine subject in the neo-liberal global economy'. Far from demonstrating Rice's 'fun side', this deeply serious observation implied that Rice's performance of womanhood in her position as US Secretary of State played a significant role in giving coherence, strength and rationale to Bush's imperialistic endeavours and, moreover, helped to buttress and solidify the USA's/the west's righteous position as defenders and promoters of global freedom and democracy. Does it matter that these very serious conclusions could dissipate into a 'lot of fun'?

The policy-makers weren't happy. They seemed perturbed by the (seemingly) academic use of the word gender instead of women. They seemed irritated by the attention to the gender of women foreign policy-makers, yet at the same time were clear that 'being women' did matter, but in ways they were unclear about, or couldn't keep track of. They were annoyed at the lack of clear answers from academics to their direct questions. What is feminism? What characterises a feminist? Can men be feminists? To be sure, critical academic work perhaps allows for more philosophical and critical interrogation than policy-makers can afford in their daily working lives, and we did only have one day to talk to each other. But there was something riveting and profound about the range of confusions, contradictions, paradoxes and irritations that rippled through the day and late into the evening which, to me, spoke reams about gender – and why we can't seem to make it work the way we (think we) want it to.

But we were there to address the 'woman question' – here is a reminder about women's place:

In phallogocentric society women get equality as long as they don't forget to stay women.[498]

Steeped in psychoanalytic angst, the otherness of woman, the difference of woman regularly materialises as a problem to be solved. The 'woman question': the title of numerous feminist-inspired books, articles and chapters explicating the puzzle of woman. Through feminist language, the question perhaps invites less significance, becoming trivial. Transmitting (feminist) arguments supported by (feminist) evidence through phallogocentric prisms of rationality and reason can readily transmute into irritation and bickering. As fat-fighter Marjorie Dawes in the TV comedy *Little Britain*[499] cannot understand the (clearly enunciated) words of the woman marked as 'foreign' in the fat-fighters group ('Indian' in the British version,[500] 'Filipina/Mexican' in the US version),[501] feminist reasoning is regularly heard as rancorous and unreasonable.

Flippancy and trivialising. The relief at being able to find fun does something quite interesting with the heavy assumptions and expectations that lace questions about women's roles as political representatives, which was the specific form of the 'woman question' on that day. The difficulty in finding the boundaries, or really keeping the boundaries intact, around women, around gender, around how much progress has been made, around how far there is to go, around how much it matters (to be a woman) and how much it doesn't, and around how much control can be exercised over how much it matters, these difficulties also reveal something very interesting about gender and about feminism.

The liberal-inspired equality agenda (one with which the foreign policy-makers would be well acquainted) infers that when women aren't noticed anymore, success will have been achieved. Equality invokes a sense of the normal, the ordinary, even the natural. Particularly distinctive about things natural is that they seem to be part of the fabric of life – they are just 'there'. This evinces a sense of somnambulant comfort so whatever they are, we tend not to notice them.[502] Yet we do keep noticing women, and we do keep forgetting that men appear very comfortably at the centre. Sometimes a spark of exasperation at this preponderance urges attention,[503] but we then forget quickly. But we keep on and on noticing women.

The keynote speech given by Nancy Soderberg at the end of the day focused on women and current security challenges. Describing herself as 'not a feminist', she began her speech with the 'old Chinese saying' – 'women hold up half the sky' – moving on to state that if women were not 'at the table' we would not be able to meet the challenges of today, whether in the context of failed states, climate change or terrorism. Soderberg was clear that there was a direct correlation between societies in conflict and poverty and the status of women. We will not have peace and prosperity, she argued, if women continued to be abused.

On a more up-beat note, she acknowledged that it is now conceivable that a woman could be US president, a sign of sure progress, though still a long way off the mark in the top political positions (also noting that women oftentimes choose not to stay the course). More broadly even, given the list of achievements since the Beijing Platform for Action, success is far from complete. Shifting seemingly seamlessly from politically powerful American women with choices to the abused women in the Congo – 'it just breaks your heart'. And of course, it does.

Soderberg was insistent that societies do better when women have equal rights. Nations become more stable, more peaceful and more secure when women are equal and when women take part. Offering Northern Ireland as an example which produced a movement for peace that was instigated from the 'bottom up', Soderberg said women 'forced the issue' and moreover proved themselves to be 'good at listening' and 'open to reconciliation'. Further still, female military personnel were better with local communities and helping with crowd control; the metaphorical gene for peace lingering closely. More broadly, the United Nations was putting much effort into giving women a greater role in peace-building; women were especially needed to restore peace in transitional societies. But she never took the 'women's issues jobs' when in Clinton's administration, she went for the 'power jobs', knowing that if she got stuck in the 'women's jobs' she'd never get out of them. The suffocating trap of woman. Returning to speak more comfortably about men, Soderberg remarked that real change was not going to happen until men accepted women as full partners. Men and women should be responsible for the range of decision-making, not leaving the 'women's issues' to women. But she was still sure that women did bring 'a different perspective' to the table.

For Soderberg, nowhere in the world was safe. Iraq, Afghanistan, London, the threat of WMDs and now cyberthreats. In the context of terrorism and global security challenges, Pakistan was, for Soderberg, the most dangerous place on Earth. Osama bin Laden was, she claimed, probably on the Pakistan–Afghanistan border.★ And Iran, North Korea, Somalia, Sudan, these were all very messy political situations.

The 'woman question'. On that day it was this: would the world be different if women had a stronger political role? My ultimate answer was no. Or at least, I could not say yes. But actually, and crucially, it's the wrong question to ask. What is assumed in its asking? What is missed by asking it? What other questionable directions might be pursued? The shape of feminism is interesting here. Though working with typologies of feminist theory is not always, or often, very helpful – it might be a useful way to begin thinking about what is at stake when considering the significance or role of women in US foreign policy. Or why it might matter, or make a difference, that there are increasing numbers of women in US foreign policy (which is generally taken to mean more women at the top in positions which men usually occupy). The contemporary liberal (feminist) position is a little confused and contradictory (perhaps illustrating a problem with typologies, it's as if we think they are real or genuinely and coherently depict some kind of truth). But let's stay with it for now.

There is something about representation that matters for liberal feminists, which is tied up with an element of symbolic importance, which is further linked to the need for a tangible illustration of gender equality. As such, women's visible presence and activity in senior and ostensibly powerful political roles suggests the success of democratic ideology and practice on a number of levels, including

---

★ This was before he was killed.

equality (opportunity and outcome) and clear evidence that the central governing body is representational of the wider polity, even if not quite fully. The temporal signs seem positive. That there is some way to go before there is full (statistical) gender representation perhaps explains why women (in US foreign policy) have not become invisible in the same way that men are. Women have not yet blended imperceptibly into this high-political fabric.

One way in which women's inevitable visibility transpires is as symbols, a familiar gendered place for women. Women's symbolic presence at this level is understood to be important not simply because they figure as role models ('for' women? all women?) but also as gendered emblems, and in this context perhaps especially of America's (the USA's) 'can do' attitude. This 'can do' attitude invokes not only, or simply, levels of personal achievement possible (women can make it to the top if . . .) but a 'can do' related to 'making a difference'. And here 'making a difference' carries with it a heavy gendered symbolism and agency which bleeds out to other women not strictly 'in' US foreign policy, but centrally part of it: Laura Bush speaking out for the women of Afghanistan presenting as the feminised voice of western reason an embodiment of democracy, freedom and justice. Lynndie England opening up space for thought about the place of torture in US foreign policy. Jessica Lynch closing that circle.

Women are still different. And oftentimes it is expected or hoped that women will act differently. When Madeleine Albright took over leadership of President's Interagency Council on Women, she was noted for 'her actions in mainstreaming gender in foreign policy, as in her efforts to reach out to and work with INGOs [international NGOs]'.[504] Is the hope that they will act differently to help women, to advance women's equality? Is the hope that they will act differently to create a different (more peaceful?) foreign policy agenda? Why would anyone hope for either of these, given that each would almost inevitably tether women – these women – right back to their gender? A liberal inflected position suggests the possibility of containing and controlling gender in theoretical evaluation and (embodied) practice. But containing gender is not so easy.

Questions about the sex of political representatives – although this is very rarely taken to mean anything other than being about women – these questions, again even with a heavy feminist intonation, have the effect of securing the hold of gender, and specifically the hold on gender in relation to women. This does not beckon a choice of rejecting the special character of woman; the category is held together by exceptionality, at least of a certain sort.

But feminism is curiously unbounded in these narratives around women representatives. The questions invoke attention to logics and practices of justice, of representation, of the symbolic importance of noticing women. But then noticing women secures gender once again. This is what the women foreign policy-makers know, or perhaps they sense it. This is not to say they don't negotiate around it skilfully, women seem extraordinarily skilful at negotiating around and playing tricks with gender. Though there is the conflict between securing gender and tricking it – we can't really make gender do what we want it to.

In the late-night discussion in the bar with Soderberg and the other foreign policy-makers, the answer for them is no, dwelling on whether women make a difference is not worth it, especially in the convoluted ways academics approached this issue. This is because it cannot provide answers, solutions, speedy responses; they want to be able to 'do' something. I suppose this is not surprising, it's their job and what they do. The successful implementation of action is the overriding goal.

So what to do? This is a question at which the policy-makers and the academics converge. We both want to know 'what to do' – or we both think this is an important consideration, and we know students generally do. There is a point to the work. But we probably think very differently about what constitutes a legitimate and useful answer.

My answers may not be of direct use to foreign policy-makers, but what use can they be? Is this even a fruitful way to think? There was such a radical divergence between 'us' and 'them', they were befuddled and bemused by the kinds of things we were saying. But then, why would they understand my/our points? I presume they haven't read a plethora of books and articles on gender/feminist theory – isn't that part of the point of an academic education? Or the intellectual remit? It isn't 'common-sense' or practical action (even if related to it).

But it's difficult to leave gender alone, sticky attachments are hard to dislodge. It remains very important to keep tracking how gender metamorphoses, and the 'new work' gender does. The ways gender materialises through the 'figure' of woman and women in US foreign policy remains noticeable. Yet still 'some' women don't seem to realise their gender:

> You never seen a naked woman before? No ma'am.[505]

Two women

> She was just a piece of data waiting for his words to write her up, to pass her down to us as social science.[506]

Telling women's stories remains consistently important within feminism. Ethnography, oral history, interviewing, surveys, archival work, data collection, these are just a few of the ways women's lives have been recovered and recorded. There are countless lost stories and lost lives outside of these retrieved ones, but there remains the hope that something important might be learned through these stories, many of which materialise only because of feminist insistence that women matter. Breathing 'voice' into the lives of women,[507] imagining that this will keep them from disappearing into the invisible dregs of history where most people's lives lie like so much sludge. Inspecting the lives of women who are not white is imagined to offer important knowledge about women, about gender, about race and about power, which it does. But what else does this selective peering into the flesh and blood lives of 'other' women do?

> Two armed groups raped more than 150 women in a village in the volatile North Kivu province in the Democratic Republic [of Congo] in a four-day spree, a United Nations official said Monday.[508]

The raping of African women (the mediated image conjures black women) by (again assumed) black African men (how many in 'two groups?') invokes, in westernised imaginaries, a mélange of fear and horror. We (white/western women?) sympathise. Though the quiet but insistent inflection of a masculine, racially ripped madness (a 'raping spree') perhaps suggests 'we' cannot really empathise, though the pornographic allure of carnage and violated bodies[509] enticingly acts as an invitation to western action.

> The United States has repeatedly condemned the epidemic of sexual violence in conflict zones round the world, and we will continue to speak for those who cannot speak for themselves.[510]

I have spoken in classes about both Sara Baartman and Sojourner Truth, introducing them as illustrative. The image of Truth as an elderly woman seated with knitting to hand – a restful image, concealing the violence and grind of slave lives[511] – along with her iconic speech, 'Ain't I A Woman' is easily accessible through internet search engines, very easy for me to access and show on a PowerPoint slide in class.[512] Images and stories about Sara Baartman, too, are easily accessed via the internet. Though, given that part of the retrieved narrative about Baartman centres on the exploitative visual display of her, reproducing an image of Baartman in a class or in a text is intellectually and emotively difficult in a complex way.[513] To show or not to show? To look (again) or not?

My students and I look, through contemporary eyes, mostly with horror and shock at the colonial and racist exploitation of Sara Baartman, hoping that this recuperation will enable the telling of stories about colonialism, racism and gender. Labelled the 'Hottentot Venus', she was paraded naked with lascivious eyes honing in on her sensualised, sexualised, large (large(r) than 'normal' white women's) labia and buttocks. These pictures are also easily accessible via the internet; so many voyeurs, so many people peering, prodding, poking.

There is a large literature on Baartman,[514] sometimes called Sara/Sarah, sometimes Saartjie (a Dutch diminutive for Sara); her original name is unknown. We have learned that this Khosian woman was shipped from Africa, along with animals and plants, to England in 1810 by Alexander Dunlop, a ship's surgeon who also exported museum specimens. Baartman was bought by a man named Hendrick Cezar (little is known about him) and the public were invited to view the 'Hottentot Venus' for two shillings. She moved to Paris in 1814 and was exhibited there for eighteen months. She died in 1815. Consequent to her death she continued to be exhibited, first through her autopsy; latterly in the exhibition of her skull, brain, skeleton and dissected genitalia. After a campaign began in 1995 for the repatriation of her remains from where they were held in the Musée de l'Homme in Paris to South Africa, she was finally returned there in 2002 and was buried as a local woman who had been returned home.[515] Minh ha clarifies this well:

> It's as if everywhere we go, we become Someone's private zoo.[516]

The man who bought Baartman and took her to Paris was an animal trainer and, though she was not kept in a cage along with the 'other animals', the sense is that she might as well have been. The entrails of racist science which were viscerally present in the autopsy report, her skull being described as more like a monkey's skull than a human one, continue to haunt twenty-first-century scientific imaginaries.

Anne Fausto-Sterling and Sadiah Qureshi are two scholars who have painstakingly traced Baartman's life. What is both poignant and sophisticated about their work is that they (try to) stop looking at Baartman and instead look more at those who have looked (and continue to look). As Fausto-Sterling comments, 'what we do know about her comes from reading beneath the surface of newspaper reports, court proceedings and scientific articles'...'we can never see her except through the eyes of the white men who described her'.[517] This shifting of attention to those who gaze – and there is still much gazing upon physiognomic differences[518] – takes us on different narrative trails, and constitutes different knowledges about Baartman. Qureshi's view that the sensationalist impact of Baartman on the nineteenth-century London entertainment-seeking publics had perhaps less to do with her physical appearance (with all the accompanying dark hints of 'black women's raw, untamed sexuality') and more to do with the abolitionist politics animating London in the early nineteenth century.[519] This part of retrieved knowledge has transpired as less popular. The good (feminist) intentions to write women back into history and to oxygenate their lives: can 'we' get it 'right?' Can 'we' extricate ourselves, our methodologies, our desires, from the discursive infection of racism and colonialism, so much of which has made our world white?[520]

Like Baartman's story, our words about Sojourner Truth have come from white people.[521] Her famous speech, made to resonate powerfully over the centuries, was remoulded in racially inflected tones to suit 'northern US interests'[522] with the hoped-for effect of relocating responsibility for slavery in the south and not the north. Yet by giving a name to one woman, 'we' hope to reveal the usually invisible mass of 'other' women. The agency and power 'we' imagine emerging consequent to the resurrection of 'exceptional' individuals[523] can further coagulate the already congealed image of the mass of 'brown other' women. The lone 'heroic Afghani woman'[524] captured in the photographs taken by Steve McCurry – or more accurately 'Afghan girl' (internet search engines will readily reveal this 'iconic' image) – suggests that power remains stickily attached to the white voices and venues that speak for/through her/them. Recall that some women don't realise their gender.

> You never seen a naked woman before? No ma'am.[525]

In Alice Walker's novel The Color Purple,[526] Celie seems not to know herself as female, given her answer 'No ma'am'. A poor, uneducated, black young woman in early twentieth-century America is perhaps not a woman at all. And she knows this, though a girl really at fourteen, but with two children already, a result of rape. Sojourner Truth also knows she is not a woman; at least, this might be imagined reading her speech through western, twenty-first-century eyes. And Condoleezza Rice – what kind of woman can she be?

Trying to separate out race from gender, or to demarcate more clearly the boundaries beyond which one might comfortably say race or gender is more salient, seems to remain important in feminist work. Though there is also strong agreement that 'race' and 'gender' are 'intersectional' markers and makers of identity, agency and power; indeed, intersectionality has become something of a preferred approach, perhaps especially in feminist IR. Yet the easiness with which the rational veneer of dialogue around race and gender is so violently ruptured hints at something important. Nell Painter's work on the persistent use by white activists of racialised representations of Sojourner Truth incurred emotively resistant responses by a range of feminist scholars.[527] The arguments and tensions that marked the World Conferences on Women and consequent debates around transnationalism since 1975 (when the last World Conference in Beijing was held) suggest that inflections and practices of western racism within feminist work have not dissipated.

> In trying to tell herself, a woman is told.[528]

The hours

> To inherit feminism can mean to inherit sadness.[529]

> *Ahmed treads dangerous ground with this thought.*

As experiences go, dreams remain enigmatic. Intensely private, even the dreamer sometimes – oftentimes – isn't let in to the secrets of dreams. Yet dreams are shared. One in particular, the 'teeth falling out' dream, is seemingly in the 'top five' of shared dreams. Infections of the teeth have been thought to cause mental disorder, a kind of seeping blood poisoning of the brain. Virginia Woolf was subjected to teeth extraction in an attempt to cure her bouts of melancholia and depression, or at least these are the names they might be given now. These connections, sharing dreams, linking tooth infection with mental illness are beguilingly corporeal.

Michael Cunningham's book *The Hours*[530] starts and ends with suicide. Virginia Woolf peacefully walks into a river near her home, filling the pockets of her coat with rocks. Richard, an ostensibly fictional character, serenely slips out of the window of his fifth-floor apartment. Dramatic and mundane, Woolf refused to dismiss the lives that others usually ignore. As Cunningham says:

> . . . she runs an errand, meets an old flame in whom she is no longer interested, takes a nap, and gives a party. That's the plot.[531]

Acceptably black[532]

> Whiteness silences itself by pretending it has no meaning.[533]

In the same week that two white men were convicted of the racist murder of teenager Stephen Lawrence eighteen years after the crime was committed,[534] the British Member of Parliament Diane Abbott got into trouble for comments she made on *Twitter*.[535] The first black woman to be elected to the British House of Commons and currently (early 2012) the Shadow Minister for Public Health, Abbott tweeted, 'white people love playing divide and rule' in a conversation about the Stephen Lawrence murder case. She was swiftly accused of making a racist remark and faced calls to resign. Conservative MP Nadhim Zahawi commented that if a white politician had made similar comments about blacks, they would have had to quit. This simple reversal belies the weighted orientation of racism.

In a subsequent TV interview, Abbott insisted her words had been taken out of context. While she was on camera, she received a phone call from the Labour party leader Ed Miliband, who told her she had let down both him and the Labour Party and demanded that she make a public apology. She promptly issued a statement saying: 'I understand people have interpreted my comments as making generalisations about white people. I do not believe in doing that. I apologise for any offence caused.' One week later, Michelle Obama was in the media spotlight reported as having said she rejected the idea that she was 'an angry black woman'.[536]

The founder of the blog *AngryBlackBitch.com*, Pamela Merritt, was invited to comment on Michelle Obama's statement for a 'Roundtable' section in the UK's *Guardian* newspaper.[537] Growing up learning that black women's anger was unacceptable, Merritt channelled her emotion into her work. Though this was consequent to her realisation that the issue wasn't really about anger at all, 'other people got angry and they didn't get treated like they were about to blow something up'. For the other members of the Roundtable, as well as for Merritt, there was still a lot to be angry about, given that black and Latina women are much more likely to suffer higher levels of poverty and a range of social deprivation in relation to other ethnic and gender categories.[538] Michelle Obama is doubtless aware of the wealth of data illustrating this. Though she is canny enough to realise that, in an institutionalised atmosphere of racism, the colour of calm reason is not black.

Writing about oppression, Marilyn Frye observed that it is a requirement for some bodies to show signs of being happy, or at least to be adjusted. Anything but the sunniest encounter invites being read as angry and hostile.[539] Sara Ahmed takes up this observation, describing how certain bodies are 'encountered as being negative'.[540] When these bodies give shape to silent violences, this can quickly expose the emaciated distance between polite silences and brutal attacks. And the one that voices this silence readily becomes perceived as the harbour of aggression. If the exposure of violence is read as the origin of violence, Ahmed claims that the violence is not exposed.[541] The figure of the 'angry black woman'[542] is one that Michelle Obama perhaps judiciously rejects, adjusting her body to fit the shape and colour of reason already there.

White-stained (reasoned) feminism has been put to effective use by a former First Lady. Laura Bush, wife of George W. Bush, gained the accolade of being the first 'First Lady' to deliver the president's weekly radio address in November 2001.[543] Speaking to a country freshly reeling from the attacks on September 11, she spoke 'on behalf' of the women of Afghanistan.[544] Her speech exuded the virtuous tones of US democratic rhetoric embellished with the reasoned hues of rights and justice: 'brutal oppression of women is a central goal of the terrorists' ('their' women can be just like 'our' women). Top-slicing rich layers of innocence and morality which have regularly kneaded western feminism into a cosseted whole, the dulcet prose delivered by Laura Bush neatly consolidated the ready-made rationale for the subsequent war in Afghanistan.

Feminist analyses of the 9/11 attacks have been prolific, much focusing on the Bush administration's callous colonisation of feminist rhetoric. The 'brown women' of Afghanistan have not been saved by the 'white men' of the USA, even when masculinised scripts are ventriloquised through the mouth of a 'white woman'. Yet the USA emerged psychically wounded after 9/11, experiencing a vicious jolt to its protected isolationist consciousness.[545] A freshly wounded site of injury surfaced from the ashes of Ground Zero: whiteness. An injured whiteness wrapped up in innocence, morality and racial purity. Feminisms infused with white attachments were unlikely to be immunised from playing an active part in recuperation strategies.

Sunera Thobani – a professor at a Canadian University – spoke out very clearly about the ways whiteness was being recast as vulnerable and endangered. It might be imagined that the public space for voicing dissent was perhaps less restricted in Canada than it had become in the squeezed political and intellectual spheres of the post-9/11 USA. Yet a speech she gave at a women's conference in Ottawa in October 2001 caused uproar in the Canadian press, accompanied by calls for her to apologise, and for her to be fired from her university.[546] In her speech, Thobani had proposed that the 'we' – the 'western we' of the USA – was deeply problematic, especially for third world women and women of colour, echoing the work of Audre Lorde, Cherríe Moraga, Gloria Anzaldúa, Hazel Carby, Chandra Talpade Mohanty, Patricia Williams, Amos and Parmar, Gayatri Chakravorty Spivak and bell hooks,[547] to mention some. As bell hooks put it in her book *Ain't I A Woman: Black Women and Feminism*,[548] when feminists use the word 'women' it invariably means 'white women'.[549] Thobani had also said in her speech that 'the path of US foreign policy is soaked in blood'. What place for western feminism in this trail of blood?

Thobani turned her attention to the work of three feminist scholars, judging it was extremely important to think about how feminist scholars were theorising the 'war on terror' consequent to 9/11.[550] She chose three books written by well known authors to consider: Judith Butler (*Precarious Life: The Powers of Mourning and Violence*),[551] Zillah Eisenstein (*Against Empire: Feminisms, Racisms, and the West*)[552] and Phyllis Chesler (*The New Anti-Semitism: The Current Crisis and What We Must Do About It*).[553] I imagine these authors would be quite differently placed in a contemporary typology of feminism: perhaps Butler as a feminist, queer, critical and poststructural theorist; Eisenstein as a feminist, socialist, anti-racist theorist; and Chesler as an equal rights advocate, and more on the political right than left (a supporter of the war on terror). Despite their quite significant differences, Thobani concludes that each of these authors, at least in these texts, plays a part in reinstalling white supremacy and white racial innocence. The journal in which Thobani's article was published invited Butler, Eisenstein and Chesler to respond. Chesler responded quite lengthily, expressing a range of emotions in her reply. Eisenstein wrote sparingly, though with emotive tones fully present. There was no (published) response from Butler, though this absence is not devoid of feeling.

'You're calling me a racist?'; this was a frequent response from white women in interviews carried out by Sarita Srivastava.[554] Tears and frustration; tears and anger. 'White women cry all the fucking time, and women of color never cry.'[555] So crying and anger are disallowed for some. Restrictions around what some bodies can do, what some bodies can feel, and how some bodies move, silt up silently, silt up incrementally, quietly, invisibly. A return to the revolving violent door of nothingness.

Hegemonic forms gain currency by being unnoticed.[556]

Invisible Whiteness

You can't see yourself walking down the street
But you notice me in every black face that passes you by.
Other white faces remain invisible to you
Because you are normal,
And I,
I am

"the Other".

Your white values are "right" and beyond reproach.
Your way of life something I "must aspire to".
But your white race privilege is what has put you where you are.
Allowing you to wear Reebox without question –
While I "must have stolen them".
You're white race privilege allows you to choose to op shop –
While I "must have to".
Your white race privilege lets you roam the department store
             unnoticed –
While I am followed by the security camera and guard.

Your whiteness makes you so invisible
That it brings you disproportionate benefits,
But still I feel sorry for you.
Because with all your extras –
You are still without the sense of place,
That I,
             "the Other"
Will always have.

Anita Heiss[557]

White

> White is a colour . . . but because it is the colour of light, and we see light all the time, we don't see its colour.[558]

Despite such transparency, white has tenaciously been equated with beauty and truth, emerging as the Enlightened translucent colour, the colour of knowledge. It is the colour of transparency, the colour of beauty,[559] and the colour of virtue.[560] White is beautiful, clean, suggestive of neutrality, of just being 'there'. White is the 'space of ordinariness'.[561] In the context of knowledge, to claim ordinariness may appear weak, powerless. Useful, usable knowledge is regularly equated with having, or being in a position of, power. Politicians, scientists, academics, for example, all offer what they know, and their ensuing judgments and predictions, from a place of expertise. Do these knowledges, these ordinary, powerful knowledges, have a colour?

The colour of power is perhaps more recognisably associated with black, especially Black Power as an aspect of racial resistance activities, as in the USA in the 1960s. Figure 18 shows two US Olympic gold and bronze medalists in the 1968

Mexico Games raising clenched fists in 'Black Power salutes' while the 'Star-Spangled Banner' played. This image was front-page news around the world at the time. As Tommie Smith and John Carlos left the podium, they were booed. They were sent back to the USA the next day.

Smith later said, 'If I win, I am an American, not a black American. But if I did something bad, then they would say I am a Negro. We are black and we are proud of being black, Black America will understand what we did tonight'. Where does the sense of Smith's claim about black understanding lie? Is the power of black knowing and being always contingent? Richard Dyer is eloquent:

> For a white person who is bad is failing to be 'white', whereas a black person who is good is a surprise, and one who is bad merely fulfills expectations.[562]

FIGURE 18 Smith and Carlos

The use of white as part of explicit racial 'resistance' strategy is also not unusual. Think of the Ku Klux Klan in the southern states of the USA, the discredited apartheid system in South Africa, or the British National Party and the English Defence League in the UK. With a 'left-critical eye', Black Power is perhaps seen as more obviously a specific and targeted form of resistance to racist/white culture. Yet for Tommie Smith and John Carlos, their own very public form of resistance seemed to tear too violently at white expectations, despite increasing social acknowledgement of the oppression of black people in late-1960s America. But even in the midst of such knowledge, a strong sense of appropriate behaviour rippled through the 'national' shock at Smith and Carlos' brazen act. Perhaps 1960s US white culture still expected 'black' behaviour to be white-respectful, to not insult white(s) by simply taking ownership of the ordinary centre.

The white power resistance activities of the Ku Klux Klan seem more borne out of expectations of what they righteously own, laced through with a seething and visceral distaste for all that is non-white. 'It's strange that their kids are so cute' – this comment from one of the racist/violent police officers in the film *Mississippi Burning*.[563] This 'exception' bespeaks well the depth of white disgust. The British National Party urges the need to 'clamp down' on the 'flood' of 'asylum seekers'[564] fuelling lightly buried fears of oozingly fluid racial contamination. 'White power' and 'black power' emerge with very different political, theoretical and personal hues. Black power evinces resistance. White power evinces righteousness.

Analysing race through white western eyes has generally tended to mean looking at 'others', most often non-white others. In classes on feminist IR, I am sometimes asked why I don't spend more time on Palestinian women, or Afghani women, or some other 'other' women. The students in my classes are overwhelmingly white. Focusing on what appears as the ordinary, the normal, so usually 'white' in the context of race, can transpire as perplexing. I think it is important to look at 'white'. But at the same time, if white is a 'social construction designed to mark the boundaries of race'[565] and race is marked by hierarchy, a simultaneous consideration of the functions served by concentrating on white and the power of white is called for.

Richard Dyer offers a salutatory thought: 'my blood runs cold at the thought that talking about whiteness could lead to the development of something called "White Studies"'.[566] If, in studying 'gender', it is a simple matter of democracy and equality to give equal attention to the supposed two halves of the gender binary, perhaps in studying 'race', or as I am thinking about it here – 'colour' – it may be a simple matter of democracy and equality to study the ubiquitous binary, 'white' and 'non-white'.

Elizabeth Sacre, an Australian psychoanalyst and writer married to a man with an African American mother, tells a story about buying a doll for her five-year-old niece (her husband's sister's child) for Christmas. The 'warm brown of the doll's skin matched that of my niece almost perfectly'.[567] On unwrapping her gift, the child flung the doll at the wall shouting, 'I don't want no white doll!' The doll, Sacre realised, was white simply by virtue of its association with her.[568]

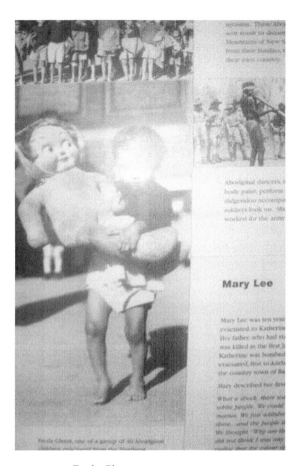

FIGURE 19   Freda Glenn

Author's photograph (© Marysia Zalewski)

Freda Glenn was one of a group of forty Aboriginal children evacuated from the Northern Territory to the eastern states by the Church Missionary Society in 1942. In Figure 19, Freda is holding a doll given to her on arrival at Spencer Street railway station in Melbourne.[569]

A report in the British tabloid newspaper *The Daily Mail* claims that 'girls are more naturally drawn to dolls as soon as they can crawl'.[570] The report was headed up with a picture of a small white, blonde-haired, smiling girl clutching a white doll. Building on the opening line, it was stated that 'there could be a biological basis for their choices. Males through evolution have been adapted to prefer moving objects, probably through hunting instincts, while girls prefer warmer colours such as pink, the colour of a newborn baby'. A white hue tinged with 'girl colour'. It takes time to notice this, or to allow it to catch your eye:

The thing that usually catches my eye, that compels me to look, is race.[571]

Taking time to care

I can feel the discomfort, perhaps.[572]

Perhaps it is easier not to care ...

... when the delegate in the audience at the first of a series of gender and IR conferences marking twenty years of scholarship on British 'Gender and IR' pointed out that 'we were still very white', I wonder what she hoped might ensue from her comment. There was a muted acknowledgment of the veracity of her observation. A perceptible sense of guilt and shame, also, I think. But such feelings are very familiar in western-focused discussions around race: guilt, shame, horror, disappointment, frustration. White people sometimes feel guilty, though feeling guilty is both not enough and part of the problem. What can white people do about racism? The wrong question perhaps; (re)locating agency in the space of hegemony – still no time to care:

> Liberal modernity's response to racism is of a piece with its failing to take race seriously.[573]

Following his election as the first black President of the USA, Barack Obama appointed Lawrence Summers as his chief economic advisor. Summers had not long left his position as President of Harvard University, whether because of his suggestion that women had less 'intrinsic aptitude' than men for science[574] is uncertain, though this was clearly a view that engendered much unrest and media attention. Yet Obama presumably judged that Summers's capacity to be a good economist outweighed the dubious rationale informing his views on women and science. This acceptability is curious. Summers also made judgments that have deep racial inflections: here are his views on the reasonableness of exporting pollution to 'less developed countries'.

> I think the economic logic behind dumping a load of toxic waste in the lowest wage country is impeccable and we should face up to that ... I've always thought that under-populated countries in Africa are vastly UNDER-polluted, their air quality is probably vastly inefficiently low compared to Los Angeles or Mexico City ... The concern over an agent that causes a one in a million change in the odds of prostate cancer is obviously going to be much higher in a country where people survive to get prostate cancer than in a country where under-5 mortality is about 200 per thousand.[575]

Summers makes no overt mention of racial difference in these comments, yet as Gilroy incisively observes, 'assumptions about racial hierarchy were active in secur-ing his combination of arguments ... the natives, whose bodies are comparatively worthless, already exist in a space of death'.[576] Logic, reason and (common) sense are sutured by finely tuned racial othering. White business as usual.

Christine Chin asks an important question. She asks: 'while some phenomena readily lend themselves to . . . gender analyses because of the inescapability of their empirical manifestations, whither race?'[577] It seems to be very hard to care, or to know how to, though 'the "who" of IR studies continues to be a select number of academics hailing primarily from the countries of the core'.[578]

The realities of racial division and hierarchy are well theorised,[579] though consistently denied and forgotten.[580] Yet the desire, the 'craving' for transformative politics around race[581] remains strong.

In a fourth-year undergraduate class we discuss ways in which masculinity as a form of conceptual logic both sutures and produces hegemonic knowledges. We consider Kimberly Hutchings' concept of masculinity as a 'cognitive shortcut'[582] through her analysis of two influential IR books: Mearsheimer's *The Tragedy of Great Power Politics*[583] and Hardt and Negri's *Empire*.[584] We also think about Judith Halberstam's work on the subtly blatant 'heterosexual conversion narratives'[585] in films such as *As Good as it Gets*,[586] *Chasing Amy*[587] and *The Opposite of Sex*.[588] These lovely examples of the labyrinthine ways white, straight masculinity bonds itself to common sense and everyday meaning are variably received by my students, who want to know how best to achieve real changes in the discriminatory enactments of gender, race and sexuality. As (mostly) young people 'socialized [and seduced] by promises of freedom',[589] they are quite certain there must be clear and sure routes through which these inequitable realities can be changed, very sure that 'better knowledge of the forces that make us will lead to their undoing',[590] though a refusal of the promises of 'white action' perhaps offers possibilities.

So, there are a range of disparate discussions about how race might be incorporated into studies of (feminist) IR (the separation here invokes a white tone). But it is still business as usual. Things need to change to take into race into account (and 'our' racist present–past), yet nothing seems to shift (much). If it did, what would this look like?

My students palpably sense and imagine the potential for happy futures. Feminist/IR scholars can (and surely do?) agree the need for engendering societies that will become marked not by racism, but a kind of, what Sara Ahmed calls, 'happy stories of diversity'.[591] But sites of analytical importance, or enquiry, or study remain stagnant. Mary Hawkesworth writes about wilful 'evidence blindness'.[592] Arlene Tickner reminds us that IR is a 'social practice'[593] and urges more attention to disciplinary gate-keeping and the necessity of moving the 'locus of enunciation'.[594] Tickner also suggests there might be a problem of 'autism' in IR, offering an embodied explanation for why it is always easy to ignore problems and perspectives that fail to resonate with the traditional worldview.[595] The students clearly care, but is there methodological room for this?

In her undergraduate class on American culture, Avery Gordon and her students make a thorough list of every possible explanation Toni Morrison gives in *The Bluest Eye*[596] for why dreams die. The list includes: the nature of white man's work, disappointment, folding up inside, the dialectics of violence and hatred, being put outdoors, the weather, deformed feet and lost teeth, nobody paying attention, furniture without memories, the unyielding soil, and 'what Morrison sometimes just calls *the thing*, the sedimented conditions that constitute what is in place in the first place'.[597] An eclectic list, but not a random one. A list with a shape of an *Exquisite Corpse*, perhaps.

> Just how much inequality is acceptable before individuals become indifferent to those who are different in status?[598]

Joan Tronto's question and subsequent work formed part of an important but regularly disregarded body of theorising within feminism which has acquired the label the 'ethic of care'. Yet care is a perilous subject for feminism, certainly strategically hazardous, and for Tronto in 1987 'philosophically stultifying'.[599] Theoretically deploying women's habitual practices, so often analytically remaindered to the dregs of ordinary life, readily morphs into 'leftovers' in the ostensibly more sophisticated realm of theorising. Though perhaps attaching philosophical and political significance to ('real') women's ways of being invited too close an alignment to the corporeal closures which the (feminine) body theoretically invites. This materialises through the ways Carol Gilligan's innovative work on moral reasoning[600] has been greedily read as claiming women are different reasoners from men. A conclusion easily tainted by the essentialist superior/inferior paradoxes this is mired in. Similarly, Sara Ruddick's subtle points about the potential for synaptic phenomenological connections between practices of mothering and peace[601] have largely, at least in the 'grand scheme' of (international) theory and politics, been relegated, theoretical 'leftovers'. Though someone else's act of destruction can turn into a magical creation.[602]

But woman isn't the question here, perhaps (theoretical) care is.

> Taking care involves work.[603]

Exquisite Corpse

> Inevitably, a work is always a form of tangible closure. But closures need not close off; they can be doors opening onto other closures and functioning as ongoing passages to an elsewhere (-within-here).[604]

In her book *Cruel Optimism*,[605] Lauren Berlant writes about political work which does not seek repair in forms recognisable in dominant terms (she discusses a range of art works, street performances and political projects).[606] These works turn away from, rather than refuse, normative models and frames. She describes such work as 'straying beneath the radar', where things go without saying not because they are censored or normative, but because it is not clear what to say.

When talking to a colleague about how I was writing my book, he asked me how I could enact an *Exquisite Corpse* by myself. 'Well, it's more of a methodological muse than anything else', I replied. The bemused look is still unnerving. Sigh. Yet the mixture of unruliness of sense, combined with the conjoining of seemingly random unconnected things which become stories in their own right, is both disturbing and joyous. Disturbing because it doesn't tell us which way to turn, or quite what to say. Joyous because one of its seriously playful messages is that nothing is foreclosed. Perhaps alternative ways of living do lurk in the 'murky waters of the counterintuitive'.[607]

I suggested in an early part of this book that I aimed to creatively betray some of the boundaries that keep feminist international relations in place. At first sight, the word 'betray' is perhaps the most disturbing one in that sentence; yet 'creatively' might be the one to pay more attention to. Though etymologically and intuitively linked with the verb 'to create', to act creatively is not about 'creating' something wholly new or heroically previously unimagined, it is not 'cut loose from the world',[608] but rather embraces both the unexpected and recognisable. To work creatively is to betray the accustomed illusion of wholeness and dramatic closure and to disrupt through a working combination of semantic, emotional, imaginative and ironic newness. It is about constantly juggling theorisation and experimentation as well as involving political engagement, disciplined commitment and copious editing work.[609] To be creative is to shift.

Over the road from the National Portrait Gallery in London, one can partake in a slice of 'English' heritage with a 'healthy' portion of bread-and-butter pudding or apple crumble with (lashings of) custard. The vat of custard is bubbling, filled to the brim, and the puddings are enticing. It's June, so the crypt of St Martin-in-the-Fields (transformed into a café[610]) is full of tourists. My sister and I promise we will return later in the year and share a portion of the crumble; decisions emergent from cultural constructions of appropriate femininity are always close to hand. In the National Portrait Gallery we decide on the contemporary exhibition which has an eclectic range of paintings and photographs. No painting of 'Kate' yet, though the one of Princes William and Harry in full military attire has a swarm of attentive viewers. 'I really dislike that image', I vent to my sister, the arbitrary wealth and privilege dripping off the shared, almost coy glance, and the sneakily strident lionisation of all things military. 'Harry doesn't look a bit like the rest of them, you know', my sister observes.

Nearing the end of the course on 'Gender, sex and death', I suggest to my undergraduate students that, if they are going to watch the royal wedding, to make sure they look out for signs of militarisation on the 'big day'. A couple of weeks before, one student remarked she had been surprised by something Cynthia Enloe had said in one of the readings, namely that most people who are militarised are civilians.[611] They begin to see and feel what they hadn't noticed they were seeing or feeling before.

The British royal wedding, the killing of Osama bin Laden, the arrest of Dominique Strauss-Kahn, the Slut Walk in Toronto, Arnie's 'love child' – just the first two 'international events' combined spawned numerous *Facebook* sites, including one which regaled – 'a Royal Wedding, the bad guy dies, a great *Disney* weekend!'. Heroes/Villains. Sex/Rape. *Facebook/Disney*. The headlines readily tell of colonialism, violence and greed, at the same time eviscerating the rabid persistence of discrimination, disgust and distaste. International politics writ large.

FIGURE 20   Kate and William

© Getty Images

Roland Bleiker re-imagines international relations as a range of pictures hanging in gallery; I think about this when looking at the photo of Kate and William (Figure 20). Few appear to have missed the similarities to the 'Charles and Diana' engagement photographs some thirty years earlier, though it is hard *not* to re-imagine these, given the eerie reincarnation of the ghost of Diana in the blue sapphire ring Kate is gazing at. With an army of judicious decision-makers in their employ, the British royal family's decision that this was the ring for Kate was not lightly made. The decision which captures the essence of Diana is the shape of a ring like a genie, with her unruliness tamed forever, reincarnated, at last, in the form of 'the good Princess', at least for a moment. Older and more canny, though, like Diana, corporeally vanishing with alarming speed. The bodies of women, dead or alive, enter a room differently. But perhaps none of this matters.

Osama Bin Laden is dead. Can I bring shampoo with me to the airport now?[612]

... the door speaks.[613]

Simmel

I know I do not learn anything when I am told what to learn.[614]

Trinh T Minh-ha

A book is a door. You open it. You step through. Do you come back?[615]

Jeanette Winterson

NOTES

1 'IRIS OF THE WORLD' – Written by Bruce Cockburn – © Rotten Kiddies Music LLC (BMI). All Rights Reserved. Lyric reproduced by kind permission of Carlin Music Corp.

2 H. Cixous, *White Ink: Interviews on Sex, Text and Politics*, Stocksfield, UK: Acumen Publishing, 2008, p. 5.

3 G. Vignale, *The Beautiful Invisible: Creativity, Imagination and Theoretical Physics*, Oxford: Oxford University Press, 2011, p. xvi.

4 b. hooks, *Feminism is for EVERYBODY*, London: Pluto Press, 2000, p. vii.

5 National Capital, Self-Guided Walking Tour, ANZAC PARADE. Online. Available HTTP: http://www.nationalcapital.gov.au/downloads/education_and_understanding/tours/Anzac_Parade_Walk.pdf (accessed 21 January 2012).

6 *Ibid*.

7 W. Larcombe, *Compelling Engagements: Feminism, Rape Law and Romance Fiction*, Annandale, NSW: Federation Press, 2005, p. 4.

8 J. Rancière, *The Emancipated Spectator*, London: Verso, 2009, p. 17.

9 "Cascade Experiment" is from *Powers of Congress* by Alice Fulton, published by Sarabande Books, Inc. © 1990, 2001 by Alice Fulton. Reprinted by kind permission of Sarabande Books and the author.

10 The 'drunken boys' were Surrealist artists including André Breton, Joan Miró and Man Ray.

11 Personal conversations with Fiona Sampson (poet) and Merlyn Riggs (artist).

12 W. Chadwick, *Women Artists and the Surrealist Movement*, London: Thames & Hudson, 2002, p. 13.

13 E. Heartney, H. Posner, N. Princenthal and S. Scott (eds), *After the Revolution: Women Who Transformed Contemporary Art*, London and New York: Prestel, 2007, p. 31.

14 C. Sylvester, *Feminist Theory and International Relations in a Postmodern Era*, Cambridge: Cambridge University Press, 1994.

15 R. Bleiker, *Aesthetics and World Politics*, Basingstoke, UK: Palgrave Macmillan, 2009.

16 M. Zalewski, 'Distracted reflections on the production, narration and refusal of feminist knowledge in International Relations', in B. Ackerly, M. Stern and J. True (eds), *Feminist Methodologies for International Relations*, Cambridge: Cambridge University Press, 2006, pp. 42–61.

17 "Cascade Experiment" is from *Powers of Congress* by Alice Fulton, published by Sarabande Books, Inc. © 1990, 2001 by Alice Fulton. Reprinted by kind permission of Sarabande Books and the author.

18   R. Dyer, *White*, London and New York: Routledge, 1997, p. 222.
19   M. Zalewski, 'Marysia Zalewski on unsettling IR, masculinity and making IR theory interesting (again)', *Theory Talks*: Theory Talk #28. Online. Available HTTP: http://www.theory-talks.org/2009/04/theory-talk-28.html (accessed 13 January 2012).
20   J. Winterson, *Why Be Happy When You Could Be Normal?* London: Jonathan Cape, 2011, p. 63. Permission kindly granted by The Peters Fraser & Dunlop Group Ltd, London.
21   "Cascade Experiment" is from *Powers of Congress* by Alice Fulton, published by Sarabande Books, Inc. © 1990, 2001 by Alice Fulton. Reprinted by kind permission of Sarabande Books and the author.
22   J. Butler, *Undoing Gender*, New York and London: Routledge, 2004, p. 205.
23   YouTube, 'Truman Show Emotional Ending'. Online. Available HTTP: http://www.youtube.com/watch?v=zBu9l_EKWVs (accessed 13 January 2012).
24   Barad, *Meeting The Universe Halfway*, p. 156.
25   In this book the following terms are used: 'international relations' (IR) refers to the study (lower case) or discipline (title case) of international relations in universities; 'international politics' refers to the broad range of international political practices that the discipline of IR purports to study; 'feminist IR' refers, at least sometimes, to the disciplinary study of international politics through feminist theory. All these definitions are problematic and exceed their boundaries.
26   V. Woolf, 'Professions for Women'. Online. Available HTTP: http://ebooks.adelaide.edu.au/w/woolf/virginia/w91d/chapter27.html (accessed 28 March 2012).
27   J. Edkins and N. Vaughan Williams (eds), *Critical Theorists and International Relations*, London: Routledge, 2009, p. 3; G. Deleuze and F. Guattari, *A Thousand Plateaus: Capitalism and Schizophrenia*, trans. Brian Massumi, London: Athlone Press, 1987.
28   D. Haraway, *Simians, Cyborgs and Women: The Reinvention of Nature*, New York: Routledge, 1991.
29   R. Cooper, 'Assemblage notes', in R.C.H. Chia (ed.), *Organized Worlds: Explorations in Technology and Organization with Robert Cooper*, London and New York: Routledge, 1998, p. 108.
30   Cixous, *White Ink*, p. 4.
31   T. Minh-Ha, *When the Moon Waxes Red*, London and New York: Routledge, p. 7.
32   Cixous, *White Ink*, p. 4.
33   M. Cunningham, *The Hours*, London and New York: Harper Perennial, 2006, p. 71.
34   S. Žižek, *Violence: Six Sideways Reflections*, London: Profile Books, 2009; K. Dunn, 'Interrogating white privilege', in J. Parpart and M. Zalewski (eds), *Rethinking the Man Question: Sex, Gender and Violence in International Relations*, London and New York: Zed Press, 2008, pp. 47–68.
35   S. Fuller, *The Intellectual*, Cambridge: Icon Books, 2005, p. 68, emphasis in original.
36   *Ibid.*, p. 69.
37   Cunningham, *The Hours*, p. 71.
38   On a notice at the exhibition door.
39   Flyer – Dundee Contemporary Arts, 'Thomas Hirschhorn, It's Burning Everywhere', 19 September–29 November 2009. Online. Available HTTP: http://www.dca.org.uk/uploads/Hirschhorn-leaflet-FINAL.pdf (accessed 13 January 2012).
40   From leaflet provided at the exhibition at Dundee Contemporary Arts.
41   N. Scheper-Hughes and P. Bourgois, *Violence in War and Peace*, Oxford: Blackwell, 2004.
42   V. Jabri, 'Shock and awe: power and the resistance of art', *Millennium: Journal of International Studies*, 2006, 34:3, 819–39.
43   R. Bleiker, 'The aesthetic turn in international political theory', *Millennium: Journal of International Studies*, 2001, 30:3, p. 510.
44   J. Butler, *Frames of War*, London: Verso, 2009; S. Žižek, *Welcome to the Desert of the Real*, London: Verso, 2002.
45   R. Grant and K. Newland (eds), *Gender and International Relations*, Milton Keynes, UK: Open University Press, 1991.

46 J.A. Tickner, *Gender in International Relations*, New York: Columbia University Press, 1992.

47 Francisco Goya, *The Disasters of War*, with new introduction by Philip Hofer, New York: Dover Publications, 1967.

48 E. Friederich, 'Anti-War Books of the 1920s: "The War Against War"'. Online. Available HTTP: http://www.greatwardifferent.com/Great_War/Kriege/Kriege_00.htm (accessed 11 June 2011).

49 S. Sontag, *Regarding the Pain of Others*, New York: Farrar, Straus and Giroux, 2003, p. 13.

50 J. Chapman and D. Chapman, *Insult to Injury*, London: SteidlMACK, 2003; *Insult to Injury* (wallpaper, Victoria & Albert Museum). Online. Available HTTP: http://collections. vam.ac.uk/item/O1154956/wallpaper-insult-to-injury (accessed 14 October 2011).

51 *Ibid.*

52 T. Morse and E. Madden, *Two Little Boys*, 1902.

53 Sontag, *Regarding the Pain of Others*, p. 37.

54 K. Weston, *Gender in Real Time: Power and Transience in a Visual Age*, New York: Routledge, 2002, p. 136.

55 BBC, 'Maids rally at ex-IMF head's court hearing'. Online. Available HTTP: http:// www.bbc.co.uk/news/world-us-canada-13675573 (accessed 18 January 2012).

56 L. Kramer, *After the Lovedeath: Sexual Violence and the Making of Culture*, Berkley, Los Angeles, London: University of California Press, 2000, p. 203.

57 Guardian Online, 'It's not just John Bercow – charm is disappearing from public life. About time too'. Online. Available HTTP: http://www.guardian.co.uk/commentisfree/ 2011/jan/15/john-bercow-charm-public-life?INTCMP=SRCH (accessed 23 March 2012).

58 Žižek, *Violence*, p. 180.

59 J. Dodd, *Violence and Phenomenology*, London: Routledge, 2009, p. 15.

60 A. Gordon, *Ghostly Matters: Haunting and the Sociological Imagination*, Minneapolis and London: University of Minnesota Press, 2001, p. 22.

61 *Ibid.*, p. 15.

62 Carroll, L., *Alice's Adventures in Wonderland and Through the Looking-Glass*, illustrated by John Tenniel, with an introduction and notes by Martin Gardner. London: Penguin Books, 1974, p. 88.

63 C. Dickens, *Hard Times*, London: Wordsworth Classics, 1995 [1845].

64 T. Docherty, *For the University: Democracy and the Future of the Institution*, London: Bloomsbury Academic, 2011; M. Evans, *Killing Thinking: The Death of Universities*, London and New York: Continuum, 2004.

65 Dickens, *Hard Times*, p. 4.

66 *Ibid.*

67 Evans, *Killing Thinking*.

68 B. Readings, *The University in Ruins*, Cambridge, MA and London: Harvard University Press, 1999, p. 133.

69 J. Glynos and D. Howarth (eds), *Logics of Critical Explanation in Social and Political Theory*, Abingdon and New York: Routledge, 2007, especially chapter 6 for further discussion of UK higher education.

70 Research Councils UK, 'Knowledge Exchange and Impact'. Online. Available HTTP: http://www.rcuk.ac.uk/kei/Pages/home.aspx (accessed 2 January 2012).

71 R. Wiegman, 'The intimacy of critique: ruminations on feminism as a living thing', *Feminist Theory*, 2010, 11:1, 79–84, p. 81.

72 BBC, 'Invisibility cloak "step closer"'. Online. Available HTTP: http://news.bbc. co.uk/1/hi/sci/tech/7553061.stm (accessed 11 August 2008).

73 C. Adler and A. Worral (eds), *Girls' Violence: Myths and Realities*, Albany, NY: State University of New York Press, 2004.

74 W. Brown, *Politics out of History*, Princeton, NJ and Oxford: Princeton University Press, 2001, p. 9.

75 Žižek, *Violence*, p. 10.

76 B. Chandramohan and S. Fallows, *Interdisciplinary Learning and Teaching in Higher Education: Theory and Practice*, London: Routledge, 2008; G.C. Spivak, *Outside in the Teaching Machine*, London and New York: Routledge, 1993; Readings, *The University in Ruins*; Evans, *Killing Thinking*.

77 F. Moten and S. Harney, 'The university and the undercommons: seven theses', *Social Text*, 2004, 79:22, 101–15.

78 Docherty, *For the University*.

79 Rancière, *The Emancipated Spectator*, p. 11.

80 C. Eschle and B. Maiguashca, 'Bridging the academic/activist divide: feminist activism and the teaching', *Millennium: Journal of International Studies*, 2006, 35:1, 119–37.

81 S. Ahmed, *Queer Phenomenology: Orientations, Objects, Others*, Durham, NC and London: Duke University Press, 2007, p. 22.

82 Butler, *Bodies that Matter: On the Discursive Limits of 'Sex'*, London and New York, 1993, p. ix.

83 Wiegman, 'The intimacy of critique', p. 84.

84 S. Gunew, 'Feminist cultural literacy: translating differences, cannibal options', in R. Wiegman (ed.), *Women's Studies on its Own*, Durham, NC and London: Duke University Press, 2002, pp. 47–65, p. 53.

85 Spivak, *Outside in the Teaching Machine*, p. 53.

86 J. Halberstam, *The Queer Art of Failure*, Durham, NC and London: Duke University Press, 2011, p. 11.

87 Moniza Alvi, 'How the Stone Found its Voice', *Split World: Poems 1990–2005* (Bloodaxe Books, 2008). Permission to reproduce kindly granted by Bloodaxe Books.

88 J. Halley, *Split Decisions: How and Why to Take a Break from Feminism*, Princeton, NJ: Princeton University Press, 2006.

89 B. Aretxaga, *Shattering Silence: Women, Nationalism and Political Subjectivity in Northern Ireland*, Princeton, NJ: Princeton University Press, 1997.

90 J. Kristeva, *Powers of Horror: An Essay in Abjection*, trans. Leon S. Roudiez, New York: Columbia University Press, 1982.

91 K. Oliver, *Women as Weapons of War: Iraq, Sex, and the Media*, New York: Columbia University Press, 2007.

92 M. Nicholson, 'What's the use of international relations?', *Review of International Studies*, 2000, 26:2, 183–98.

93 Bleiker, *Aesthetics and World Politics*.

94 A. Wendt, *Social Theory of International Politics*, Cambridge: Cambridge University Press, 1999.

95 United Nations Development Programme, *The Millennium Development Goals*. Online. Available HTTP: http://www.undp.org/content/undp/en/home/mdgoverview.html (accessed 12 January 2012).

96 Huffington Post, 'Obama Prague speech on nuclear weapons'. Online. Available HTTP: http://www.huffingtonpost.com/2009/04/05/obama-prague-speech-on-nu_n_183219. html (accessed 05 February 2012).

97 K. Hudson, 'Obama's nuclear test'. Online. Available HTTP: http://www.newstates man.com/international-politics/2009/01/obama-nuclear-poland-czech (accessed 17 September 2009).

98 *Dr Strangelove or: How I Learned to Stop Worrying and Love the Bomb*, Dir. Stanley Kubrick, Columbia Pictures, 1964.

99 Nicholson, 'What's the use of international relations?', p. 191.

100 *Ibid.*, p. 184.

101 C. Eschle and B. Maiguashca, 'Feminist scholarship, bridge-building and political affinity', *International Relations*, 2009, 23:1, 127–34.

102 Spivak, *Outside in the Teaching Machine*, p. 53.

103 D. Haraway, *Primate Visions: Gender, Race, and Nature in the World of Modern Science*, London and New York, Verso, 1992, p. 316.

104 S. Drakulić, *They Would Never Hurt a Fly: War Criminals on Trial in The Hague*. London: Penguin Books, 2003, p. 22.

105 J. Law, *After Method: Mess in Social Science Research*, London and New York: Routledge, 2004; Glynos and Howarth, *Logics of Critical Explanation*.

106 Minh-Ha, *When the Moon Waxes Red*, pp. 88, 91.

107 J. Gallop, *Thinking Through the Body*, New York: Columbia University Press, 1988 (this is the title of a sub-section in her chapter 'The anal body', p. 33).

108 K. Engle, *Seeing Ghosts: 9/11 and the Visual Imagination*, Montreal, Kingston and London: McGill–Queen's University Press, 2009, p. 7.

109 B. Subramaniam, 'Snow Brown and the Seven Detergents: a metanarrative on science and the scientific method', in M. Wyer, M. Barbercheck, D. Giesman, H. Öztürk and M. Wayne (eds), *Women, Science and Technology*, London: Routledge, 2001, pp. 36–41, p. 36.

110 *Ibid.*, p. 39.

111 This might include inductive argument, logical deduction, critical theory, participant observation, interviewing techniques, rational choice theory and so on.

112 D.E. Smith, *The Everyday World as Problematic: A Feminist Sociology*, Boston: Northeastern University Press, 1987.

113 C. Enloe, 'The mundane matters', *International Political Sociology*, 2011, 5:4, p. 447.

114 C. Enloe, 'Margins, silences and bottom rungs: how to overcome the underestimation of power in the study of international relations', in S. Smith, K. Booth and M. Zalewski (eds), *International Theory: Positivism and Beyond*, Cambridge: Cambridge University Press, 1996, pp. 186–202.

115 R. Hubbard, *The Politics of Women's Biology*, New Brunswick, NJ: Rutgers University Press, 1990.

116 J. Ussher, *Women's Madness: Misogyny or Mental Illness?*, Hemel Hempstead, UK: Harvester Wheatsheaf, 1991.

117 K. Davis, "Reclaiming women's bodies: colonialist trope or critical epistemology?', *Sociological Review*, 2007, 55:1, 50–54, p. 52.

118 M. Hawkesworth, *Feminist Inquiry*, New Brunswick, NJ: Rutgers University Press, 2006.

119 C. Hemmings, 'Telling feminist stories', *Feminist Theory*, 2005, 6:2, 115–39.

120 H. Arendt, *On Violence*, New York and London: Harcourt, 1970, p. 11.

121 Hawkesworth, *Feminist Inquiry*, p. 1.

122 Weston, *Gender in Real Time*, p. 39.

123 L. Irigaray, *This Sex Which Is Not One*, Ithaca, NY: Cornell University Press, 1985, p. 150.

124 T. Brennan, *The Transmission of Affect*, Ithaca, NY and London: Cornell University Press, 2004, p. 1.

125 Ahmed, *Queer Phenomenology*, p. 163.

126 See the range of C. Enloe's work, also R. Bleiker, 'Forget international relations theory', *Alternatives*, 1997, 22, 57–85.

127 Butler, *Frames of War*, p. 11.

128 L. Mangan [adapted], 'Last word', 2 November 2005, back page.

129 Eschle and Maiguashca, 'Feminist scholarship' and 'Bridging the academic/activist divide'.

130 Eschle and Maiguashca, 'Bridging the academic/activist divide'.

131 *Ibid.*, p. 123.

132 P. Williams, *The Alchemy of Race and Rights*, Cambridge, MA: Harvard University Press, 1991, p. 49.

133 Gordon, *Ghostly Matters*, p. 3.

134 *Ibid.*

135 *Ibid.*, p. 32.

136 *Ibid.*, p. 45.

137 *Ibid.*, p. 10.

138 Cunningham, *The Hours*, p. 87.

139 Haraway, *Simians, Cyborgs, and Women*, p. 178.

140 S. Gunne, and Z. Brigley Thompson (eds), *Feminism, Literature and Rape Narratives*, London: Routledge, 2009, p. 15. See also Heartney *et al.* (eds), *After the Revolution*. See

also Kipton Art, 'Marina Abramović, "The Artist is Present"'. Online. Available HTTP: http://blogfiles.kiptonart.com/labels/Marian%20Abramovic.html (accessed 29 April 2010).

141 G. de Montigny, *Social Working: An Ethnography of Front-line Practice*, Toronto: Toronto University Press, 1995, p. 223.

142 A native-born American; enslaved in the early part of her life (b. 1797, d. 1883). I return to speak about Truth later in the book.

143 T.T. Minh-ha, 'Difference: A Special Third World Women Issue', *Feminist Review*, 1987, 25, 5–22, p. 18.

144 *Ibid.*

145 *Ibid.*, p. 16.

146 Halberstam, *The Queer Art of Failure*, p. 139.

147 Irigaray, *This Sex Which Is Not One*.

148 L. Sjoberg, 'Gender and personal pedagogy: some observations', *International Studies Perspectives*, 2007, 8:3, 336–9, p. 336.

149 M. Hawkesworth, 'The semiotics of premature burial: feminism in a postfeminist age', *Signs: Journal of Women in Culture and Society*, 2004, 29:4, 961–85, p. 972.

150 R. Wiegman, 'Dear Ian', *Duke Journal of Gender, Law and Policy*, 2004, 11:93, 93–120, p. 94.

151 Sjoberg, 'Gender and personal pedagogy', p. 336.

152 M. Zalewski, 'Where is woman in international relations?: "To return as a woman and be heard"', *Millennium: Journal of International Studies*, 1999, 127:4, 847–67.

153 M. Zalewski, '"Women's troubles" again in IR', Forum on Gender and International Relations, *International Studies Review*, 2003, 5:2, 291–4; M. Stern and M. Zalewski, 'Feminist fatigue(s): reflections on feminism and familiar fables of militarization', *Review of International Studies*, 2009, 35:3, 611–30; M. Zalewski, 'Distracted reflections on the production, narration and refusal of feminist knowledge in International Relations', in B. Ackerly, M. Stern and J. True (eds), *Feminist Methodologies for International Relations*, Cambridge: Cambridge University Press, 2006, pp. 42–61.

154 M. Lloyd, *Judith Butler: From Norms to Politics*, Cambridge: Polity Press, 2007, p. 4.

155 J. Squires and J. Weldes, 'Beyond being marginal: gender and international relations in Britain', *British Journal of Politics and International Relations*, 2007, 9:2, 185–203, p. 190.

156 L. Sjoberg, 'Gendered realities of the immunity principle: why gender analysis needs feminism', *International Studies Quarterly*, 2006, 50, 889–910.

157 Squires and Weldes, 'Beyond being marginal'.

158 I still find myself doing this even as I simultaneously suggest that the 'gender in/and international relations module' (or some other critically inspired course) might be interestingly installed as the core theory course. Also see discussion on teaching gender in *International Studies Perspectives*: 'Pedagogy Forum on Mainstreaming Gender into the IR Curriculum' 2007, 8:3, 315–43. See also K. Shaw and R.B.J. Walker, 'Situating academic practice: pedagogy, critique and responsibility', *Millennium: Journal of International Studies*, 2006, 35:1, 155–65.

159 Z. Eisenstein, *Against Empire: Feminisms, Racism and the West*, London: Zed Books, 2004, p. 189.

160 R. West, 'Mr. Chesterton in Hysterics', *The Clarion*, November 14, 1913.

161 Wikipedia, 'Feminism'. Online. Available HTTP: http://en.wikipedia.org/wiki/Feminism (accessed 12 January 2012).

162 Guardian Online, 'David Willetts blames feminism over lack of jobs for working men'. Online. Available HTTP: http://www.guardian.co.uk/politics/2011/apr/01/david-willetts-feminism-lack-of-jobs (accessed 14 June 2011).

163 M. Phillips, 'These "Slut Walks" prove feminism is now irrelevant to most women's lives'. Online. Available HTTP: http://www.dailymail.co.uk/debate/article-2002887/Slut-Walks-prove-feminism-irrelevant-womens-lives.html?ito=feeds-newsxml (accessed 14 June 2011).

164   Lloyd, *Judith Butler*, p. 4.

165   Squires and Weldes, 'Beyond being marginal', p. 190.

166   M. G. Dietz, 'Current controversies in feminist theory', *Annual Review of Political Science*, 6, 2003, 399–431, p. 399.

167   Wiegman, 'The intimacy of critique', p. 82.

168   Wikipedia, 'Feminism'.

169   P. Robertson, quotes, *Think Exist*. Online. Available HTTP: http://thinkexist.com/quotes/pat_robertson (accessed 12 January 2012).

170   Bleiker, 'The aesthetic turn', p. 531.

171   S. Ahmed, *The Promise of Happiness*, Durham, NC and London: Duke University Press, 2011, p. 65.

172   Irigaray, *This Sex Which Is Not One*, p. 150.

173   A. McRobbie, *The Aftermath of Feminism: Gender, Culture and Social Change*, London: Sage, 2009.

174   *Ibid.*

175   Sex Discrimination Act.

176   British Criminal Records Check directed by the UK's Home Office. http://www.homeoffice.gov.uk/agencies-public-bodies/crb

177   Telegraph Online, 'Britons spend half their waking hours using technology, finds Ofcom'. Online. Available HTTP: http://www.telegraph.co.uk/technology/news/7952091/Britons-spend-half-their-waking-hours-using-technology-finds-Ofcom.html (accessed 20 August 2010).

178   S. de Beauvoir, *The Second Sex*, trans. H.M. Parshley, London: Vintage, 1952 [1949], p. xxxi.

179   W. Brown, *Edgework: Critical Essays on Knowledge and Politics*, Princeton, NJ: Princeton University Press, 2005, p. 99.

180   P. Uwineza and E. Pearson, *Sustaining Women's Gains in Rwanda: The Influence of Indigenous Culture and Post-Genocide Politics*. Online. Available HTTP: http://www.scribd.com/doc/39669384/Sustaining-Women%E2%80%99s-Gains-in-Rwanda-Indigenous-Culture-Post-Genocide-Politics (accessed 11 March 2012).

181   Inter-Parliamentary Union, 'Women in national parliaments'. Online. Available HTTP: http://www.ipu.org/wmn-e/classif.htm (accessed 5 January 2012).

182   Centre for Sustainable International Development, University of Aberdeen. Online. Available HTTP: http://www.abdn.ac.uk/sustainable-international-development/events/338 (accessed 12 January 2012).

183   M. Wollstonecraft, *A Vindication of the Rights of Woman, with Strictures on Political and Moral Subjects*, London: Dover Publications, 1996[1792].

184   de Beauvoir, *The Second Sex*.

185   A vast range of feminist literature demonstrates this, here is a small selection of examples: H. Abelove, M.A. Barale and D.M. Halperin (eds), *The Lesbian and Gay Studies Reader*, London: Routledge, 1993; L. Martin Alcoff and E. Mendieta, *Identities: Race, Class, Gender and Nationality*, Oxford: Blackwell Publishing, 2003; N. Hartsock, *Money, Sex and Power*, Boston: Northeastern University Press, 1985; S. Harding, *The Science Question in Feminism*, Milton Keynes, UK: Open University Press, 1986; M. Hawkesworth, 'Knowers, knowing, known: feminist theory and claims of truth', *Signs*, 1989, 14, 533–56; Gilligan, C., *In a Different Voice: Psychological Theory and Women's Development*, Cambridge, MA: Harvard University Press, 1982; S. Ruddick, *Maternal Thinking: Towards a Politics of Peace*, Boston: Beacon Press, 1989; C. Pateman, *The Sexual Contract*, Oxford: Polity Press, 1988; M. Lederman and I. Bartsch (eds), *The Gender and Science Reader*, London: Routledge, 2001; P. Hill Collins, *Black Feminist Thought*, Boston: Unwin Hyman, 1990; Williams, *The Alchemy of Race and Rights*; A. Fausto-Sterling, *Myths of Gender: Biological Theories about Women and Men*, New York: Basic Books, 1985.

186   Minh-ha, *When the Moon Waxes Red*, p. 188.

187   N. Tuana, *The Less Noble Sex*, Bloomington: Indiana University Press, 1993; R. Tong, *Feminist Thought: A More Comprehensive Introduction*, Boulder, CO: Westview Press, 2009.

188 K.E. Ferguson, *The Man Question: Visions of Subjectivity in Feminist Theory*, Berkeley and Oxford: University of California Press, 1993.

189 C. Hemmings, *Why Stories Matter: The Political Grammar of Feminist Theory*, Durham, NC: Duke University Press, 2011.

190 See A.M. Jaggar, *Feminist Politics and Human Nature*, Brighton, UK: Harvester Press, 1983.

191 See D. Fuss, *Essentially Speaking: Feminism, Nature and Difference*, London and New York: Routledge, 1989, and M.G. Dietz, 'Current controversies in feminist theory', p. 408.

192 Harding, *The Science Question in Feminism*; Hartsock, *Money, Sex and Power*; Gilligan, *In a Different Voice*; J.C. Tronto, 'Beyond gender difference to a theory of care', *Signs: Journal of Women in Culture and Society*, 1987, 12:4, 644–63; Ruddick, *Maternal Thinking*.

193 Gilligan, *In a Different Voice*.

194 Ruddick, *Maternal Thinking*.

195 S. Moller Okin, *Women in Western Political Thought*, Princeton, NJ: Princeton University Press, 1979.

196 Gilligan, *In a Different Voice*.

197 J. Butler, *Gender Trouble*, New York and London: Routledge, 1990, p. 2.

198 *Sustaining Women's Gains in Rwanda*. Authored by Peace Uwineza and Elizabeth Pearson, edited by Elizabeth Powley. The Institute of Inclusive Security: Hunt Alternatives Fund, 2009.

199 L.J. Shepherd, *Gender Matters in Global Politics*, London: Routledge, 2009, p. 3.

200 Minh-ha, *When the Moon Waxes Red*, p. 94.

201 Halberstam, *The Queer Art of Failure*, p. 14.

202 A.C. Grayling, 'The last word on confusion', *The Guardian*, Saturday Review, 4 May 2002.

203 S. Hall, 'Old and new identities', in A.D. Kind (ed.), *Culture, Globalization and the World-System*, London: Macmillan, 1991, pp. 42–69.

204 Halberstam, *The Queer Art of Failure*.

205 *Ibid.*, p. 16.

206 G. Pollock, *Differencing the Canon: Feminist Desire and the Writing of Art's Histories*, London and New York: Routledge, 1997, p. 13.

207 Ahmed, *Queer Phenomenology*, p. 22.

208 Halberstam, *The Queer Art of Failure*, p. 10.

209 See R.J. Ellis, '"Problems may cut right across the borders", why we cannot do without interdisciplinarity', in B. Chandramohan and S. Fallows (eds), *Interdisciplinary Learning and Teaching in Higher Education: Theory and Practice*, London: Routledge, 2009, p. 9.

210 *Ibid.*, p. 5.

211 Docherty, *For the University*.

212 *Ibid.*, p. 3.

213 Evans, *Killing Thinking*.

214 Glynos and Howarth, *Logics of Critical Explanation*, p. 171.

215 Halley, *Split Decisions*, p. 20.

216 Gunew, 'Feminist cultural literacy', p. 49.

217 Halberstam, *The Queer Art of Failure*, p. 13.

218 Wiegman, *Women's Studies on its Own*.

219 *Ibid.*, p. 5.

220 Hall, 'Old and new identities', p. 43.

221 *Lost in Translation*, Dir. Sofia Coppola, Focus Features, 2003.

222 Script-O-Rama, 'Lost In Translation Script – Dialogue Transcript'. Online. Available HTTP: http://www.script-o-rama.com/movie_scripts/l/lost-in-translation-script-tran script.html (accessed 19 July 2012).

223 Quoted in Ellis, '"Problems may cut right across the borders", p. 9.

224 Minh-ha, *When the Moon Waxes Red*, p. 104.

225 N. Crawford, 'Feminist futures: science fiction, utopia, and the art of possibilities in world politics', in J. Weldes (ed.), *To Seek Out New Worlds: Exploring Links between Science Fiction and World Politics*, London: Palgrave Macmillan, 2003, p. 199.

226   A comment made by Sandra Harding from the audience in a panel at the annual convention of the International Studies Association in 2006.

227   Budapest Tourist Guide, 'Budapest Statue Park: Szobor Park'. Online. Available HTTP: http://www.budapest-tourist-guide.com/budapest-statue-park.html (accessed 12 January 2012).

228   *Children of Men*, Dir. Alfonso Cuaro (based on the novel by P.D. James), Universal Pictures, 2006.

229   YouTube, 'Žižek on *Children of Men*'. Online. Available HTTP: http://www.youtube.com/watch?v=pbgrwNP_gYE (accessed 20 October 2010).

230   Butler, *Undoing Gender*, p. 205.

231   United Nations Women, 'UN creates new structure for empowerment of women'. Online. Available HTTP: http://www.unwomen.org/2010/07/un-creates-new-structure-for-empowerment-of-women (accessed 30 July 2010).

232   Butler, *Undoing Gender*, p. 204.

233   K. Hutchings, '1988 and 1998: contrast and continuity in feminist international relations', *Millennium: Journal of International Studies*, 2008, 37:1, 97–105, p. 100.

234   *Ibid.*, p. 104.

235   *Ibid.*, p. 102.

236   *Ibid.*, p. 101.

237   F. Fukuyama, 'Women and the evolution of world politics', *Foreign Policy*, 1998, 77:5, 24–40.

238   *Ibid.*, p. 25.

239   *Ibid.*, p. 36.

240   *Rise of the Planet of the Apes*, Dir. Rupert Wyatt, Twentieth Century Fox, 2011. The main plot line of previous films in this genre.

241   Halberstam, *The Queer Art of Failure*, p. 35.

242   Haraway, *Primate Visions*.

243   Minh-ha, *When the Moon Waxes Red*, p. 6.

244   F. Howe, *The Winter Sun: Notes on a Vocation*, Minnesota: Graywolf Press, 2009. Permission kindly granted by The Permissions Company, Inc., rights agency for Graywolf Press.

245   C. Enloe, *The Morning After: Sexual Politics at the End of the Cold War*, Berkley and Los Angeles: University of California Press, 1993, p. 1.

246   *Ibid.*

247   *Ibid.*, p. 2.

248   *Ibid.*

249   Mentioned in the vignette 'And feminism is…' (the first of three) on page 29.

250   L. Sjoberg, 'Emotion and the feminist IR researcher', *International Studies Review*, The Forum, C. Sylvester (ed.), 2011, 13:4, 687–708, p. 699.

251   Carroll, *Alice's Adventures in Wonderland*, p. 88.

252   *Ibid.*, p. 90.

253   M. Zalewski, A. Brew, M. Riggs, C. Clare, C. Hackett, H.M. Kinsella and C. Clare (eds), '20 years of British gender and international relations: crafting the past–present–future', *International Feminist Journal of Politics*, 2009, 11:3, 305–33; L. Sjoberg (ed.), *Gender and International Security: Feminist Perspectives*, London and New York: Routledge, 2010.

254   A small selection of this literature includes: C. Cohn, 'Sex and death in the rational world of defense intellectuals', *Signs*, 1988, 12:4, 687–718; C. Enloe, *Bananas, Beaches and Bases: Making Feminist Sense of International Politics*, London: Pandora Press, 1989; Grant and Newland, *Gender and International Relations*; V.S. Peterson (ed.), *Gendered States: Feminist (Re)Visions of International Relations Theory*, Boulder, CO: Lynne Rienner, 1992; V.S. Peterson and A. Sisson Runyan, *Global Gender Issues*, Boulder, CO: Westview, 1993 (2nd edn) and 2010 (3rd edn); J.J. Pettman, *Worlding Women: A Feminist International Politics*, New York: Routledge, 1996; Sylvester, *Feminist Theory and International Relations in a Postmodern Era*; S. Whitworth, *Feminism and International Relations*, Basingstoke, UK: Macmillan, 1994.

255   J.J. Pettman, *Worlding Women*.

256   Peterson and Sisson Runyan, *Global Gender Issues*.

257   *Ibid.*, p. 20. Image courtesy of the United Nations, 'The state of the world's women 1985', illustrator Wendy Hoile, 1993.

258   Though I am wary of typologising feminism, the legacy and continuing contested impact of what we can call radical feminism (see Jaggar, *Feminist Politics and Human Nature*; B.A. Crow (ed.), *Radical Feminism: A Documentary Reader*, New York: New York University Press, 2000) is too important not to mention.

259   Enloe, 'Margins, silences and bottom rungs'.

260   Weston, *Gender in Real Time*, p. 9.

261   Squires and Weldes, 'Beyond being marginal'; C. Sylvester, 'Whither the international at the end of IR?', *Millennium: Journal of International Studies*, 2007, 35:3, 551–73.

262   M. Zalewski, '"Women's troubles" again in IR'; 'Feminism and international relations: an exhausted conversation?', in F. Harvey and M. Brecher (eds), *Critical Paradigms in International Studies*, Michigan: University of Michigan Press, 2002, 330–41; J.A. Tickner, 'You just don't understand: troubled engagements between feminists and IR theorists', *International Studies Quarterly*, 1997, 41: 4: 611–32; J. Steans, 'Engaging from the margins: feminist encounters with the "mainstream" of international relations', *British Journal of Politics and International Relations*, 2003, 5:3, 428–54.

263   A. Jones, 'Does "gender" make the world go around?', *Review of International Studies*, 1996, 22:4, 405–29; R. Keohane, 'Beyond dichotomy: conversations between international relations and feminist theory', *International Studies Quarterly*, 1998, 42:1, 193–8; Squires and Weldes, 'Beyond being marginal'.

264   See for example the range of Cynthia Enloe's work.

265   S. Roy, 'Melancholic politics and the politics of melancholia: the Indian women's movement', *Feminist Theory*, 2009, 10:3, 341–57.

266   See B. D'Costa and K. Lee-Koo, *Gender and Global Politics in the Asia-Pacific*, London: Palgrave Macmillan, 2009.

267   C. Brown, 'IR theory in Britain – the New Black?', *Review of International Studies*, 32, 677–87.

268   Irigaray, *This Sex Which Is Not One*, p. 185.

269   Dorothea Tanning. Online. Available HTTP: http://www.dorotheatanning.org (accessed 12 January 2012).

270   Chadwick, *Women Artists and the Surrealist Movement*, p. 138.

271   *Ibid.*, p. 135.

272   Alice Fulton, *Shy One*, quoted in Barad, *Meeting The Universe Halfway*; Fulton, *Cascade Experiment: Selected Poems*.

273   Dorothea Tanning. Online. Available HTTP: http://www.dorotheatanning.org (accessed 12 January 2012).

274   Chadwick, *Women Artists and the Surrealist Movement*, p. 123.

275   N. Henry, *War and Rape: Law, Memory and Justice*, London: Routledge, 2011, p. 108.

276   Sontag, *Regarding the Pain of Others*, p. 7.

277   Enloe, 'The mundane matters', p. 447.

278   *Rendition*, Dir. Gavin Hood, Anonymous Content, 2007.

279   *2012*, Dir. Roland Emmerich, Columbia Pictures, 2012.

280   See J. Horowitz's *Apocalypto Now*. Online. Available HTTP: http://www.museen koeln.de/museum-ludwig/download/ML_Horowitz_Flyer%20%281%29.pdf (accessed 12 February 2012).

281   *The Road*, Dir. John Hillcoat, Dimension Films, 2010.

282   *The Book of Eli*, Dirs Albert Hughes and Allen Hughes, Alcon Entertainment, 2010.

283   *The Day After Tomorrow*, Dir. Roland Emmerich, Twentieth Century Fox, 2004.

284   *The Day the Earth Stood Still*, Dir. Scott Derrickson, Twentieth Century Fox, 2008.

285   *War of the Worlds*, Dir. Steven Spielberg, Paramount Pictures, DreamWorks SKG, 2005.

286   *I Am Legend*, Dir. Francis Lawrence, Warner Bros., 2007.

287 *Invasion*, Dir. Oliver Hirschbiegel, Warner Bros., 2007.

288 *Children of Men*.

289 *Rise of the Planet of the Apes*.

290 Žižek, *Violence*; D. Dunn, 'The Incredibles: an ordinary day tale of a superpower in the post 9/11 World', *Millennium: Journal of International Studies*, 34:2, 2006, 559–62.

291 Ruddick, *Maternal Thinking*.

292 S.P. Huntington, 'The clash of civilizations?, *Foreign Affairs*, 1993, 72:3, 22–49.

293 F. Fukuyama, *The End of History and the Last Man*, London: Hamish Hamilton, 1992.

294 See United Nations Women, Fourth World Conference on Women. Online. Available HTTP: http://www.un.org/womenwatch/daw/beijing/platform (accessed 11 March 2012).

295 United Nations Security Council Resolutions 1325, 2000; 1820, 2008; 1888, 2009; 1889, 2009.

296 United Nations Educational, Scientific and Cultural Organization, 'Gender mainstreaming'. Online. Available HTTP: http://portal.unesco.org/en/ev.php-URL_ID=46723&URL_DO=DO_TOPIC&URL_SECTION=201.html (accessed 12 January 2012).

297 R. Sorenau and D. Hudson, 'Feminist scholarship in international relations and the politics of disciplinary emotion', *Millennium: Journal of International Studies*, 2008, 37:1, 123–51, p. 123.

298 BBC, 'Bombs and beatings: life among the Taliban'. Online. Available HTTP: http://news.bbc.co.uk/1/hi/world/south_asia/8499578.stm (accessed 5 February 2010).

299 A. Jenkins, 'Politics', in *In the Hot-House*, London: Chatto & Windus, 1988. Permission kindly granted by Chatto & Windus.

300 S. Truth, 'Ain't I a woman?', adapted by E. Stetson. Online. Availabe HTTP: http://www.womenwriters.net/domesticgoddess/truth.htm (accessed 11 March 2012).

301 W. Vrasti, 'The strange case of ethnography and international relations', *Millennium: Journal of International Studies*, 2008, 37:2, 279–301.

302 United Nations Security Council Resolutions 1325, 2000; 1820, 2008; 1888, 2009; 1889, 2009.

303 US Department of State, 'Secretary Clinton's remarks on women, peace and security'. Online. Available HTTP: http://www.state.gov/secretary/rm/2011/12/179173.htm (accessed 10 January 2012).

304 *Hollow Man*, Dir. Paul Verheoven, Columbia Pictures, 2000.

305 Inter-Parliamentary Union, 'Women in national parliaments'. Online. Available HTTP: http://www.ipu.org/wmn-e/classif.htm (accessed 5 January 2012).

306 Guardian Online, 'Shocking lack of women top company directors, says report'. Online. Available HTTP: http://www.guardian.co.uk/business/2011/oct/13/shocking-lack-women-directors-ftse (accessed 5 January 2012).

307 New York Times, 'For soldiers, death sees no gender lines'. Online. Available HTTP: http://www.nytimes.com/2011/06/22/world/asia/22afghanistan.html?_r=2&pagewanted=all (accessed 29 December 2011).

308 M. Lloyd, '(Women's) human rights: paradoxes and possibilities', *Review of International Studies*, 2007, 33:1, 91–103.

309 J. Oestreich, 'Teaching gender and international relations', *International Studies Perspectives*, 2007, 8:3, 326–9, p. 329.

310 Telegraph Online, 'Wooten Bassett: bikers honour dead'. Online. Available HTTP: http://www.telegraph.co.uk/news/uknews/defence/7442432/Wooten-Bassett-bikers-honour-dead.html (accessed 29 March 2010).

311 W. Brown, *States of Injury*, Princeton, NJ and Oxford: Princeton University Press, 1995, xi.

312 M. Lloyd, *Beyond Identity Politics*, London: Sage, 2005, p. 2.

313 Žižek, *Violence*, p. 73.

314 F. Fanon, *Black Skin, White Masks*, London: Pluto Press, 1986.

315 Times Higher Education, 'It is a popularity contest, sisters'. Online. Available HTTP: http://www.timeshighereducation.co.uk/story.asp?sectioncode=26&storycode=413763&c=1 (accessed 13 October 2010).

316 A. Ronell, 'Deviant payback: the aims of Valerie Solanos', in V. Solanos, *SCUM MANIFESTO*, London: Verso, 2009, 1–31, p. 16.

317 W. Brown, *States of Injury*, Princeton, NJ and Oxford: Princeton University Press, 1995, p. xii.

318 Brown, *Edgework*, p. 101.

319 P. Lather, 'Postbook: working the ruins of feminist ethnography', *Signs: Journal of Women in Culture and Society*, 2001, 27:1, 199–227, p. 214.

320 L. Berlant, *Cruel Optimism*, Durham, NC: Duke University Press, 2011, p. 1.

321 Quoted in B. Hanssen, *Critique of Violence*, London and New York: Routledge, p. 220. The quote is from one of Elfriede Jelenik's characters (Carmilla) in one of her plays, *Illness or Modern Woman*.

322 K. Bumiller, *In an Abusive State: How Neoliberalism Appropriated the Feminist Movement against Sexual Violence*, Durham, NC and London: Duke University Press, 2008, p. 23.

323 Minh-ha, *When the Moon Waxes Red*, p. 83.

324 M. Hawkesworth, 'The semiotics of premature burial', p. 962.

325 V. Woolf, *Three Guineas*, London: The Hogarth Press, 1986.

326 H. Eisenstein, *Feminism Seduced: How Global Elites Use Women's Labor and Ideas to Exploit the World*, Boulder, CO: Paradigm Publishers, 2009.

327 http://news.bbc.co.uk/1/hi/world/europe/8501181.stm (accessed 2 December 2010).

328 J. Halley, *Split Decisions*.

329 A. McRobbie, *The Aftermath of Feminism: Gender, Culture and Social Change*, London: Sage, 2009

330 Minh-ha, *When the Moon Waxes Red*, p. 104.

331 Gordon, *Ghostly Matters*, p. 197.

332 All Voices, 'Glasgow Scotland joins latest addition of slutwalks around the globe'. Online. Available HTTP: http://www.allvoices.com/contributed-news/9301620-glasgow-scotland-joins-latest-addition-of-slutwalks-around-the-globe (accessed 20 June 2011); https://www.facebook.com/slutwalkdelhi (accessed 8 January 2012).

333 BBC, 'Politics'. Aired 12 June 2011.

334 Business Insider, 'French radio: The lawyers were "surprised" at how unattractive the maid was'. Online. Available HTTP: http://www.businessinsider.com/dsk-lawyers-were-surprised-at-how-unattractive-maid-was-2011-5 (accessed 14 June 2011).

335 A quip made by a friend in relation to judges and women 'in the dock'.

336 See M. Zalewski, '"I don't even know what gender is". A discussion of the relationship between gender mainstreaming and feminist theory', *Review of International Studies*, 2010, 36, 3–27.

337 Former trainer for the International Rescue Committee (IRC), in conversation with Nina Hall, Dili, 23 November 2007. Quoted in N. Hall and J. True, 'Gender mainstreaming in a post-conflict state', in B. D'Costa and K. Lee-Koo (eds), *Gender and Global Politics in the Asia-Pacific*, London: Palgrave Macmillan, 2009, pp. 159–74, p. 164.

338 M. Jauhola, 'Building back better? – negotiating normative boundaries of gender mainstreaming and post-tsunami reconstruction in Nanggroe Aceh Darussalam, Indonesia', *Review of International Studies*, 2010, 36, 29–50, p. 36.

339 Also interesting is the making of the statement into a question. See Janet Halley's discussion of Judith Butler and 'the question of sexual difference' in *Split Decisions*, p. 217.

340 G. Youngs, D. Lisle and M. Zalewski, 'Three readings of *G.I. Jane*', *International Feminist Journal of Politics*, 1999, 1:3, 476–81; L.R. Williams, 'Ready for action: *G.I. Jane*, Demi Moore's body and the female combat movie', in Y. Tasker (ed.), *Action and Adventure Cinema*, London: Routledge, 2004, pp. 169–85; T. Carver, "*G.I. Jane*: what are the "manners" that "maketh a man"?' *British Journal of Politics and International Relations*, 2007, 9:2, 313–17.

341 This includes conventional popular culture such as Hollywood movies, but also involves the 'global gender industry', which includes, for example, NGOs (see Stern and Zalewski, 'Feminist fatigue(s)').

342 Halley, *Split Decisions*, p. 22.

343 United Nations Women, 'Beijing and its follow-up'. Online. Available HTTP: http://www.un.org/womenwatch/daw/beijing/ (accessed 12 January 2012). See discussion in J. Butler, 'The end of sexual difference?', in E. Bronfen and M. Kavka (eds), *Feminist Consequences: Theory for the New Century*, New York: Columbia University Press, 2001.

344 The impact of 'gender theory' and the ensuing 'blurring of gender roles' has most recently been identified as a concern more serious than the destruction of the rainforests by the Pope in his New Year address for 2008. See BBC, 'Pope attacks blurring of gender'. Online. Available HTTP: http://news.bbc.co.uk/1/hi/world/europe/7796663.stm (accessed 6 January 2009).

345 Convention on the Elimination of All Forms of Discrimination Against Women. Adopted in 1979 by the UN General Assembly. See http://www.un.org/womenwatch/daw/cedaw/

346 United Nations Security Council Resolution 1889, 2009.

347 United Nations Office on Drugs and Crime, 'Human trafficking fuels violence against women'. Online. Available HTTP: http://www.unodc.org/unodc/en/frontpage/2009/November/human-trafficking-fuels-violence-against-women.html (accessed 3 March 2010).

348 http://uk.reuters.com/article/2011/05/23/uk-jimmychoo-idUKTRE74L1OZ20110523 (accessed 5 September 2011).

349 M. Zalewski, '"I don't even know what gender is"'.

350 'UN celebrates a "watershed day" for women', *The Independent on Sunday*, 4 July 2010, p. 4.

351 Halberstam, *The Queer Art of Failure*, p. 12.

352 Minh-ha, *When the Moon Waxes Red*, p. 22.

353 Irigaray, *This Sex Which Is Not One*, p. 45.

354 Online. Available HTTP: http://www.upf.edu/pcstacademy/_docs/200411_environment1.pdf (accessed 12 February 2012).

355 *The Song of Bernadette*, Dir. Henry King, Twentieth Century Fox, 1946.

356 http://www.script-o-rama.com/movie_scripts/d/day-after-tomorrow-script-transcript.html (accessed 12 July 2012).

357 http://cleolinda.livejournal.com/110923.html 22.10.10 – no longer available.

358 Minh-ha, *When the Moon Waxes Red*, p. 108.

359 Ronell, 'Deviant payback', p. 15.

360 Solanos, *SCUM MANIFESTO*, p. 37.

361 *Ibid.*, p. 35.

362 *Ibid.*, p. 38.

363 *Ibid.*, p. 45.

364 *Ibid.*, p. 54.

365 M. Wittig, 'One is not born a woman', in L.M. Alcoff and E. Mendieta (eds), *Identities: Race, Class, Gender, and Nationality*, Oxford: Blackwell, 2003, pp. 158–62, p. 160.

366 S. Brownmiller, *Against Our Will: Men, Women and Rape*, New York: Random House, 1975.

367 See discussion in Hawkesworth, *Feminist Inquiry*, chapter 5.

368 Brownmiller, *Against Our Will*, p. 109.

369 BBC, 'Libbers'. Online. Available HTTP: http://www.bbc.co.uk/programmes/b00rbkkp (accessed March 2010). 'Acclaimed filmmaker Vanessa Engle turns her attention to sexual politics in a three-part documentary series about feminism and its impact on women's lives today'. Shown on the UK's BBC in March 2010.

370 YouTube, 'American Psycho – Business Card Scene'. Online. Available HTTP: http://www.youtube.com/watch?v=cISYzA36-ZY (accessed 12 January 2012).

371 Script-O-Rama, 'American Psycho Script Transcript'. Online. Available HTTP: http://www.script-o-rama.com/movie_scripts/a/amercan-psycho-script-transript-bale.html (accessed 12 January 2012).

372 M. Kimmel, 'Globalization and its mal(e)contents: the gendered moral and political economy of terrorism', *International Sociology*, 2003, 18, 603–20, p. 617.

373   M. Stern and M. Eriksson Baaz, 'Why do soldiers rape? Masculinity, violence and sexuality in the armed forces in the Congo (DRC)', *International Studies Quarterly*, 2009, 53, 495–518, p. 500.

374   Ronell, 'Deviant payback', p. 13.

375   R. Connell, 'Preface: the man questions, gender and global power', in J. Parpart and M. Zalewski (eds), *Rethinking the Man Question: Sex, Gender and Violence in International Relations*, London: Zed Press, 2008, viii–xiv, p. xi.

376   Carver, 'G.I. Jane'.

377   Ronell, 'Deviant payback', p. 37.

378   *Ibid.*, p. 8.

379   *Ibid.*, p. 3.

380   J. Bourke, *Rape: Sex, Violence, History*, London: Virago Press. 2007, p. 5.

381   A. Dworkin, *Life and Death: Unapologetic Writings on the Continuing War Against Women*, London and New York: Simon & Schuster, 1997, p. 53.

382   G. Corea, *The Mother Machine: Reproductive Technologies from Artificial Insemination to Artificial Wombs*, London: Women's Press, 1998, p. 281.

383   Bourke, *Rape: Sex, Violence, History*; Henry, *War and Rape*; Gunne and Brigley Thompson, *Feminism, Literature and Rape Narratives*; Stern and Eriksson Baaz, 'Why do soldiers rape?'.

384   Henry, *War and Rape*.

385   S. Jeffrey, *Industrial Vagina*, London: Routledge, 2008.

386   *Taken*, Dir. Pierre Morel, Europa Corp., 2008.

387   *Lilya 4-Ever*, Dir. Lukas Moodysson, Memfis Films, 2002.

388   E. Martin, *The Woman in the Body*, Milton Keynes, UK: Open University Press, 1988, p. 201.

389   Drakulić, *They Would Never Hurt a Fly*, p. 179.

390   Women in Black. Online. Available HTTP: http://www.womeninblack.org/en/history (accessed 12 January 2012).

391   Fukuyama, 'Women and the evolution of world politics', p. 39. See also L.H.M. Ling, 'Hypermasculinity on the rise, again: a response to Fukuyama on women and world politics', *International Feminist Journal of Politics*, 2:2, 277–86.

392   http://www.unwomen.org/2010/10/un-women-executive-director-michelle-bachelet-commends-security-council-for-renewed-progress-on-women-peace-and-security/ (accessed 28 March 2012).

393   *Monster*, Dir. Patty Jenkins, Media 8 Entertainment, 2003.

394   Halley, *Split Decisions*, p. 33.

395   See articles in special issue of *International Feminist Journal of Politics*, on 'Comparative gender mainstreaming', 2005, 7:4; also A. McRobbie, *The Aftermath of Feminism: Gender, Culture and Social Change*, London: Sage, 2009.

396   Halley, *Split Decisions*.

397   A. Jones, *Gender Inclusive: Essays on Violence, Men, and Feminist International Relations*, London: Routledge, 2009.

398   Ahmed, *The Promise of Happiness*, p. 198.

399   Halberstam, *The Queer Art of Failure*, p. 15.

400   YouTube, 'Žižek on *Children of Men*'.

401   Žižek, *Welcome to the Desert of the Real*.

402   Žižek, *Violence*.

403   See, for example, http://www.funny-joke-rating.com/best-jokes/top_30_best_jack_bauer_jokes.html (accessed 11 March 2012).

404   The first series of *24* was aired in 2002. Since then there have been 8 seasons (plus *Redemption*). 'Jack Bauer for President' T-shirts are available for purchase. The distinctive telephone ring tone of the Counter Terrorism Unit is available to download for mobile/cell phones.

405   Though the US emerges as representing 'the globe' – reflecting a common self-perception of its own international role.

406 The series began in 2002.

407 See *Facebook* site http://www.facebook.com/pages/Jack-Bauer-for-President/120686 134617188 (accessed 11 March 2012).

408 Funny Joke Rating, '24 New Jack Bauer Jokes'. Online. Available HTTP: http:// www.funny-joke-rating.com/New-Jokes/24_New_Jack_Bauer_Jokes.html (accessed 29 November 2010).

409 There are many intriguing enactments of gender in *24* – notably the 'complementary' masculinity of President David Palmer (in seasons 1–5 – who we are led to believe is the US's first black President. The femininity of Jack's nineteen-year-old daughter Kim is also intriguing (regularly needing Dad to help her out of a mess). For readings on *24* see S. Peacock (ed.), *Reading 24: TV Against the Clock*, London: New York: I.B. Tauris, 2007 and R. Minter (ed.), *Jack Bauer for President: Terrorism and Politics in 24*, Dallas, TX: Benbella Books, 2008.

410 Funny Joke Rating, '24 New Jack Bauer Jokes'.

411 P. Hardcastle, '19', *Paul Hardcastle*, 1985.

412 The Soldiers, *Coming Home*, 2009.

413 C. Cockburn, *From Where we Stand: War, Women's Activism and Feminist Analysis*, London: Zed Books, 2007, p. 257.

414 *World Trade Center*, Dir. Oliver Stone, Paramount Pictures, 2006.

415 *Children of Men.*

416 Halberstam, *The Queer Art of Failure*, p. 15.

417 L. Sjoberg and C. Gentry, *Mothers, Monsters, Whores: Women's Violence in Global Politics*, London and New York: Zed Books, 2007, p. 25.

418 United Nations UNiTE Secretary General's campaign to end violence against women, 'Network of Men Leaders'. Online. Available HTTP: http://www.un.org/en/women/ endviolence/network.shtml (accessed 12 January 2012).

419 See, for example, http://www.hrw.org/news/2011/10/10/dr-congo-prosecute-atrocities-exposed-un (accessed 25 March 2012).

420 Guardian Online, 'Congo women relive terror of mass rape: "this is our cry for help"'. Online. Available HTTP: http://www.guardian.co.uk/world/2010/oct/12/congo-unitednations (accessed 14 October 2010).

421 C.P. Gilman, *Herland*, Kindle edn, Digireads.com, 2004. Permission kindly granted by Digireads.com Publishing.

422 Kramer, *After the Lovedeath*, p. 2.

423 http://www.facebook.com/pages/Real-Men-Dont-Rape/293949751004 (accessed 27 March 2012).

424 Kramer, *After the Lovedeath*, p. 203.

425 Ronell, 'Deviant payback', p. 5.

426 United Nations, UNiTE to end violence against women. 'Network of men leaders'. Online. Available HTTP: http://un.org/en/women/endviolence/network.shtml (accessed 12 January 2012)..

427 W. Brown, *Regulating Aversion: Tolerance in the Age of Identity and Empire*, Princeton, NJ: Princeton University Press, 2006.

428 United Nations, 'Network of Men Leaders'.

429 Ronnell, 'Deviant payback', p. 3.

430 P. Melzer, *Alien Constructions: Science Fiction and Feminist Thought*, Austin: University of Texas Press, 2006, p. 2.

431 K. Waltz, *Man the State and War: A Theoretical Analysis*, New York: Columbia University Press, 1959.

432 *International Relations*, 23:2, 2009.

433 15 October 2009 at 1:21 am.

434 15 October 2009 at 3:41 am.

435 http://merln.ndu.edu/archivepdf/nss/state/36915.pdf (accessed 27 March 2012).

436 Pettman, *Worlding Women*, p. 7.

437 J.B. Elshtain, 'Woman, the state, and war', *International Relations*, 2009, 23:2, 289–303.

438 L. Sjoberg, 'Gender, the state, and war redux: feminist international relations across the "levels of analysis"', *International Relations*, 2011, 25:1, 108–134.

439 Enloe, *Bananas, Beaches and Bases*, p. 6.

440 Bleiker, 'The aesthetic turn', p. 517.

441 Ronell, 'Deviant payback', p. 3.

442 Crawford, 'Feminist futures', p. 207.

443 Ronell, 'Deviant payback', p. 3.

444 Fiona Sampson, *Rough Music*, Carcanet Press Limited, 2010. Permission kindly granted by Carcanet Press Limited.

445 Brownmiller, *Against Our Will*, p. 186.

446 *Ibid*.

447 Waltz, K., *Man the State and War: a theoretical analysis*, New York: Columbia University Press, 1959.

448 *Ibid*., p. 46.

449 See Henry, *War and Rape*.

450 S.L. Dyvik, 'Gendered war and reconstruction: the politics of representation and the "liberation" of Afghan women', paper presented at the Standing Group on International Relations Conference, Stockholm, September 2010. See also Henry, *War and Rape*.

451 See Bourke, *Rape: Sex, Violence, History*, p. 13.

452 C. Enloe, *The Curious Feminist*, Berkeley: University of California Press, 2004, p. 99.

453 Stern and Eriksson Baaz, 'Why do soldiers rape?'

454 Solanos, *SCUM MANIFESTO*, p. 74.

455 *Dr Jekyll and Mr Hyde*, Dir. Rouben Mamoulian, Paramount Pictures, 1931; R.L. Stevenson, *Strange Case of Dr Jekyll and Mr Hyde*, London: Longman, 1886.

456 M. Wollstonecraft, *A Vindication of the Rights of Woman, with Strictures on Political and Moral Subjects*, London: Dover Publications, 1996 [1792].

457 Solanos, *SCUM MANIFESTO*.

458 S. Marcus, 'Fighting bodies, fighting words: a theory and politics of rape protection', in J. Butler and J. Scott (eds), *Feminists Theorize the Political*, New York and London: Routledge, 1992, pp. 385–403.

459 Gunne and Brigley Thompson, *Feminism, Literature and Rape Narratives*, p. xix.

460 *Horrible Bosses*, Dir. Seth Gordon, Newline Cinema, 2011.

461 Halberstam, *The Queer Art of Failure*, see chapter 2.

462 At least this was the line in the version I viewed on a flight.

463 *The Accused*, Dir. Jonathan Kaplan, Paramount Pictures, 1998.

464 Bumiller, *In an Abusive State*.

465 Graphic Witness, 'Political realities: prints by Sue Coe, 1977–'. Online. Available HTTP: http://www.graphicwitness.org/coe/prnpol.htm (accessed 12 January 2012).

466 Bumiller, *In an Abusive State*, pp. 25–6.

467 See discussion about *The Accused* in K. Boyle *Media and Violence*, London: Sage, 2005.

468 Bumiller, *In an Abusive State*, p. 46.

469 *Ibid*.

470 Boyle, *Media and Violence*, p. 141.

471 Bumiller, *In an Abusive State*, p. 10.

472 Kramer, *After the Lovedeath*, p. 203.

473 Bumiller, *In an Abusive State*; Gunne and Brigley Thompson, *Feminism, Literature and Rape Narratives*.

474 Henry, *War and Rape*.

475 Secretary Clinton's Statement on Reports of Mass Rape in the Democratic Republic of the Congo, 25 August 2010. http://blogs.state.gov/index.php/site/entry/clinton_statement_rape_drc (accessed 25 March 2012).

476 S. Srivastava, '"You're calling me a racist?" The moral and emotional regulation of anti-racism and feminism', *Signs: Journal of Women in Culture and Society*, 2005, 31:1, 29–62.

477   United Nations, UNiTE to end violence against women.

478   T. Morrison, *The Bluest Eye*, London: Vintage Books, 1999.

479   *Ibid.*, p. 128.

480   *Gone with the Wind*, Dir. Victor Fleming, Warner Bros., 1939.

481   Z. Waxman, 'Testimony and silence: sexual violence and the holocaust', in Gunne and Brigley Thompson, *Feminism, Literature and Rape Narratives*, p. 122.

482   Kramer, *After the Lovedeath*, p. 62.

483   T. Carver, 'Conclusion', in Shepherd, *Gender Matters*, 347–50.

484   Winterson, *Why Be Happy When You Could Be Normal?*, p. 58.

485   Rancière, *The Emancipated Spectator*, p. 17.

486   See http://www.xtimeline.com/evt/view.aspx?id=87805

487   Halberstam, *The Queer Art of* Failure, p. 133. See also B. Hanssen, *Critique of Violence*, p. 211.

488   E. Jelinek, *The Piano Teacher*, London: Serpent's Tail, 2001.

489   Kramer, *After the Lovedeath*, p. 8.

490   Wittig, 'One is not born a woman', p. 162.

491   *The Sunday Times*, 'Les Sarkozettes', 6 May 2007.

492   http://news.bbc.co.uk/1/hi/uk_politics/4698222.stm (accessed 27 March 2012).

493   Wittig, 'One is not born a woman', p. 3.

494   S. Hunt, 'Let women rule', *Foreign Affairs*, 2007, 86:3, 109–20, p. 109.

495   Peterson, *Gendered States*.

496   Sjoberg, 'Emotion and the feminist IR researcher'.

497   N. Pratt, 'What do women foreign policy leaders mean for gender and for international relations? The case of Condoleezza Rice', unpublished paper, www2.warwick.ac.uk/fac/soc/pais/people/pratt/research

498   P. MacCormack, 'Unnatural alliances', in C. Nigianni and M. Storr (eds), *Deleuze and Queer Theory*, Edinburgh: Edinburgh University Press, 2009, pp. 134–49, p. 144.

499   S. Bendelack, *Little Britain*, Series 1–3, London: BBC, Pinewood Studios, 2003.

500   http://www.youtube.com/watch?v=qcVZg2tVswk – no longer available.

501   YouTube, 'Marjory Dawes tells Rosie O'Donnell What's What'. Online. Available HTTP: http://www.youtube.com/watch?v=jgODHapn5L4 (accessed 12 January 2012).

502   A. Oakley, *Adventures of a Broken Body*, Bristol: Policy Press, 2007; Ahmed, *Cultural Politics of Emotion*.

503   http://thegrindstone.com/office-politics/why-are-there-no-women-at-davos-531/ (accessed 28 March 2012).

504   J. True and M. Mintrom, 'Transnational networks and policy diffusion: the case of gender mainstreaming', *International Studies Quarterly*, 2002, 45:1, 27–57, p. 35.

505   A. Walker, *The Color Purple*, London: Orion Publishing Group, 2009, p. 51. Permission to reproduce kindly granted.

506   Gordon, *Ghostly Matters*, p. 185.

507   Srivastava, '"You're calling me a racist?"'.

508   http://www.hindustantimes.com/world-news/africa/More-than-150-women-raped-in-Congolese-village-says-UN/Article1-591083.aspx (accessed 25 March 2012).

509   Sontag, *Regarding the Pain of Others*.

510   Secretary Clinton's Statement on reports of mass rape in the Democratic Republic of the Congo, 25 August 2010. http://blogs.state.gov/index.php/site/entry/clinton_statement_rape_drc (accessed 25 March 2012).

511   See M. Daigle, 'Sexuality, the discourse of "prostitution", and governance of bodies in post-Soviet Cuba', 2012, PhD thesis, Aberystwyth University, p. 32.

512   Online. Available HTTP: http://www.google.co.uk/images?hl=en&expIds=17259,27586,28025&xhr=t&q=sojourner+truth&cp=6&um=1&ie=UTF-8&source=og&sa=N&tab=wi&biw=1408&bih=636 (accessed 25 March 2012).

513   A. Fausto-Sterling, *Sexing the Body*, New York: Basic Books, 2000.

514   See for example S. Qureshi, 'Displaying Sara Baartman, the "Hottentot Venus"', *History of Science*, 2004, 42, 234–57; Fausto-Sterling, *Sexing the Body*; Clifton Crais and Pamela

Scully, *Sara Baartman and the Hottentot Venus: A Ghost Story and a Biography*, Durham, NC: Princeton University Press, 2008; N. Gordon-Chipembere, *Representation and Black Womanhood: The Legacy of Sarah Baartman*, London: Palgrave Macmillan, 2011.

515 Qureshi, 'Displaying Sara Baartman'.

516 T. T. Minh-ha, 'Difference: A Special Third World Women Issue', p. 7.

517 Lederman and Bartsch, *The Gender and Science Reader*, pp. 350–53.

518 C. Chin, 'Claiming race and gracelessness in international studies', *International Studies Perspectives*, 2009, 10:1, 92–98, p. 93.

519 Qureshi, 'Displaying Sara Baartman', p. 240.

520 Ahmed, *The Promise of Happiness*.

521 N. Painter, quoted in Hawkesworth, *Feminist Inquiry*, p. 126.

522 *Ibid.*, p. 127.

523 Butler, *Precarious Life*.

524 Dyvik, 'Gendered war and reconstruction'.

525 Walker, *The Colour Purple*, p. 45.

526 *Ibid.*

527 Hawkesworth, *Feminist Inquiry*, p. 127.

528 Minh-ha, *When the Moon Waxes Red*, p. 5.

529 Ahmed, *The Promise of Happiness*, p. 75.

530 Cunningham, *The Hours*; *The Hours*, Dir. Stephen Daldry, Paramount, 2002.

531 *Ibid.*

532 Angry Black Bitch. Online. Available HTTP: http://www.cafepress.com/angryblackbitch (accessed 12 January 2012). There is a choice of merchandise at the *Angry Black Bitch* boutique imprinted with these words: 'Acceptably Black: clean, non-threatening, speaks well'.

533 Z. Eisenstein, *Against Empire: Feminisms, Racism and the West*, London: Zed Books, 2004, p. 59.

534 Guardian Online, 'Stephen Lawrence verdict: Dobson and Norris guilty of racist murder'. Online. Available HTTP: http://www.guardian.co.uk/uk/2012/jan/03/stephen-lawrence-verdict-guilty-murder (14 January 2012).

535 Mail Online, 'The moment Miliband phoned race row MP Diane Abbott to say: apologise or I'll sack you'. Online. Available HTTP: http://www.dailymail.co.uk/news/article-2082527/Diane-Abbott-Twitter-race-row-MP-faces-calls-resign-racist-tweet.html (accessed 14 January 2012).

536 CBS News, 'Michelle Obama says people have inaccurately cast her as "an angry black woman"'. Online. Available HTTP: http://www.cbsnews.com/8301-250_162-57356780/michelle-obama-says-people-have-inaccurately-cast-her-as-an-angry-black-woman (accessed 14 January 2012).

537 The Guardian, Roundtable, 'Yes, we are angry and proud of it', 13 January 2012, p. 32.

538 See http://minorityhealth.hhs.gov/templates/browse.aspx?lvl=2&lvlID=51 (accessed 25 March 2012).

539 M. Frye, *The Politics of Reality: Essays in Feminist Theory*, New York: Crossing Press, 1983.

540 Ahmed, *The Promise of Happiness*, p. 66.

541 *Ibid.*, p. 170.

542 A. Lorde, 'The master's tools will never dismantle the master's house', in C. Moraga and G. Anzaldua (eds), *This Bridge Called My Back: Writings By Radical Women of Color*, New York: Women of Color Press, 1983; hooks, *Feminism is for EVERYBODY*.

543 Los Angeles Times, 'Laura Bush address state of Afghan Women'. Online. Available HTTP: http://articles.latimes.com/2001/nov/18/news/mn-5602 (accessed 10 May 2010).

544 See discussion in Eisenstein, *Against Empire*, chapter 7.

545 Butler, *Undoing Gender*.

546 S. Thobani, Presentation to Ottawa Women's Resistance Conference, 1 October 2001. Online. Available HTTP: http://englishmatters.gmu.edu/issue6/911exhibit/emails/sunera_thobani.htm (accessed 12 January 2012).

547 V. Amos and P. Parmar, 'Challenging imperial feminism', *Feminist Review*, 1984, 17, 3–19; H. Carby, 'White woman listen! Black feminism and the boundaries of sisterhood',

in Centre for Contemporary Cultural Studies (ed.), *The Empire Strikes Back: Race and Racism in 1970s Britain*, London: Hutchinson, 1982; Lorde, 'The master's tools'; C.T. Mohanty, *Feminism without Borders: Decolonizing Theory, Practicing Solidarity*, Durham, NC: Duke University Press, 2003; Williams, *The Alchemy of Race and Rights*; Spivak, *Outside in the Teaching Machine*; hooks, *Feminism is for EVERYBODY*.

548   b. hooks, *Ain't I A Woman: Black Women and Feminism*, London: Pluto Press, 1992.

549   *Ibid.*

550   S. Thobani, 'White wars: Western feminisms and the "War on Terror"', *Feminist Theory*, 2007, 8:2, 169–85; P. Chesler and Z. Eisenstein, 'Responses to Sunera Thobani's "White wars: Western feminisms and the 'War on Terror'"', *Feminist Theory*, 2007, 8:2, 227–35.

551   Butler, *Precarious Life*.

552   Eisenstein, *Against Empire*.

553   P. Chesler, *The New Anti-Semitism: The Current Crisis and What We Must Do About It*, New York: Jossey-Bass, 2005.

554   Srivastava, '"You're calling me a racist?"'.

555   *Ibid.*, p. 42

556   Ahmed, *Queer Phenomenology*.

557   A. Heiss, 'Invisible whiteness', in *I'm Not Racist, But…*, Cambridge: Salt Publishing, 2007. Permission kindly granted by arrangement with Anita Heiss c/- Curtis Brown (Aust) Pty Ltd.

558   Dyer, *White*, p. 46.

559   McRobbie, *The Aftermath of Feminism*.

560   Dyer, *White*, p. 72.

561   *Ibid.*, p. 223.

562   *Ibid.*, p. 63.

563   *Mississippi Burning*, Dir. Alan Parker, Orion Pictures, 1989.

564   British National Party, 'Immigration'. Online. Available HTTP: http://www.bnp.org. uk/policies/immigration (accessed 20 May 2011).

565   M. Berger, *White Lies: Race and the Myth of Whiteness*, New York: Farrar, Strauss and Giroux, 2000, p. 286.

566   Dyer, *White*, p. 10.

567   Berger, *White Lies*, p. 140.

568   Story relayed in Berger, *White Lies*.

569   Photo and detail taken at the War Museum in Canberra.

570   Mail Online, 'Why girls are naturally drawn to dolls as soon as they can crawl'. Online. Available HTTP: http://www.dailymail.co.uk/sciencetech/article-1266364/Why-girls-naturally-drawn-dolls-soon-crawl.html (accessed 20 May 2011).

571   Berger, *White Lies*, p. 215.

572   Ahmed, *Queer Phenomenology*, p. 163.

573   D.T. Goldberg, *Racist Culture: Philosophy and the Politics of Meaning*, Oxford: Blackwell, 1993, p. 7.

574   BBC, 'Harvard to boost women scientists'. Online. Available HTTP: http://news.bbc. co.uk/1/hi/education/4556299.stm (accessed 19 June 2011).

575   Quoted in P. Gilroy, *After Empire: Melancholia or Convivial Culture?*, London: Routledge, 2004, p. 11.

576   Gilroy, *After Empire*, p. 12.

577   Chin, 'Claiming race and racelessness in international studies', p. 93.

578   A. Tickner, 'Seeing international relations differently – notes from the 3rd world', *Millennium*, 2003, 32:2, p. 296.

579   Pettman, *Worlding Women*.

580   Gilroy, *After Empire*, p. ix.

581   G. Chowdhry and S. Rai, 'The geographies of exclusion and the politics of inclusion: race-based exclusions in the teaching of international relations', *International Studies Perspectives*, 2009, 10:1, 84–91, p. 90.

582 K. Hutchings, 'Cognitive short cuts', in Parpart and Zalewski, *Rethinking the Man Question*, pp. 23–46.

583 J. Mearsheimer, *The Tragedy of Great Power Politics*, New York: W.W. Norton, 2001.

584 M. Hardt and A. Negri, *Multitude: War and Democracy in the Age of Empire*, London: Penguin, 2006.

585 J. Halberstam, 'The good, the bad, and the ugly: men, women, and masculinity', in J. Kegan Gardiner (ed.), *Masculinity Studies and Feminist Theory*, New York: Columbia University Press, 2002, pp. 344–67.

586 *As Good as It Gets*, Dir. James L. Brooks, TriStar Pictures, 1997.

587 *Chasing Amy*, Dir. Kevin Smith, Miramax, 1997.

588 *The Opposite of Sex*, Dir. Don Roos, Rysher Entertainment, 1998.

589 Chin, 'Claiming race and racelessness in international studies', p. 98.

590 Wiegman, 'The intimacy of critique', p. 83.

591 S. Ahmed, 'A phenomenology of whiteness', *Feminist Theory*, 2007, 8:2, 149–68, p. 164.

592 Hawkesworth, *Feminist Inquiry*, see chapter 5.

593 Tickner, 'Seeing international relations differently', p. 300.

594 *Ibid.*, p. 297.

595 *Ibid.*, p. 300.

596 T. Morrison, *The Bluest Eye*, London: Vintage Books, 1999.

597 Gordon, *Ghostly Matters*, p. 4.

598 Tronto, 'Beyond gender difference', p. 661.

599 *Ibid.*, p. 646.

600 Gilligan, *In a Different Voice*.

601 Ruddick, *Maternal Thinking*.

602 N. Rhode, 'Nina Rhode: Friendly Fire', Dundee Contemporary Arts, 21 May–31 July 2011. Online. Available HTTP: http://www.dca.org.uk/uploads/Nina-gallery-leaflet.pdf (accessed 27 March 2012).

603 Ahmed, *Queer Phenomenology*, p. 23.

604 Minh-Ha, *When the Moon Waxes Red*, p. 15.

605 Berlant, *Cruel Optimism*, p. 249.

606 See, for example, http://www.ultrared.org/publicrecord/directory.html (accessed 3 March 2012); http://www.archive.org/details/Fifteen_Sounds_of_the_War_on_the_Poor_vol1-6289 (accessed 3 March 2012).

607 Halberstam, *The Queer Art of Failure*, p. 2.

608 K. Hastrup, 'Agency, anticipation and creativity', in E. Hallam and T. Ingold (eds), *Creativity and Cultural Improvisation*, Oxford and New York: Berg, 2007, pp. 193–206, p. 200.

609 W. Vrasti, 'The strange case of ethnography', p. 288.

610 St Martin in the Fields, 'Café in the Crypt'. Online. Available HTTP: http://www2.stmartin-in-the-fields.org/page/cafe2010/cafe.html (accessed 12 January 2012).

611 C. Enloe, *Globalization and Militarism: Feminists make the Link*, New York: Rowman & Littlefield, 2007, p. 4.

612 Online. Available HTTP: http://www.facebook.com/pages/Bin-Laden-dead-Does-this-mean-I-can-bring-shampoo-the-airport-now/197817743595347

613 G. Simmel, 'Bridge and door', *Theory, Culture and Society*, 11:5, 5–10, p. 7.

614 Minh-Ha, *When the Moon Waxes Red*, p. 109.

615 Winterson, *Why Be Happy When You Could Be Normal?*, p. 38. Permission kindly granted by The Peters Fraser & Dunlop Group Ltd, London.

BIBLIOGRAPHY

Print and online

Adler, C. and Worral, A. (eds), *Girls' Violence: Myths and Realities*, Albany, NY: State University of New York Press, 2004.

Ahmed, S., *The Cultural Politics of Emotion*, Edinburgh: Edinburgh University Press, 2004.

—— 'A phenomenology of whiteness', *Feminist Theory*, 2007, 8:2, 149–68.

—— *Queer Phenomenology: Orientations, Objects, Others*, Durham, NC and London: Duke University Press, 2007.

—— *The Promise of Happiness*, Durham, NC and London: Duke University Press, 2011.

All Voices, 'Glasgow Scotland joins latest addition of slutwalks around the globe'. Online. Available HTTP: http://www.allvoices.com/contributed-news/9301620-glasgow-scotland-joins-latest-addition-of-slutwalks-around-the-globe (accessed 20 June 2011).

Alvi, M., *How the Stone Found Its Voice*, Tarset, UK: Bloodaxe Books, 2005.

Amos, V. and P. Parmar, 'Challenging imperial feminism', *Feminist Review*, 1984, 17, 3–19.

Angry Black Bitch. Online. Available HTTP: http://www.cafepress.com/angryblackbitch (accessed 12 January 2012).

Arendt, H., *On Violence*, New York and London: Harcourt, 1970.

Aretxaga, B., *Shattering Silence: Women, Nationalism and Political Subjectivity in Northern Ireland*, Princeton, NJ: Princeton University Press, 1997.

Barad, K., *Meeting The Universe Halfway*, Durham, NC and London: Duke University Press, 2007.

BBC, 'Bombs and beatings: life among the Taliban'. Online. Available HTTP: http://news.bbc.co.uk/1/hi/world/south_asia/8499578.stm (accessed 5 February 2010).

—— 'Girl violence increasing – report'. Online. Available HTTP: http://news.bbc.co.uk/1/hi/uk/137049.stm (accessed 11 August 2008).

—— 'Harvard to boost women scientists'. Online. Available HTTP: http://news.bbc.co.uk/1/hi/education/4556299.stm (accessed 19 June 2011).

—— 'Invisibility cloak "step closer"'. Online. Available HTTP: http://news.bbc.co.uk/1/hi/sci/tech/7553061.stm (accessed 11 August 2008).

—— 'Libbers'. Online. Available HTTP: http://www.bbc.co.uk/programmes/b00rbkkp (accessed March 2010).

—— 'Michelle Obama: "I'm no angry black woman"'. Online. Available HTTP: http://www.bbc.co.uk/news/world-us-canada-16515834 (accessed 26 November 2012).

—— 'Politics'. Aired 12 June 2011.

—— 'Pope attacks blurring of gender'. Online. Available HTTP: http://news.bbc.co.uk/1/hi/world/europe/7796663.stm (accessed 6 January 2009).

de Beauvoir, S., *The Second Sex*, trans. H.M. Parshley, London: Vintage, 1952[1949].

Berger, M., *White Lies: Race and the Myth of Whiteness*, New York: Farrar, Strauss and Giroux, 2000.

Berlant, L., *Cruel Optimism*, Durham, NC: Duke University Press, 2011.

Bleiker, R., 'Forget IR theory', *Alternatives*, 1997, 22, 57–85.

—— 'The aesthetic turn in international political theory', *Millennium: Journal of International Studies*, 2001, 30:3, 509–33.

—— *Aesthetics and World Politics*, Basingstoke, UK: Palgrave Macmillan, 2009.

Bourke, J., *Rape: Sex, Violence, History*, London: Virago Press, 2007.

Boyle, K., *Media and Violence*, London: Sage, 2005.

Brennan, T., *The Transmission of Affect*, Ithaca, NY and London: Cornell University Press, 2004.

British National Party, 'Immigration'. Online. Available HTTP: http://www.bnp.org.uk/policies/immigration (accessed 20 May 2011).

Bronfen, E. and Kavka, M. (eds), *Feminist Consequences: Theory for the New Century*, New York: Columbia University Press, 2001.

Brown, C., 'IR theory in Britain – the New Black?', *Review of International Studies*, 32, 677–87.

Brown, W., *States of Injury*, Princeton, NJ and Oxford: Princeton University Press, 1995.

—— *Politics out of History*, Princeton, NJ and Oxford: Princeton University Press, 2001.

—— *Edgework: Critical Essays on Knowledge and Politics*, Princeton, NJ and Oxford: Princeton University Press, 2005.

—— *Regulating Aversion: Tolerance in the Age of Identity and Empire*, Princeton, NJ: Princeton University Press, 2006.

Brownmiller, S., *Against Our Will: Men, Women and Rape*, New York: Random House, 1975.

Budapest Tourist Guide, 'Budapest Statue Park: Szobor Park'. Online. Available HTTP: http://www.budapest-tourist-guide.com/budapest-statue-park.html (accessed 12 January 2012).

Bumiller, K., *In an Abusive State: How Neoliberalism Appropriated the Feminist Movement against Sexual Violence*, Durham, NC and London: Duke University Press, 2008.

Business Insider, 'French radio: The lawyers were "surprised" at how unattractive the maid was'. Online. Available HTTP: http://www.businessinsider.com/dsk-lawyers-were-surprised-at-how-unattractive-maid-was-2011-5 (accessed 14 June 2011).

Butler, J., *Gender Trouble*, New York and London: Routledge, 1990.

—— *Bodies That Matter: On the Discursive Limits of 'Sex'*, London and New York, Routledge, 1993.

—— 'The end of sexual difference?', in E. Bronfen and M. Kavka (eds), *Feminist Consequences: Theory for the New Century*, New York: Columbia University Press, 2001.

—— *Precarious Life: The Powers of Mourning and Violence*, London and New York: Verso, 2004.

—— *Undoing Gender*, New York and London: Routledge, 2004.

—— *Frames of War*, London: Verso, 2009.

Carby, H., 'White woman listen! Black feminism and the boundaries of sisterhood', in Centre for Contemporary Cultural Studies (ed.), *The Empire Strikes Back: Race and Racism in 1970s Britain*, London: Hutchinson, 1982.

Carlagirl Photo, *Hottentot Venus Bibliography*. Online. Available HTTP: http://carlagirl.net/artists-links/hottentot-venus-bibliography/ (accessed 1 March 2010).

Carroll, L., *Alice's Adventures in Wonderland and Through the Looking-Glass*, illustrated by John Tenniel, with an introduction and notes by Martin Gardner. London: Penguin Books, 1974.

Carver, T., 'G.I. Jane: what are the "manners" that "maketh a man"?', *British Journal of Politics and International Relations*, 2007, 9:2, 313–17.

—— 'Conclusion', in Laura J. Shepherd, *Gender Matters in Global Politics*, London: Routledge, 2009, pp. 347–50.

Centre for Sustainable International Development, University of Aberdeen. Online. Available HTTP: http://www.abdn.ac.uk/sustainable-international-development/events/338 (accessed 12 January 2012).

Chadwick, W., *Women Artists and the Surrealist Movement*, London: Thames & Hudson, 2002.

Chandramohan, B. and S. Fallows, *Interdisciplinary Learning and Teaching in Higher Education: Theory and Practice*, London: Routledge, 2009.

Chapman, D. and J. Chapman, *Insult to Injury* (wallpaper, Victoria & Albert Museum). Online. Available HTTP: http://collections.vam.ac.uk/item/O1154956/wallpaper-insult-to-injury (accessed 14 October 2011).

—— *Insult to Injury*, London: SteidlMACK, 2003.

Chesler, P. and Z. Eisenstein, 'Responses to Sunera Thobani's "White wars: Western feminisms and the 'War on Terror'"', *Feminist Theory*, 2007, 8:2, 227–35.

Chin, C., 'Claiming race and racelessness in international studies', *International Studies Perspectives*, 2009, 10:1, 92–98.

Chowdhry, G. and S. Rai, 'The geographies of exclusion and the politics of inclusion: race-based exclusions in the teaching of international relations', *International Studies Perspectives*, 2009, 10:1, 84–91.

Cixous, H., *White Ink: Interviews on Sex, Text and Politics*, Stocksfield, UK: Acumen Publishing, 2008.

Cockburn, C. *From Where we Stand: War, Women's Activism and Feminist Analysis*, London: Zed Books, 2007.

Cohn, C., 'Sex and death in the rational world of defense intellectuals', *Signs*, 1988, 12:4, 687–718.

Connell, R. W., *Masculinities*, Cambridge: Polity Press, 1995.

—— 'Preface: the man questions, gender and global power', in J. Parpart and M. Zalewski (eds), *Rethinking the Man Question: Sex, Gender and Violence in International Relations*, London: Zed Press, 2008, viii–xiv.

Cooper, R., 'Assemblage notes', in R.C.H. Chia (ed.), *Organized Worlds: Explorations in Technology and Organization with Robert Cooper*, London and New York: Routledge, 1998.

Corea, G., *The Mother Machine: Reproductive Technologies from Artificial Insemination to Artificial Wombs*, London: Women's Press, 1998.

Crais, C. and P. Scully, *Sara Baartman and the Hottentot Venus: A Ghost Story and a Biography*, Durham, NC: Princeton University Press, 2008.

Crawford, N., 'Feminist futures: science fiction, utopia, and the art of possibilities in world politics', in J. Weldes (ed.), *To Seek Out New Worlds: Exploring Links between Science Fiction and World Politics*, London: Palgrave Macmillan, 2003.

Crow, B.A. (ed.), *Radical Feminism: A Documentary Reader*, New York: New York University Press, 2000.

Cunningham, M., *The Hours*, London and New York: Harper Perennial, 2006.

D'Costa, B. and K. Lee-Koo, *Gender and Global Politics in the Asia-Pacific*, London: Palgrave Macmillan, 2009.

Daigle, M., 'Sexuality, the discourse of "prostitution", and governance of bodies in post-Soviet Cuba', 2012, PhD thesis, Aberystwyth University.

Davis, K., 'Reclaiming women's bodies: colonialist trope or critical epistemology?', *Sociological Review*, 2007, 55:1, 50–54.

Deleuze, G. and F. Guattari, *A Thousand Plateaus: Capitalism and Schizophrenia*, trans. Brian Massumi, London: Athlone Press, 1987.

Deleuze, G. and C. Parent, *Dialogues*, London: Athlone Press, 1987.

Dickens, C., *Hard Times*, London: Wordsworth Classics, 1995[1845].

Dietz, M.G., 'Current controversies in feminist theory', *Annual Review of Political Science*, 6, 2003, 399–431.

Diken, B. and C. Bagge Lausten, 'Becoming abject: rape as a weapon of war', *Body & Society*, 11:1, 111–28.

Docherty, T., *For the University: Democracy and the Future of the Institution*, London: Bloomsbury Academic, 2011.

Dodd, J., *Violence and Phenomenology*, London: Routledge, 2009.

Drakulić, S., *They Would Never Hurt a Fly: War Criminals on Trial in The Hague*, London: Penguin, 2003.

Dundee Contemporary Arts, 'Thomas Hirschhorn, It's Burning Everywhere', 19 September–29 November 2009. Online. Available HTTP: http://www.dca.org.uk/uploads/Hirschhorn-leaflet-FINAL.pdf (accessed 13 January 2012).

Dunn, D., 'The Incredibles: an ordinary day tale of a superpower in the post 9/11 World', *Millennium: Journal of International Studies*, 34:2, 2006, 559–62.

Dunn, K., 'Interrogating white privilege', in J. Parpart and M. Zalewski (eds), *Rethinking the Man Question: Sex, Gender and Violence in International Relations*, London and New York: Zed Press, 2008, pp. 47–68.

Dworkin, A., *Life and Death: Unapologetic Writings on the Continuing War Against Women*, London and New York: Simon & Schuster, 1997.

Dyer, R., *White*, London and New York: Routledge, 1997.

Dyvik, S.L., 'Gendered war and reconstruction: the politics of representation and the "liberation" of Afghan women', paper presented at the Standing Group on International Relations Conference, Stockholm, September 2010.

Edkins, J. and N. Vaughan Williams (eds), *Critical Theorists and International Relations*, London: Routledge, 2009.

Eisenstein, H., *Feminism Seduced: How Global Elites Use Women's Labor and Ideas to Exploit the World*, Boulder, CO: Paradigm Publishers, 2009.

Eisenstein, Z., *Against Empire: Feminisms, Racism and the West*, London: Zed Books, 2004.

Ellis, R.J., '"Problems may cut right across the borders", why we cannot do without interdisciplinarity', in B. Chandramohan and S. Fallows (eds), *Interdisciplinary Learning and Teaching in Higher Education: Theory and Practice*, London: Routledge, 2009, p. 9.

Elshtain, J.B., 'Women, the state, and war', *International Relations*, 23:2, 2009, 289–303.

Engle, K., *Seeing Ghosts: 9/11 and the Visual Imagination*, Montreal, Kingston and London: McGill–Queen's University Press, 2009.

Enloe, C., *Bananas, Beaches and Bases: Making Feminist Sense of International Politics*, London: Pandora Press, 1989.

—— *The Morning After: Sexual Politics at the End of the Cold War*, Berkley and Los Angeles: University of California Press, 1993.

—— 'Margins, silences and bottom rungs: how to overcome the underestimation of power in the study of international relations', in S. Smith, K. Booth and M. Zalewski (eds), *International Theory: Positivism and Beyond*, Cambridge: Cambridge University Press, 1996, pp. 186–202.

—— *The Curious Feminist: Searching for Women in a New Age of Empire*, Berkeley and London: University of California Press, 2004

—— *Globalization and Militarism: Feminists Make the Link*, New York: Rowman & Littlefield, 2007.

Eschle, C. and B. Maiguashca, 'Bridging the academic/activist divide: feminist activism and the teaching', *Millennium: Journal of International Studies*, 2006, 35:1, 119–37.

—— 'Feminist scholarship, bridge-building and political affinity', *International Relations*, 2009, 23:1, 127–34.

Evans, M., *Killing Thinking: The Death of Universities*, London and New York: Continuum, 2004.

Fanon, F., *Black Skin, White Masks*, London: Pluto Press, 1986.

Fausto-Sterling, A., *Sexing the Body*, New York: Basic Books, 2000.

Ferguson, K.E., *The Man Question: Visions of Subjectivity in Feminist Theory*, Berkeley and Oxford: University of California Press, 1993.

Finlayson, A. and J. Valentine (eds), *Politics and Post-Structuralism: An Introduction*, Edinburgh: Edinburgh University Press, 2002.

Flax, J., 'Postmodernism and gender relations in feminist theory', *Signs: Journal of Women in Culture and Society*, 1987, 12:4, 621–43.

Friederich, E., 'Anti-War Books of the 1920s: "The War Against War"'. Online. Available HTTP: http://www.greatwardifferent.com/Great_War/Kriege/Kriege_00.htm (accessed 11 June 2011).

Frye, M., *The Politics of Reality: Essays in Feminist Theory*, New York: Crossing Press, 1983.

Fukuyama, F., 'Women and the evolution of world politics', *Foreign Policy*, 1998, 77:5, 24–40.

—— *The End of History and the Last Man*, London: Hamish Hamilton, 1992.

Fuller, S., *The Intellectual*, Cambridge: Icon Books, 2005.

Fulton, A., *Cascade Experiment: Selected Poems*, New York and London: W.W. Norton, 2004.

Funny Joke Rating, '24 New Jack Bauer Jokes'. Online. Available HTTP: http://www.funny-joke-rating.com/New-Jokes/24_New_Jack_Bauer_Jokes.html (accessed 29 November 2010).

Fuss, D., *Essentially Speaking: Feminism, Nature and Difference*, London and New York: Routledge, 1989.

Gallop, J., *Thinking Through the Body*, New York: Columbia University Press, 1988.

Gilligan, C., *In a Different Voice: Psychological Theory and Women's Development*, Cambridge, MA: Harvard University Press, 1982.

Gilman, C.P., *Herland*, Kindle edn, Digireads.com, 2004.

Gilroy, P., *After Empire: Melancholia or Convivial Culture?*, London: Routledge, 2004.

Glynos, J. and D. Howarth (eds), *Logics of Critical Explanation in Social and Political Theory*, Abingdon and New York: Routledge, 2007.

Goldberg, D.T., *Racist Culture: Philosophy and the Politics of Meaning*, Oxford: Blackwell, 1993.

Gordon, A., *Ghostly Matters: Haunting and the Sociological Imagination*, Minneapolis and London: University of Minnesota Press, 2001.

Gordon-Chipembere, N., *Representation and Black Womanhood: The Legacy of Sarah Baartman*, London: Palgrave Macmillan, 2011.

Goya, F., *The Disasters of War*, with new introduction by Philip Hofer, New York: Dover Publications, 1967.

Grant, R. and K. Newland (eds), *Gender and International Relations*, Milton Keynes, UK: Open University Press, 1991.

Graphic Witness, 'Political realities: prints by Sue Coe, 1977–'. Online. Available HTTP: http://www.graphicwitness.org/coe/prnpol.htm (accessed 12 January 2012).

Grosz, E., *The Nick of Time: Politics, Evolution, and the Untimely*, Durham, NC and London: Duke University Press, 2007.

The Guardian, Roundtable, 'Yes, we are angry and proud of it', 13 January 2012, p. 32.

Guardian Online, 'Congo women relive terror of mass rape: "this is our cry for help"'. Online. Available HTTP: http://www.guardian.co.uk/world/2010/oct/12/congo-unit ednations (accessed 14 October 2010).

—— 'David Willetts blames feminism over lack of jobs for working men'. Online. Available HTTP: http://www.guardian.co.uk/politics/2011/apr/01/david-willetts-feminism-lack-of-jobs (accessed 14 June 2011).

—— '"Shocking" lack of women top company directors, says report'. Online. Available HTTP: http://www.guardian.co.uk/business/2011/oct/13/shocking-lack-women-directors-ftse (accessed 5 January 2012).

—— 'Stephen Lawrence verdict: Dobson and Norris guilty of racist murder'. Online. Available HTTP: http://www.guardian.co.uk/uk/2012/jan/03/stephen-lawrence-verdict-guilty-murder (accessed 14 January 2012).

—— 'It's not just John Bercow – charm is disappearing from public life. About time too'. Online. Available HTTP: http://www.guardian.co.uk/commentisfree/2011/jan/15/john-bercow-charm-public-life?INTCMP=SRCH (accessed 23 March 2012).

—— Mangan, L. [adapted], 'Last word', 2 November 2005, back page.

Guillaume, X. (ed.) *et al.*, 'Forum: The international as an everyday practice', *International Political Sociology*, 2011, 5:4, 446–62.

Gunew, S., 'Feminist cultural literacy: translating differences, cannibal options', in R. Wiegman (ed.), *Women's Studies on Its Own*, Durham, NC and London: Duke University Press, 2002, pp. 47–65.

Gunne, S. and Z. Brigley Thompson (eds), *Feminism, Literature and Rape Narratives*, London: Routledge, 2009.

Halberstam, J., 'The good, the bad, and the ugly: men, women, and masculinity', in J. Kegan Gardiner (ed.), *Masculinity Studies and Feminist Theory*, New York: Columbia University Press, 2002, pp. 344–67.

—— *The Queer Art of Failure*, Durham, NC and London: Duke University Press, 2011.

Hall, N. and J. True, 'Gender mainstreaming in a post-conflict state', in B. D'Costa and K. Lee-Koo (eds), *Gender and Global Politics in the Asia-Pacific*, London: Palgrave Macmillan, 2009, pp. 159–74.

Hall, S., 'The local and the global: globalization and ethncity', in A.D. King (ed.), *Culture, Globalization and the World-System*, London: Macmillan.

Halley, J., *Split Decisions: How and Why to Take a Break from Feminism*, Princeton, NJ: Princeton University Press, 2006.

Hanssen, B., *Critique of Violence: Between Poststructuralism and Critical Theory*, London and New York: Routledge, 2000.

Haraway, D.J., *Simians, Cyborgs and Women: The Reinvention of Nature*, New York: Routledge, 1991.

—— *Primate Visions: Gender, Race, and Nature in the World of Modern Science*, London: Verso, 1992.

—— *Modest_Witness@Second_Millennium. FemaleMan©_Meets_OncoMouse™*, New York and London: Routledge, 1997.

Harding, S., *The Science Question in Feminism*, Milton Keynes, UK: Open University Press, 1986.

Hardt, M. and A. Negri, *Multitude: War and Democracy in the Age of Empire*, London: Penguin, 2006.

Hartsock, N., *Money Sex and Power*, Boston: Northeastern University Press, 1985.

Hastrup, K., 'Agency, anticipation and creativity', in E. Hallam and T. Ingold (eds), *Creativity and Cultural Improvisation*, Oxford and New York: Berg, 2007, pp. 193–206.

Hawkesworth, M., 'Knowers, knowing, known: feminist theory and claims of truth', *Signs: Journal of Women in Culture and Society*, 1989, 14, 533–56.

—— 'The semiotics of premature burial: feminism in a postfeminist age', *Signs: Journal of Women in Culture and Society*, 2004, 29:4, 961–85.

—— *Feminist Inquiry*, New Brunswick, NJ: Rutgers University Press, 2006.

Heartney, E., H. Posner, N. Princenthal and S. Scott (eds), *After the Revolution: Women who Transformed Contemporary Art*, London and New York: Prestel, 2007.

Heiss, A., *I'm Not Racist, But…*, Cambridge: Salt Publishing, 2007.

Hekman, S., *Private Selves, Public Identities: Reconsidering Identity Politics*, University Park, PA: Pennsylvania State University Press, 2004.

Hemmings, C., 'Telling feminist stories', *Feminist Theory*, 2005, 6:2, 115–39.

—— *Why Stories Matter: The Political Grammar of Feminist Theory*, Durham, NJ and London: Duke University Press, 2011.

Henry, N., *War and Rape: Law, Memory and Justice*, London: Routledge, 2011.

Hill Collins, P., *Black Feminist Thought*, Boston: Unwin Hyman, 1990.

Hirschhorn, T., 'It's Burning Everywhere', Exhibition at Dundee College of Arts, 19 September–29 November, 2009.

hooks, b., *Ain't I a Woman: Black Women and Feminism*, London: Pluto Press, 1992.

—— *Feminism is for EVERYBODY*, London: Pluto Press, 2000.

Horowitz, J., *Apocalypto Now*. Online. Available HTTP: http://www.museenkoeln.de/museum-ludwig/download/ML_Horowitz_Flyer%20%281%29.pdf (accessed 12 February 2012).

Howe, F., *The Winter Sun: Notes on a Vocation*, Saint Paul, MN: Graywolf Press, 2009.

Hubbard, R., *The Politics of Women's Biology*, New Brunswick, NJ: Rutgers University Press, 1990.

Hudson, K., 'Obama's nuclear test'. Online. Available HTTP: http://www.newstatesman.com/international-politics/2009/01/obama-nuclear-poland-czech (accessed 17 September 2009).

Huffington Post, 'Obama Prague speech on nuclear weapons'. Online. Available HTTP: http://www.huffingtonpost.com/2009/04/05/obama-prague-speech-on-nu_n_183219.html (accessed 05 February 2012).

Hunt, L., *Inventing Human Rights: A History*. New York: W.W. Norton, 2007.

Hunt, S., 'Let women rule', *Foreign Affairs*, 2007, 86:3, 109–20.

Huntington, S.P., 'The clash of civilizations?', *Foreign Affairs*, 1993, 72:3, 22–49.

—— *The Clash of Civilizations? The Debate*, London: W.W. Norton, 1996.

Hutchings, K., 'Cognitive short cuts', in J. Parpart and M. Zalewski (eds), *Rethinking the Man Question: Sex, Gender and Violence in International Relations*, London: Zed Press, 2008, pp. 23–46.

—— '1988 and 1998: contrast and continuity in feminist international relations', *Millennium: Journal of International Studies*, 2008, 37:1, 97–105.

International Feminist Journal of Politics, special issue on 'Comparative gender mainstreaming', 2005, 7:4.

International Studies Perspectives, 'Pedagogy Forum on Mainstreaming Gender into the IR Curriculum', 2007, 8:3, 315–43.

Inter-Parliamentary Union, 'Women in national parliaments'. Online. Available HTTP: http://www.ipu.org/wmn-e/classif.htm (accessed 5 January 2012).

Irigaray, L., *This Sex Which Is Not One*, Ithaca, NY: Cornell University Press, 1985.

Jabri, V., 'Shock and awe: power and the resistance of art', *Millennium: Journal of International Studies*, 2006, 34:3, 819–39.

Jaggar, A.M., *Feminist Politics and Human Nature*, Brighton, UK: Harvester Press, 1983.

Jauhola, M., 'Building back better? – negotiating normative boundaries of gender mainstreaming and post-tsunami reconstruction in Nanggroe Aceh Darussalam, Indonesia', *Review of International Studies*, 2010, 36, 29–50.

Jeffrey S., *Industrial Vagina*, London: Routledge, 2008.

Jelinek, E., *The Piano Teacher*, London: Serpent's Tail, 2001.

Jenkins, A., 'Politics', in *In the Hot-House*, London: Chatto & Windus, 1988.

Jones, A. 'Does 'gender' make the world go around?', *Review of International Studies*, 1996, 22:4, 405–29.

—— *Gender Inclusive: Essays on Violence, Men, and Feminist International Relations*, London: Routledge, 2009.

Keohane, R., 'Beyond dichotomy: conversations between international relations and feminist theory', *International Studies Quarterly*, 1998, 42:1, 193–8.

Kimmel, M., 'Globalization and its mal(e)contents: the gendered moral and political economy of terrorism', *International Sociology*, 2003, 18, 603–20.

Kipton Art, 'Marina Abramović, "The Artist is Present"'. Online. Available HTTP: http://blogfiles.kiptonart.com/labels/Marian%20Abramovic.html (accessed 29 April 2010).

Kramer, L., *After the Lovedeath: Sexual Violence and the Making of Culture*, Berkley, Los Angeles, London: University of California Press, 2000.

Kristeva, J., *Powers of Horror: An Essay in Abjection*, trans. Leon S. Roudiez, New York: Columbia University Press, 1982.

Larcombe, W., *Compelling Engagements: Feminism, Rape Law and Romance Fiction*, Annandale, NSW: Federation Press, 2005.

Lather, P., 'Postbook: working the ruins of feminist ethnography', *Signs: Journal of Women in Culture and Society*, 2001, 27:1, 199–227.

Law, J., *After Method: Mess in Social Science Research*, London and New York: Routledge, 2004.

Lederman, M. and I. Bartsch (eds), *The Gender and Science Reader*, London: Routledge, 2001.

Ling, L.H.M., 'Hypermasculinity on the rise, again: a response to Fukuyama on women and world politics', *International Feminist Journal of Politics*, 2:2, 277–86.

Lloyd, M., *Beyond Identity Politics*, London: Sage 2005.

—— *Judith Butler: From Norms to Politics*, Cambridge: Polity Press, 2007.

Lorde, A., 'The master's tools will never dismantle the master's house', in C. Moraga and G. Anzaldua (eds), *This Bridge Called my Back: Writings by Radical Women of Color*, New York: Women of Color Press, 1983.

Los Angeles Times, 'Laura Bush addresses state of Afghan women'. Online. Available HTTP: http://articles.latimes.com/2001/nov/18/news/mn-5602 (accessed 10 May 2010).

MacCormack, P., 'Unnatural alliances', in C. Nigianni and M. Storr (eds), *Deleuze and Queer Theory*, Edinburgh: Edinburgh University Press, 2009, pp. 134–49.

McRobbie, A., *The Aftermath of Feminism: Gender, Culture and Social Change*, London: Sage, 2009.

Mail Online, 'The moment Miliband phoned race row MP Diane Abbott to say: apologise or I'll sack you'. Online. Available HTTP: http://www.dailymail.co.uk/news/article-2082527/Diane-Abbott-Twitter-race-row-MP-faces-calls-resign-racist-tweet.html (accessed 14 January 2012).

—— 'Why girls are naturally drawn to dolls as soon as they can crawl'. Online. Available HTTP: http://www.dailymail.co.uk/sciencetech/article-1266364/Why-girls-naturally-drawn-dolls-soon-crawl.html (accessed 20 May 2011).

Malik, K., 'Universalism and difference in discourses of race', *Review of International Studies*, 2001, 26:5: 156.

Marcus, S., 'Fighting bodies, fighting words: a theory and politics of rape protection', in J. Butler and J. Scott (eds), *Feminists Theorize the Political*, New York and London: Routledge, 1992, pp. 385–403.

Martin, E., *The Woman in the Body*, Milton Keynes, UK: Open University Press, 1987.

Mearsheimer, J., *The Tragedy of Great Power Politics*, New York: W.W. Norton, 2001.

Melzer, P., *Alien Constructions: Science Fiction and Feminist Thought*, Austin: University of Texas Press, 2006.

Minh-ha, T.T., 'Difference: A Special Third World Women Issue', *Feminist Review*, 1987, 25, 5–22.

—— *When the Moon Waxes Red: Representation, Gender and Cultural Politics*, London and New York: Routledge, 1991.

Minter, R. (ed.), *Jack Bauer for President: Terrorism and Politics in 24*, Dallas, TX: Benbella Books, 2008.

Moller Okin, S., *Women in Western Political Thought*, Princeton, NJ: Princeton University Press, 1979.

de Montigny, G., *Social Working: An Ethnography of Front-line Practice*, Toronto: Toronto University Press, 1995.

Moraga, C. and G. Anzaldua, *This Bridge Called My Back: Writings by Radical Women of Color*, New York: Women of Color Press, 1983.

Morrison, T., *The Bluest Eye*, London: Vintage Books, 1999.

Moten, F. and S. Harney, 'The university and the undercommons: seven theses', *Social Text*, 2004, 79:22, 101–15.

National Capital, Self-Guided Walking Tour, ANZAC PARADE. Online. Available HTTP: http://www.nationalcapital.gov.au/downloads/education_and_understanding/tours/Anzac_Parade_Walk.pdf (accessed 21 January 2012).

New York Times, 'For soldiers, death sees no gender lines'. Online. Available HTTP: http://www.nytimes.com/2011/06/22/world/asia/22afghanistan.html?_r=2&pagewanted=all (accessed 29 December 2011).

Nicholson, M., 'What's the use of international relations?', *Review of International Studies*, 2000, 26:2, 183–98.

Oakley, A., *Fracture: Adventures of a Broken Body*, Bristol: Policy Press, 2007.

Oestreich, J., Teaching gender and international relations', *International Studies Perspectives*, 2007, 8:3, 326–9.

Oliver, K., *Women as Weapons of War: Iraq, Sex, and the Media*, New York: Columbia University Press, 2007.

Painter, N.I., *Sojourner Truth: A Life: A Symbol*, New York: W.W Norton, 1996.

Parpart, J. and M. Zalewski (eds), *Rethinking the Man Question: Sex, Gender and Violence in International Relations*, London: Zed Press, 2008.

Pateman, C., *The Sexual Contract*, Oxford: Polity Press, 1988.

Peacock, S. (ed.), *Reading 24: TV Against the Clock*, London and New York: I.B. Tauris, 2007.

Peterson, V.S. (ed.), *Gendered States: Feminist (Re)Visions of International Relations Theory*, Boulder, CO: Lynne Rienner, 1992.

Peterson, V.S. and A. Sisson Runyan, *Global Gender Issues*, Boulder, CO: Westview, 1993 (2nd edn), 2010 (3rd edn).

Pettman, J.J., *Worlding Women: A Feminist International Politics*, New York: Routledge, 1996.

Phillips, A., *Multiculturalism Without Culture*, Princeton, NJ and Oxford: Princeton University Press, 2007.

Phillips, M., 'These "Slut Walks" prove feminism is now irrelevant to most women's lives'. Online. Available HTTP: http://www.dailymail.co.uk/debate/article-2002887/Slut-Walks-prove-feminism-irrelevant-womens-lives.html?ito=feeds-newsxml (accessed 14 June 2011).

Pollock, G., *Differencing the Canon: Feminist Desire and the Writing of Art's Histories*, London and New York: Routledge, 1997.

Qureshi, S., 'Displaying Sara Baartman, the "Hottentot Venus"', *History of Science*, 2004, 42, 234–57.

Rancière, J., *The Emancipated Spectator*, London: Verso, 2009.

Readings, B., *The University in Ruins*, Cambridge, MA and London: Harvard University Press, 1999.

Research Councils UK, 'Knowledge exchange and impact'. Online. Available HTTP: http://www.rcuk.ac.uk/kei/Pages/home.aspx (accessed 2 January 2012).

Rhode, N., 'Nina Rhode: Friendly Fire', Dundee Contemporary Arts, 21 May–31 July 2011. Online. Available HTTP: http://www.dca.org.uk/uploads/Nina-gallery-leaflet.pdf (accessed 27 March 2012).

Robertson P., quotes, *Think Exist*. Online. Available HTTP: http://thinkexist.com/quotes/pat_robertson (accessed 12 January 2012).

Ronell, A., 'Deviant payback: the aims of Valerie Solanos', in V. Solanos, *SCUM MANIFESTO*, London: Verso, 2009, 1–31.

Roy, S., 'Melancholic politics and the politics of melancholia: the Indian women's movement', *Feminist Theory*, 2009, 10:3, 341–57.

Ruddick, S., *Maternal Thinking: Towards a Politics of Peace*, Boston: Beacon, 1989.

St Martin in the Fields, 'Café in the Crypt'. Online. Available HTTP: http://www2.stmartin-in-the-fields.org/page/cafe2010/cafe.html (accessed 12 January 2012).

Sampson, F., *Rough Music*, London: Carcanet, 2011.

Scheper-Hughes, N. and P. Bourgois, *Violence in War and Peace*, Oxford: Blackwell, 2004.

Script-O-Rama, '*American Psycho* script transcript'. Online. Available HTTP: http://www.script-o-rama.com/movie_scripts/a/amercan-psycho-script-transript-bale.html (accessed 12 January 2012).

Shaw, K. and R.B.J. Walker, 'Situating academic practice: pedagogy, critique and responsibility', *Millennium: Journal of International Studies*, 2006, 35:1, 155–65.

Shepherd, L.J. (ed.), *Gender Matters in Global Politics: A Feminist Introduction to International Relations*, London and New York: Routledge, 2010.

Simmel, G., 'Bridge and door', *Theory, Culture and Society*, 11:5, 5–10.

Sjoberg, L., 'Gendered realities of the immunity principle: why gender analysis needs feminism', *International Studies Quarterly*, 2006, 50, 889–910.

—— 'Gender and personal pedagogy: some observations', *International Studies Perspectives*, 2007, 8:3, 336–9.

—— (ed.), *Gender and International Security: Feminist Perspectives*, London and New York: Routledge, 2010.

—— 'Emotion and the feminist IR researcher', *International Studies Review*, The Forum, C. Sylvester (ed.), 2011, 13:4, 687–708, pp. 699–705.

—— 'Gender, the state, and war redux: feminist international relations across the "levels of analysis"', *International Relations*, 2011, 25:1, 108–134.

Sjoberg, L. and C. Gentry, *Mothers, Monsters, Whores: Women's Violence in Global Politics*, London and New York: Zed Books, 2007.

Smith, D.E., *The Everyday World as Problematic: A Feminist Sociology*, Boston: Northeastern University Press, 1987.

Solanos, V., *SCUM MANIFESTO*, London and New York: Verso, 2004.

Sontag, S., *Regarding the Pain of Others*, New York: Farrar, Straus and Giroux, 2003.

Sorenau, R. and D. Hudson, 'Feminist scholarship in international relations and the politics of disciplinary emotion', *Millennium: Journal of International Studies*, 2008, 37:1, 123–51.

Spivak, G.C., *Outside in the Teaching Machine*, London and New York: Routledge, 1993.

Squires, J. and J. Weldes, 'Beyond being marginal: gender and international relations in Britain', *British Journal of Politics and International Relations*, 2007, 9:2, 185–203.

Srivastava, S., '"You're calling me a racist?" The moral and emotional regulation of antiracism and feminism', *Signs: Journal of Women in Culture and Society*, 2005, 31:1, 29–62.

Steans, J., 'Engaging from the margins: feminist encounters with the "mainstream" of international relations', *British Journal of Politics and International Relations*, 2003, 5:3, 428–54.

Stern, M. and M. Eriksson Baaz, 'Why do soldiers rape? Masculinity, violence and sexuality in the armed forces in the Congo (DRC)', *International Studies Quarterly*, 2009, 53, 495–518.

Stern, M. and M. Zalewski, 'Feminist fatigue(s): reflections on feminism and familiar fables of militarization', *Review of International Studies*, 2009, 35:3, 611–30.

Stevenson, R.L., *Strange Case of Dr Jekyll and Mr Hyde*, London: Longman, 1886.

Subramaniam, B., 'Snow Brown and the Seven Detergents: a metanarrative on science and the scientific method', in M. Wyer, M. Barbercheck, D. Giesman, H. Öztürk and M. Wayne (eds), *Women, Science and Technology*, London: Routledge, 2001, pp. 36–41.

Sunday Times, 'Les Sarkozettes', 6 May 2007.

Sylvester, C., *Feminist Theory and International Relations in a Postmodern Era*, Cambridge: Cambridge University Press, 1994.

—— 'Whither the international at the end of IR?', *Millennium: Journal of International Studies*, 2007, 35:3, 551–73.

Tanning, D. Dorothea Tanning. Online. Available HTTP: http://www.dorotheatanning.org (accessed 12 January 2012).

Telegraph Online, 'Britons spend half their waking hours using technology, finds Ofcom'. Online. Available HTTP: http://www.telegraph.co.uk/technology/news/7952091/Britons-spend-half-their-waking-hours-using-technology-finds-Ofcom.html (accessed 20 August 2010).

—— 'Wooten Bassett: bikers honour dead'. Online. Available HTTP: http://www.telegraph.co.uk/news/uknews/defence/7442432/Wooten-Bassett-bikers-honour-dead.html (accessed 29 March 2010).

Thobani, S., Presentation to Ottawa Women's Resistance Conference, 1 October 2001. Online. Available HTTP: http://englishmatters.gmu.edu/issue6/911exhibit/emails/sunera_thobani.htm (accessed 12 January 2012).

—— 'White wars: Western feminisms and the "War on Terror"', *Feminist Theory*, 2007, 8:2, 169–85.

Tickner, A., 'Seeing IR differently – notes from the 3rd world', *Millennium: Journal of International Studies*, 2003, 32:2, 295–324.

Tickner, J.A., *Gender in International Relations*, New York: Columbia University Press, 1992.

—— 'You just don't understand: troubled engagements between feminists and IR theorists', *International Studies Quarterly*, 1997, 41: 4: 611–32.

Times Higher Education, 'It is a popularity contest, sisters'. Online. Available HTTP: http://www.timeshighereducation.co.uk/story.asp?sectioncode=26&storycode=413763&c=1 (accessed 13 October 2010).

Tong, R., *Feminist Thought: A More Comprehensive* Introduction, Boulder, CO: Westview Press, 2009.

Tronto, J.C., 'Beyond gender difference to a theory of care', *Signs: Journal of Women in Culture and Society*, 1987, 12:4, 644–63.

True, J. and M. Mintrom, 'Transnational networks and policy diffusion: the case of gender mainstreaming', *International Studies Quarterly*, 2002, 45:1, 27–57.

Tuana, N., *The Less Noble Sex*, Bloomington: Indiana University Press, 1993.

United Nations, UNiTE to end violence against women. Online. Available HTTP: http://un.org/en/women/endviolence (accessed 12 January 2012).

—— 'Network of men leaders'. Online. Available HTTP: http://un.org/en/women/endviolence/network.shtml (accessed 12 January 2012).

United Nations Development Programme, *Millennium Development Goal 3*. Online. Available HTTP: http://www.undp.org/content/undp/en/home/mdgoverview/mdg_goals/mdg3 (accessed 12 January 2012).

—— *The Millennium Development Goals*. Online. Available HTTP: http://www.undp.org/content/undp/en/home/mdgoverview.html (accessed 12 January 2012).

United Nations Educational, Scientific and Cultural Organization, 'Gender mainstreaming'. Online. Available HTTP: http://portal.unesco.org/en/ev.php-URL_ID=46723&URL_DO=DO_TOPIC&URL_SECTION=201.html (accessed 12 January 2012).

United Nations Office on Drugs and Crime, 'Human trafficking fuels violence against women'. Online. Available HTTP: http://www.unodc.org/unodc/en/frontpage/2009/November/human-trafficking-fuels-violence-against-women.html (accessed 3 March 2010).

United Nations Security Council, Resolution 1325, 2000.

—— Resolution 1820, 2008.

—— Resolution 1888, 2009.

—— Resolution 1889, 2009.

United Nations Women, 'Beijing and its follow-up'. Online. Available HTTP: http://www.un.org/womenwatch/daw/beijing (accessed 12 January 2012).

—— 'UN creates new structure for empowerment of women'. Online. Available HTTP: http://www.unwomen.org/2010/07/un-creates-new-structure-for-empowerment-of-women (accessed 30 July 2010).

US Department of State, 'Secretary Clinton's remarks on women, peace and security'. Online. Available HTTP: http://www.state.gov/secretary/rm/2011/12/179173.htm (accessed 10 January 2012).

Ussher, J., *Women's Madness: Misogyny or Mental Illness?*, Hemel Hempstead, UK: Harvester Wheatsheaf, 1991.

Vignale, G., *The Beautiful Invisible: Creativity, Imagination and Theoretical Physics*, Oxford: Oxford University Press, 2011.

Vrasti, W., 'The strange case of ethnography and international relations', *Millennium: Journal of International Studies*, 2008, 37:2, 279–301.

Walker, A., *The Color Purple*, London: Women's Press, 1983.

Waltz, K., *Man the State and War: A Theoretical Analysis*, New York: Columbia University Press, 1959.

Wendt, A., *Social Theory of International Politics*, Cambridge: Cambridge University Press, 1999.

West, R., 'Mr. Chesterton in Hysterics', *The Clarion*, November 14, 1913.

Weston, K., *Gender in Real Time: Power and Transcience in a Visual Age*, New York: Routledge, 2002.

Whitworth, S., *Feminism and International Relations*, Basingstoke, UK: Macmillan, 1994.

Wiegman, R., *Women's Studies on Its Own*, Durham, NC and London: Duke University Press, 2002.

—— 'Dear Ian', *Duke Journal of Gender, Law and Policy*, 2004, 11:93, 93–120.

—— 'The intimacy of critique: ruminations on feminism as a living thing', *Feminist Theory*, 2010, 11:1, 79–84.

Wikipedia, 'Feminism'. Online. Available HTTP: http://en.wikipedia.org/wiki/Feminism (accessed 12 January 2012).

Williams, L.R., 'Ready for action: *G.I. Jane*, Demi Moore's body and the female combat movie', in Y. Tasker (ed.), *Action and Adventure Cinema*, London: Routledge, 2004, pp. 169–85.

Williams, P., *The Alchemy of Race and Rights*, Cambridge, MA: Harvard University Press, 1991.

Winterson, J., *Why Be Happy When You Could Be Normal?*, London: Jonathan Cape, 2011.

Wittig, M., 'One is not born a woman', in L.M. Alcoff and E. Mendieta (eds), *Identities: Race, Class, Gender, and Nationality*, Oxford: Blackwell, 2003, pp. 158–62.

Wollstonecraft, M., *A Vindication of the Rights of Woman, with Strictures on Political and Moral Subjects*, London: Dover Publications, 1996[1792].

Women in Black, 'A Short History of Women in Black'. Online. Available HTTP: http://www.womeninblack.org/en/history (accessed 12 January 2012).

Youngs, G., Lisle, D. and Zalewski, M., 'Three readings of *G.I. Jane*', *International Feminist Journal of Politics*, 1999, 1:3, 476–81.

Zalewski, M., 'Tampons and cigars: (no) escaping sexual difference in *G.I. Jane*', *International Feminist Journal of Politics*, 1999, 1:3, 479–81.

—— 'Where is woman in international relations?: "To return as a woman and be heard"', *Millennium: Journal of International Studies*, 1999, 127:4, 847–67.

—— 'Feminism and international relations: an exhausted conversation?', in F. Harvey and M. Brecher (eds), *Critical Paradigms in International Studies*, Michigan: University of Michigan Press, 2002, 330–41.

—— '"Women's troubles" again in IR', Forum on Gender and International Relations, *International Studies Review*, 2003, 5:2, 291–4.

—— 'Distracted reflections on the production, narration and refusal of feminist knowledge in International Relations', in B. Ackerly, M. Stern and J. True (eds), *Feminist Methodologies for International Relations*, Cambridge: Cambridge University Press, 2006, pp. 42–61.

—— '"I don't even know what gender is". A discussion of the relationship between gender mainstreaming and feminist theory', *Review of International Studies*, 2010, 36, 3–27.

—— 'Marysia Zalewski on unsettling IR, masculinity and making IR theory interesting (again)', *Theory Talks*: Theory Talk #28. Online. Available HTTP: http://www.theory-talks.org/2009/04/theory-talk-28.html (accessed 13 January 2012).

Zalewski, M., A. Brew, M. Riggs, C. Clare, C. Hackett, H.M. Kinsella and C. Clare (eds), '20 years of British gender and international relations: crafting the past–present–future', *International Feminist Journal of Politics*, 2009, 11:3, 305–33.

Žižek, S., *Welcome to the Desert of the Real*, London: Verso, 2002.

—— *Violence: Six Sideways Reflections*, London: Profile Books, 2008.

Cinema

2012, Dir. Roland Emmerich, Columbia Pictures, 2012.
As Good As It Gets, Dir. James L. Brooks, TriStar Pictures, 1997.
Chasing Amy, Dir. Kevin Smith, Miramax, 1997.
Children of Men, Dir. Alfonso Cuaro, based on the novel by P.D. James, Universal Pictures, 2006.
Dr Jekyll and Mr Hyde, Dir. Rouben Mamoulian, Paramount Pictures, 1931.
Dr Strangelove or: How I Learned to Stop Worrying and Love the Bomb, Dir. Stanley Kubrick, Columbia Pictures, 1964.
G.I. Jane, Dir. Ridley Scott, Caravan Pictures, 1997.
Gone with the Wind, Dir. Victor Fleming, Warner Bros., 1939.
Hollow Man, Dir. Paul Verheoven, Columbia Pictures, 2000.
Lilya 4-Ever, Dir. Lukas Moodysson, Memfis films, 2002.
Little Britain, Series 1–3, Dir. Steve Bendelack, BBC, 2003.
Lost in Translation, Dir. Sofia Coppola, Focus Features, 2003.
Mississippi Burning, Dir. Alan Parker, Orion Pictures, 1989.
Monster, Dir. Patty Jenkins, Media 8 Entertainment, 2003.
Rendition, Dir. Gavin Hood, Anonymous Content, 2007.
Rise of the Planet of the Apes, Dir. Rupert Wyatt, Twentieth Century Fox, 2011.
Taken, Dir. Pierre Morel, Europa, 2008.
Terminator, Dir. James Cameron, MGM, 1984.
Terminator 3, Dir. Jonathan Mostow, Columbia TriStar, 2003.
The Book of Eli, Dirs Albert Hughes and Allen Hughes, Alcon Entertainment, 2010.
The Day After Tomorrow, Dir. Roland Emmerich, Twentieth Century Fox, 2004.
The Day the Earth Stood Still, Dir. Scott Derrickson, Twentieth Century Fox, 2008.
The Hours, Dir. Stephen Daldry, Paramount, 2002.
The Opposite of Sex, Dir. Don Roos, Rysher Entertainment, 1998.
The Road, Dir. John Hillcoat, Dimension Films, 2010.
The Song of Bernadette, Dir. Henry King, Twentieth Century Fox, 1946.
The Truman Show, Dir. Peter Weir, Paramount, 1998.
War of the Worlds, Dir. Steven Spielberg, Paramount Pictures, DreamWorks SKG, 2005.
World Trade Center, Dir. Oliver Stone, Paramount Pictures, 2006.

Music

Cockburn, B., 'The trouble with normal is that it always gets worse', *The Trouble with Normal*, True North Records, 2007 [1983].
Morse, T. and E. Madden, *Two Little Boys*, 1902.
The Soldiers, *Coming Home*, Warner Music, 2009.

YouTube videos

'American Psycho – Business Card Scene'. Online. Available HTTP: http://www.youtube.com/watch?v=cISYzA36-ZY (accessed 12 January 2012).
'Marjory Dawes tells Rosie O'Donnell What's What'. Online. Available HTTP: http://www.youtube.com/watch?v=jgODHapn5L4 (accessed 12 January 2012).
'Truman Show Emotional Ending'. Online. Available HTTP: http://www.youtube.com/watch?v=zBu9l_EKWVs (accessed 13 January 2012).
'Žižek on *Children of Men*'. Online. Available HTTP: http://www.youtube.com/watch?v=pbgrwNP_gYE (accessed 20 October 2010).

INDEX

Note: illustrations are indicated by page numbers in **bold**.